# THE COUNSELLOR'S GUIDE TO
# PARKS INNER CHILD THERAPY

*HUMAN HORIZONS SERIES*

THE COUNSELLOR'S GUIDE
TO
# PARKS INNER
# CHILD THERAPY

## PENNY PARKS

*A CONDOR BOOK*
*SOUVENIR PRESS (E&A) LTD*

First published 1994 by Souvenir Press
(Educational & Academic) Ltd,
43 Great Russell Street, London WC1B 3PA

Reprinted 1998
Reprinted 2006

ISBN 0 285 63172 1

Photoset by Rowland Phototypesetting Ltd,
Bury St Edmunds, Suffolk

Printed in Great Britain by
CPD (Wales) Ltd, Ebbw Vale

Extracts from the Authorised Version of the Bible
(The King James Bible), the rights in which are vested in
the Crown, are reproduced by permission of the
Crown's Patentee, Cambridge University Press.

# Contents

# Acknowledgements

I would like to thank my closest friend and colleague, Pamela Hayes, for her creative expertise and contributions to the book, for her help with editing and for her loyal and caring support.

My thanks also go to Clare Rushworth and Pippa Smyth—both are very special and valued friends who cheerfully took the time to plough through the manuscript to anglicise and edit.

I would also like to express my sincere appreciation and respect to those individuals who have contributed their personal work as sample material, in order to give counsellors a clearer understanding of PICT.

# Introduction

Psychotherapists and counsellors in Western society who work in the field of childhood abuse have recognised the positive value of 'inner child' work. Parks Inner Child Therapy (PICT) is a flexibly structured approach to inner child work, which works through the 'today' adult to assist resolution of trauma within the 'past' child part to create inner harmony and balance.

PICT is a powerful and versatile therapy model package that can be most easily described as an evolving form of rapid cognitive therapy with a foundation in Transactional Analysis that incorporates Neuro-Linguistic Programming (NLP) to aid rapid positive change. PICT was originally created to specifically help people recover from the trauma and damage of sexual, physical and emotional abuse during childhood (such harm may have been caused deliberately, caused by neglect, or by inadequate parenting which was not intentional), but it has been found that PICT is equally effective for a wide range of emotional problems such as ritual abuse, food/drug/alcohol abuse, depression and anxiety, phobias, Dissociative Identity Disorders, CBD, self harm, PTSD & more.

In 1990 I published the book *Rescuing the 'Inner Child'* (Souvenir Press) which introduced the PICT model. It was designed to be a self-help book to assist people who had experienced childhood abuse. In the introduction I described the people who should use the book in collaboration with a counsellor and advised them not to attempt to tackle their problems alone. This second book is designed for counsellors who wish to work with clients using aspects of the PICT method. Of course, those counsellors who wish to be fully qualified PICT therapists and use the full array of 'tools' will attend the PICT Advanced Practitioner Training. By virtue of its purpose, the self-help book only contained information that could be used independently by a layperson. It was PICT in its most basic form. Consequently, additional information and tools that can be used by counsellors who wish to utilise some aspects of the PICT method outside of the full training. It does not contain the full form of PICT that is available in the training course, nor the advanced features that do not require disclosure of traumatic details.

PICT is an evolving model of therapy with ongoing refinements and changes. Since 1998, the most significant feature of PICT is that it can bring about change compassionately because there is little or no need to disclose the details of traumatic events. No longer are specific techniques required to recover repressed traumatic memories, which in some cases re-traumatise clients and, at the least, are time consuming. PICT addresses the effects of the trauma (whether the trauma is in conscious memory or not) rather than focusing on the detail of an event and therefore allows the client to retain their privacy, dignity and to work comfortably to bring about beneficial changes in their lives. PICT contains thorough, quick and effective techniques that can lead to lasting change.

Most clients enjoy the methods and are quickly aware of their achievements. PICT therapy can be relaxing and satisfying, with times for laughter to counterbalance the more serious moments.

Although this book is entitled *The Counsellor's Guide*, it can still be of use to people wishing to use it as a self-help guide (with the obvious limitations) or simply as an information source. It is not, however, suggested as a replacement for counsellor training. The intended use of the book is for trained counsellors to gain insight and tools to add to their repertoire; for people who are struggling to reach recovery on their own and wish to learn more about what they can do for themselves and what they will need help to achieve; for those needing more information about the effects and treatment of childhood abuse; as a reference tool for those completing the PICT Advanced Practitioner Training (see details at end of book).

# 1 Effects of Childhood Trauma

> When children experience trauma at the hands of trusted adults (especially family members) their emotional link with the adult world is severed, creating an emotional 'stop on time'. They are then left with three companions: guilt, fear and feelings of inadequacy. These three companions can stay on throughout their adult life governing part or all of their decision making.
>
> (Penny Parks, *Rescuing the 'Inner Child'*)

Upon hearing this information, most people who have experienced abuse will readily agree and verify to you the presence within of guilt, fear and feelings of inadequacy. Explain to your clients that to remove the 'three companions' you will need to access the Child part of them where those feelings originated and are still trapped. Accessing the Child part will enable them to reconnect that 'severed emotional link' with the adult world. This reconnection can assist your clients to repair the damage done during childhood and consequently begin to experience a better quality of life. The reconnection is between the person's Child part and Adult part.

## WHAT SORT OF TRAUMA/ABUSE?

The information in this book applies to those who have experienced emotional, physical or sexual abuse. Contrary to common assumptions, a person who experiences emotional abuse can suffer from the same problems and symptoms as someone who has suffered sexual abuse. In some cases, that includes sexual dysfunction. For instance, if a person's parents were sexually restricted, their verbal and behavioural messages would mirror that restriction. Their children would receive the message that just thinking about bodies, let alone sex, is bad. Those children may easily have grown up with some sort of sexual dysfunction or restriction simply as a result of emotional abuse or poor parenting.

There is little difference between the symptoms and problems of people who were emotionally abused and those who were physically or sexually abused—their exact experiences differ, but their limiting symptoms are similar. The information and techniques in this book can be used for a broad spectrum of abuse, from poor parenting to ritualistic abuse.

## WHAT IS SELF-TALK?

The following is an excerpt from the Written Assessment of one of my students on the PICT Training Course, Kath Teasdale, from Liskeard, Cornwall. Her task was to write an explanation of self-talk, the thought processes involving inner dialogue between Parent, Adult and Child parts. She did such a beautiful job of explaining it, I felt it was an appropriate introduction to explaining our Parent, Adult and Child parts.


Kath Teasdale


### *Self-talk*
Every person has three aspects within themselves—the parent, adult and child, which develop as we grow up. The adult is our reasoning part, which gathers information, enables us to manage our life, to make realistic assessments and to be assertive. To do this it needs sound information available. When working well, the parent is our teaching part. Modelled on our memory of our own parents and elders, it monitors our actions, protects us from harm, teaches about life and acknowledges our efforts without criticism or judgment. The child's job is to be spontaneous, curious, creative and fun, thus

enabling us to experiment, innovate and play. Together these parts are intended to function as a balanced team, meeting the challenges of life.

If a person has experienced traumatic childhood events or inadequate parenting the inner messages will be damaged, preventing the team from functioning correctly. The damaged adult will be ill-informed, unassertive, and a poor, indecisive manager. The damaged parent will be full of blame and criticism that disables us and undermines our efforts. We will punish ourselves for any deviation from the high standards we set ourselves with this critical parent voice. We can often recognise it as a sarcastic 'Jiminy Cricket' that sits on our shoulder. The damaged child will feel fearful, guilty, angry and become locked in self-sabotaging patterns that leave us feeling helpless and inadequate.

In this way we develop incorrect pictures of ourselves and others. We may expect too much or too little of ourselves, fail to recognise our genuine achievements and underestimate our good qualities. Our thought talk (self-talk) becomes full of confusion and self-criticism. Our relationship with ourselves and with others becomes problematical.

PICT acts to reconnect the broken emotional link with the adult world by correcting the information in the adult. The adult in turn can correctly inform, support and love the inner child. This process corrects mistaken beliefs, frees the child from fear and anger, enabling it once again to experience the spontaneity and fun it was intended to. With correct information the adult functions more strongly and supportively, the child learns to trust and the parent can take up its correct non-judgmental role. Together they learn to identify and diffuse unhealthy parent messages as they arise.

## ADULT, PARENT AND CHILD

Transactional Analysis, as developed by Eric Byrne, is built on the basic model that every person has three aspects within—the Adult, the Parent and the Child. When I first began my search for healing I found Transactional Analysis familiar because I was very aware of my Child part and also very aware of the damaged Parent part. Unfortunately, my Adult part was fairly insignificant. I immediately applied the Transactional Analysis form of therapy but found that it did not extend far enough for me. So it was at that time that, armed with the knowledge of the Adult, Parent and Child, I began my pioneering route towards healing and ultimately developed PICT.

The three aspects of Parent, Child and Adult can be recognised by listening to our self-talk—our thought talk. The Adult and Parent are often hard to distinguish apart at first, because they are both coming from thoughts that sound 'grown-up', whereas the Child is fairly easy to identify because the thoughts sound 'childlike'. In other words, our self-talk containing the Adult and Parent parts will be structured and worded in 'grown-up' terminology; the Child talk will be structured and worded as a child speaks. Each of these three aspects or parts have a job.

### Adult
The Adult's job is to be an information gatherer, have a strong assertive voice, be a strong manager (of our life circumstances), make realistic assessments (of self and others) and be executor over the other two aspects.

### Parent
The Parent's job is to teach, monitor actions and behaviours and to give acknowledgement of accomplishments. (All of these are done with a non-judgmental tone or attitude in the healthy Parent.) Teaching pertains to self and others. We 'teach' ourselves each time we try a new recipe or follow directions to put together a bookshelf and we 'teach' others each time we explain to someone else how to prepare the same recipe or assemble a similar bookshelf. Monitoring actions and behaviours pertains to our awareness of things needing to be done; in our thoughts we say, 'Remember the keys.' 'Oh, it's raining, bring in the washing.' 'It might rain, bring the umbrella.' Acknowledgement of accomplishment pertains to recognising our efforts, whether successful or

not. The Parent part can express acknowledgement by saying to self, 'Good job!', 'Well done!' when a goal is achieved,
or 'Great effort!' when a goal is tried but not attained. The
Parent part expresses similar comments to others concerning
their efforts.

### Child

The Child's jobs are spontaneity, creativity, curiosity and a
sense of fun. Individuals who say aloud, and in their
thoughts, 'I'll try it!' 'Let's go and see!' are expressing typical
spontaneous Child statements. 'Look what I've made [dis-
covered].' 'I want to try this new way' are typical Child
creative statements. 'Let's see how this works.' 'I've got a
good idea to try' are typical statements made by the curious
Child part. A sense of fun comes in many shapes but is
characterised by a great pleasure in laughter and in sharing
laughter with others.

### Damaged Adult

If an individual has experienced very poor parenting or had
his emotional link severed by trauma/abuse (emotional,
physical or sexual) during childhood, the Adult, Parent and
Child aspects become damaged and are not able to function
in a healthy manner.

  The damaged Adult will be ill-informed, be either aggressive or passive, be unable to manage or change life circumstances, make unrealistic assessments of self and be unable
to take charge of the other two aspects (Parent and Child).
Decisions will be taken by the most powerful aspect at any
given time or 'voted' on. Voting may work for our general
society but it is not useful for our inner emotional functioning, which needs the appropriate aspect (Adult) to be
in charge or confusion reigns. [Your clients will be very
familiar with feelings of confusion.] It is part of the Adult's
job to be in charge, to make the final decision, to veto
suggestions by a damaged Parent or Child part—it is easy
to see why an ineffective Adult aspect would be unable to
function properly in these areas.

*Parks Inner Child Therapy*

**Damaged Parent**
The damaged Parent will send messages that are accusing, blaming, punishing and name calling. These messages came from the significant adults in your client's childhood, i.e. parents, teachers, relatives or childminders. Generally speaking, the bulk of influence comes from parents. The messages (heard in our thought talk/self-talk) will sound very much like the exact things parents, for instance, actually said—even to the use of 'you' statements rather than 'I' statements, i.e. 'You are so clumsy!' 'Look what you've done now!' 'Did you think they would really like *you*?!' The tone will be either sarcastic or judgmental. A damaged Parent aspect can make life miserable and hopeless, robbing your client of his or her individuality and potential. The three tasks of the Parent will be executed in a damaging, sarcastic and judgmental attitude.

*Note*: The Parent and Adult are always difficult to distinguish between at first, but one rule of thumb to use is this— the damaged Parent message is *always* accusing, blaming or name calling. No matter how convinced clients may be that it is their 'Adult' which dislikes the 'Child', that is *never* true. The Adult can only be non-judgmental towards the Child, it is the damaged Parent who 'dislikes, hates' and consequently makes accusing, blaming statements about the Child. It will be vital to establish this truth for your clients and you will no doubt need to repeat it, and help them re-identify it, many times.

**Damaged Child**
A damaged Child is fearful, angry and self-sabotaging and carries the guilt, fear and feelings of inadequacy previously mentioned. When challenges face your client, the damaged Child self-talk will contain messages reflecting fear such as: 'I can't, I'm afraid.' 'I want to hide.' 'Don't ask me. I can't do it!' When faced with disappointments your client will feel angry and the damaged Child self-talk will be messages such as: 'I'll get back at you!' 'Everyone hates me!' 'Hurt people before they hurt you!' 'I hate everyone!' Disappointment can also activate damaged Child self-talk in the self-sabotage area with statements such as: 'I deserve it—I'm bad (dirty,

ruined, contaminated).' 'I shouldn't be happy.' 'I'll never be happy.' Most often self-talk contains fluctuations between the three: fear, anger and self-sabotage.

See the self-talk chart (p. 18) for more examples of healthy vs. damaged Adult/Parent/Child messages. Use it also as a handout to clients or as a quick checklist to remind yourself of the jobs each part does and how to recognise where damaged messages are coming from (which part is manifesting).

## RECONNECTING THE EMOTIONAL LINK

The severed emotional link with the adult world can be reconnected, but not with the person's actual parents. Instead it will be with the Adult your client is now. The person's Adult can give correct information, support and love to the damaged inner Child, subsequently changing the Child's mistaken beliefs about self and desensitising traumatic memories. The Child aspect can then become healthy and happy, enabling the person to experience more spontaneity and fun, thus developing his or her creativity and curiosity.

The Adult part will receive the information, to be given to the Child, from you, the counsellor. The information should then be immediately written to the Child (or planted directly into the unconscious mind if using visualisation techniques), so that you actually witness the Adult gaining strength, knowledge and stability simultaneously with the Child. The Parent part of your client will change and develop by witnessing the exchange between Adult and Child, with just the occasional letter written to the Parent part when an issue is particularly difficult.

These three aspects, Parent, Child and Adult, are a part of everyone, although most people are never aware of how they operate or that changes can be made in that operation, if needed. In order to implement change, your client will first need to understand the individuality of these aspects. In other words, the aspects will need to be separated out and addressed individually, but once healthy functioning is achieved, the Parent, Child and Adult aspects will blend

## SELF-TALK EXAMPLES: DAMAGED VS. HEALTHY

| Damaged parent voice | Ineffective adult | Damaged child voice |
|---|---|---|
| Accusing, blaming, punishing, and name calling. | Ill informed, unassertive voice, and no control. | Fearful, angry and self-sabotaging. |
| Look what you've done now! You ruin everything. I shouldn't expect anything different from you! Did you think you could really do it? You made your bed, now lie in it. You will never be any different. Stupid! Clumsy! | I guess kids who are abused asked for it, that's what people say. Mum and Dad must be right. Other people know more than me. I don't like what they say, but I can't stop them. I don't know my rights. | I can't, I'm afraid. Don't be angry, I'll do it. I want to hide. I'll get back at you! Don't trust anyone! Hurt people before they hurt you! Everyone hates me! I'm bad, dirty, ruined, and contaminated so I deserve it. I'm bad, etc., I shouldn't be happy. |

| Healthy parent voice | Effective adult | Secure child voice |
|---|---|---|
| Teaching, monitoring, acknowledgement (non-judgmental voice tone). | Information gatherer, strong assertive voice, strong manager, makes realistic assessments. | Spontaneous, creative, curious, fun. |
| That works like this. Give this a try. Here is a good way. This may be useful. Don't forget the keys. It's raining, do you have the umbrella? You have worked hard, good job. You did your best, good effort. You were very assertive, well done! | If I don't know, I shall find out. I enjoy learning. I respect others rights. I respect my rights. I am responsible for myself. I soon recognise damaged parent and child messages and defuse them. I am in charge of my life, and I feel happy and strong doing so. | I'll try it! Let's go and see. I've got a good idea to try! Look what I've made (discovered). Let's see how this works. I want to try this new way. Let's be silly. I like making you laugh. I like laughing. |

back into smooth, appropriate and natural behaviour, with their individuality being only occasionally apparent.

## THREE DIVISIONS

There are three other divisions within your client that need to evolve back into one.

*First*—A damaged, problem-ridden person, resulting from the abuse.

*Second*—The 'coping' person he often pretends to be in order to function in the world, i.e. hold employment, manage social interactions.

*Third*—The person he would have been if the negative effects of the abuse had never happened.

Clients will be very familiar with the first, damaged person and also familiar with the second, 'coping' person. The 'coping' person is experienced as a sense of wearing an emotional mask which enables the client to appear normal, rather than problem-ridden—a pretence. The mask-wearing time will vary with individuals, some having it in place for much longer periods of time than others can manage. Those able to keep the mask in place for longer periods of time may not even be seen by their colleagues as having any problems, whereas the person who cannot wear the mask for very long will be well known as problem-ridden.

Explain to your client that your work together will be to reach in and draw that third person forward—the person he would have been had the negative effects of childhood abuse never happened, the person he would have developed into had he experienced healthy parenting. Usually the client will have very little awareness of the third person's presence, but that should grow as you work together. What you are aiming for is the person he should have been, to be the total person he is—no longer experiencing damage and consequently no longer needing the 'mask' behaviour.

Making the reconnection between Adult and inner Child, and giving the Child the information, support and love that should have been received when the traumatic events happened, frees the person to be who he or she would have been if abuse had never happened.

## EXAMPLES OF THE EFFECTS OF CHILDHOOD ABUSE

### Letters

I received a letter from a man named Stephen, who is on his recovery journey. He wanted to share what he had written about his feelings and experiences, with a view to educating and/or assisting others. He called this written piece 'Climbing from the Darkness'. Often those who are beginning to come out of their pain feel a need to help others who are even further behind. Stephen's written piece mirrors this feeling. It also demonstrates the most difficult part of the journey for him—acknowledging and facing the memories. This may not be every victim's difficulty. His piece also assumes that there is skilled help available when people do come forward, which is, sadly, not always the case. Stephen's letter clearly states the confusion and emotional pain victims of abuse (emotional, physical or sexual) experience and demonstrates their silent cries for someone to intervene. It is a clear picture of the long-lasting effects of abuse.

### *Climbing from the Darkness*

PREFACE

The words written herein are those of a male victim. They try to express my beliefs and fears. The aim is to help others and by so doing ease some of my pain. I am now 38 years old and am now being helped. Please read the words with an open mind and heart.

### *One Touch into Hell*

Sexual abuse starts with the first touch. That touch can send the victim into a hell of pain, fear and isolation. Leaving a victim to feel alone; that there is no way out; that he is the only one; and that he will not be believed.

Nobody has the right to begin this pain for the victim—
it only takes that one touch. All children have a right to
be and to feel safe. Society needs to find a way to protect
them. Those who are already victims, whether still a child
or now an adult, can and must be helped to overcome the
pain, fear and confusion.

The body can be hurt, the mind numbed. The horror
lives on in the mind even long after the touching has
stopped. The victim must know that he can get help, the
body repaired, the mind unlocked. Many feelings can be
lost: the ability to love and be loved. How can a victim
grow to love and make love when sex and touch were
used to torture him? Unlocking the mind can be achieved
by talking, by someone listening and believing. If not, the
victim can begin to believe that he is sick, a freak, worthless, when it is the abuser who should feel this way.

Abusers come in many forms: father, mother, brother,
sister, uncle, aunt—anyone who has access to the child
inside or outside the family. If the abuser is within the
family, the victim is caught in many ways: to talk may
hurt others in the family, he may not be believed, he may
be put in care. The fear of breaking up the family makes
the victim feel that in some way he is the one who is wrong
and not the abuser. This is not so. The victim begins to
keep more and more silent and may start to act badly (e.g.
staying out of school, causing trouble, etc.). These are all
signs of a troubled mind (not necessarily of sexual abuse).
When nobody asks what's wrong, then the victim starts
to feel even more isolated and betrayed. The sense of
betrayal deepens with time and itself becomes confused,
thus creating even more self-doubt and a weakening of
the spirit. If the child is not listened to, or is too frightened
to get help, as the years go by the world seems to gang
up against him, each failure in his life compounds the
self-doubt. Feelings become even more difficult to unlock.
If one is a male, things such as media profiles of potential
abusers help to create self-doubt, e.g. adult males most
likely to abuse are those who were themselves abused as
children and are now unable to form adult relationships.
This describes male child victims, while female victims are

portrayed as likely to become promiscuous or to turn to prostitution out of low self-esteem. These stereotypes, although sometimes true, only serve to keep the victim from coming out of his shell.

So where do the answers lie? Prevention is always better than cure, prevention can only come through education and understanding. Teachers could be trained to look for the signs, e.g. children who skip school, who are sullen or withdrawn, too quiet or causing trouble, in poor physical health, misusing drugs, etc. The media could help to create a more open attitude so that victims and those who may feel likely to abuse can seek help. Many charitable organisations now offer counselling, but governments (not just in the UK), seem to lack the courage to deal with these areas of human behaviour. It seems that we, the victims, are not worth the investment. This itself hurts the victim.

### From One Touch into Hell
### Two Steps back to Life

The beginning of the return from childhood sexual and other abuse takes two steps: the first is to cry out for the help you need, the second is to have the courage to face the past. The help is becoming more available, the courage must come from within. You do have that courage—to have survived this far proves this. But the victim is entitled to more than just survival, you have a right to be happy and fulfilled in your life.

Others do care; so take your courage and contact the helpers (e.g. doctors, counsellors, helplines, etc.). You will overcome the pain, trauma and fear. You have a right to your freedom and life, so do it, do it now! You can have the courage. It is not easy. Be patient. Give yourself the time to release the pain, it will ease. Then you can take back control of your life and go forward and attain the peace of mind and joy that is your right.

*Freedom: the Return
from One Touch into Hell*

We now approach the time of freedom when we, the victims, can finally put the past away and take our lives back into our own hands. We have now, with help, striven hard, long and painfully, for our true rights. We, the victims, understand the pain that others may go through, so we have the best chance of understanding the anguish of others. I feel it is my duty to those who are now suffering to help. I can do little, but I will try to do what I can. To you, the victims: please come forward—you can and will be helped.

To those who feel that you may abuse or have abused: you can get help as well, but you must come forward. All people have the right to be part of the whole of society, but all must live within its rules. We must all think of the future, and children are the future. Our need to care for them and protect and guide them safely on the path of life is the most important part of all our lives. Our duty both to ourselves and to others is never to surrender to those who would damage the lives of others and by so doing, damage the future of the children.

Although my words deal with child abuse, it must not be forgotten that many adults are suffering abuse. You also count, and you can get the protection you deserve and the help and understanding that you need, so please come forward and contact the helpers: you can do it. Do it for yourself and for the future. Perhaps one day I can write a fourth part, when my own darkness has lifted. To those who read this: you are helping me; thank you.

Stephen

**Poetry**

Many victims of abuse write their pain out in the form of poetry. The following poems were written by a male, Chris, before he found help on his healing journey. They were written when he felt hopeless and trapped. The feelings described are very typical for both male and female. As you read these two poems, keep in mind that this man did come through his despair to emerge triumphantly on the other side. He is now an effective, qualified counsellor, studying research into counselling development and contemplating doing a doctorate on the subject.

### The Vessel

The vessel stands alone.
It seems so out of place
Amongst the fine blown glass
And cut crystal
Which grace the rest of the table.

It is empty.
Only dust gathers,
Clinging to its jam jar walls.
It does not taste the rich wines
Which are plentifully poured
Into the rest of the vessels.

It appears dull,
The light dimly shining through
Its dusty shape.
It is ugly.
Why not remove it, smash it?

And yet, why though?
Neglect alone has left it so.
If cleaned and polished it
Could gleam like its fellows.
Care could make it shine.

It would not sour fine wine
Nor curdle milk.
Flowers could rest in its gentle support.
Its smooth, kind rim

Could softly caress the finest lips,
If it would be taken up.

But instead the solitary vessel stands
In lonely isolation, gathering dirt,
Used occasionally to clean brushes.
Not even rinsed, but not complaining.
It could be so beautiful.
Why disregard it?


## A Journey's End


I know I cannot win
I stare defeat in the face.
Fate like a haggard old woman
Sits in a corner and mocks me
Rocking back and forth in her mirth.

No rest, no peace, no happiness
My mind is turmoil, want to scream.
Pain spreads like gangrene,
Yet invisible.
No tangible evidence of my suffering,
I near the door.

At the end of the passage
The door faces me in cold disdain.
It knows I cannot open it.
Behind me the hag's cackles
Ring like a testament to my weakness.

I have long travelled the passage.
At first my instincts bade me stop
But there is no door other than
My present tormentor.
Nausea engulfs me yet I remain still.

The master of the labyrinth
Knows the game must end.
This poor pathetic nobody has
To make the choice or
Be forever damned.

To remain outside the portal,
Starving gradually and dying in agony,
Or to turn the handle
And play out the final stage.
Still the hag cackles.

I am no fool.
The end is clear to me.
My untiring journey has been
As futile as it has been arduous.
Only the vain hope of a paradise beyond
Has given me the strength to get this far.

Now the cold reality stares spitefully
At my insignificant form.
But I realise there can be
No other way.
I must end my agony before I perish.

Twin visions flash through my mind.
An Eden where joy sings like
A thousand nightingales
Or a cold bleak wilderness where
I will meet my death in anguish.

I know I am worthy of the
Green meadows and rich orchards
But the laughter in my ears
Tells me that I am condemned
To the wasteland.

The next poem was sent to me by a young woman, Nancy,
who is in the early stages of coming to terms with the abuse

she experienced. You can see in it a good example of the first two parts of the three divisions (damaged person, mask person, person meant to be) discussed on page 19.

### The Pain He Caused

She needs to run, to get away from the pain inside, with
  her everyday.
She hurts so much deep down inside, she feels she wants
  to run and hide.
Hide from the world and the cruel ones within, hide from
  the people, who are no better than him.
She wants to get out, scream, shout and cry, 'He's the
  one who made my life a lie'.
He stole her childhood when she was so small, back when
  she was no more than two foot tall.

Now she is older, her life has grown colder, no one to
  love her, no one to hold her, she wants to die, now she
  is older.
The tablets they sit there night and day, she sometimes
  wishes they'd go away.
She sits and counts them one by one, and often thinks,
  it would be fun, to take them all out of the pot, and
  into her belly they would drop.

The pain would be gone, not just for the day, but forever
  and ever and that's okay.
No more hiding inside the gin, no more playing
  happy-go-lucky from the outside in.
The drink and the tablets would take away the pain, the
  pain he caused her again and again.

## SYMPTOMS OF ABUSE

Below are the most common symptoms and problems faced by adults who were abused during childhood. This is not a complete list, just the most common problems. The response to abuse varies, people will have a few or many of these difficulties. These symptoms/problems all stem from the mistaken/limiting beliefs each person developed as a result of childhood abuse. With each symptom I have listed possible mistaken beliefs that might match up. However, never assume that any belief is accurate until you present it to your client and see that the response/recognition is congruent (as explained in Chapter Two).

Also, remember that some of these mistaken beliefs will be so familiar that they become invisible to your clients. Although they may even be using the exact wording of the belief as they speak to you, (i.e. 'It's all my fault, everything is always my fault'), it may still come as a shock to them when you put it into the same words and reflect it back. People are seldom aware of the mistaken beliefs that control their behaviour and life.

### Lack of confidence
The most common symptom; stemming from erroneous beliefs developed in childhood of guilt and an innate sense of 'badness', defective. [Mistaken beliefs may be: 'I'm not good enough.' 'I'm defective.' 'I'm ruined.' 'I'm bad.' 'It's all my fault.']

### Low self-esteem
This feeling is usually associated with people's outward appearance, believing they are ugly and repulsive, regardless of what they actually look like or what positive input they may receive. [Mistaken beliefs may be: 'I'm not good enough.' 'I'm ruined.' 'I'm contaminated.' 'I'm bad.']

### Strong feelings of inadequacy
A belief of innate 'badness' prohibits personal achievement; that in turn is followed by self-sabotage. This person's vocabulary will be full of 'I can't' statements. [Mistaken beliefs may be: 'I'm bad.' 'I ruin everything.' 'I can't win.' 'I don't deserve happiness.' 'It's always my fault.']

**Inability to trust**
When trust in a respected and trusted adult, particularly a parent, is broken at an early age, children quickly learn that the adults around cannot be trusted. That situation experienced during childhood becomes a generalised belief something like: 'No one can be trusted' and continues to affect their adult life, prohibiting or restricting intimate or close relationships.

Often victims of abuse will sabotage friendships and intimate relationships by initiating a cut-off from the person they care about. It is easier to cut off and hurt yourself before others have a chance, particularly when you believe the hurt is inevitable. This cutting off is often done by setting unrealistic tests for the person cared for. When the test is failed, the person's belief that no one can be trusted is strengthened. That in turn strengthens the feeling/belief that it is safer to stay behind emotional walls.

Others believe that they will not be accepted if people know about the abuse. Although most are crying out for love and acceptance, their fear and erroneous belief system keeps them trapped within themselves, feeling isolated and hopeless. [Mistaken beliefs may be: 'No one can be trusted.' 'I can't trust myself.' 'People will hurt me.' 'There is no safety.' 'To feel is to be unsafe/vulnerable.' 'I can never tell.' 'I can never be known.' 'I'll always be trapped with hurt—there is no way out.']

**Problem relationships**
Other symptoms, i.e. sexual dysfunction, inability to touch, inability to trust, etc., cause serious relationship problems. Many victims of abuse choose abusive or inadequate partners because damaged personalities feel more familiar and 'normal' to them. This is because the experience of growing up in a dysfunctional family causes dysfunctional people to seem familiar and it is natural to be drawn to what is familiar.

Some people choose an inadequate partner as a result of believing that their own 'unworthiness' prohibits a partnership with a 'nice' person. [Mistaken beliefs may be: 'I'm bad.' 'I'm ruined.' 'I don't deserve happiness.' 'I should be punished.' 'I don't count.' 'I'm not good enough.' 'No one can be trusted.']

### Sexual dysfunction
Approximately two-thirds of people who are sexually abused as children are sexually repressed, while the remainder are often promiscuous. Many lack accurate sexual knowledge and therefore do not have proper information about their body functions or sexual organs. Many have become frightened of their sexuality, believing that their bodies are dirty or shameful. Some have had many sexual experiences but have not shared love with those partners. Others may use sex as a way of gaining acceptance or as a manipulative tool (learned behaviour). Still others put up a mental block concerning their sexuality, sex no longer matters.

There are some who enjoy a full sex life. However, these are usually people who were given some support and proper information at the time of (or since) the abuse and who have a supportive, emotionally healthy and loving partner. [Mistaken beliefs may be: 'I'm bad, dirty, ruined.' 'I'm defective.' 'I don't count.' 'I'm contaminated.' 'I'm not important.']

### Food/drug/alcohol abuse
Food abuse can be manifested by conditions such as anorexia or bulimia. Some people who have experienced abuse sometimes hold the erroneous belief that they will not have to face their sexuality if they are unattractive. It is also another form of self-punishment. Those who are obese may also use food as a form of comfort and their excess weight as a defence against feeling small and vulnerable. Drug or alcohol abuse can be used as a form of self-punishment, a dulling buffer, a comfort/crutch or a memory-blocking device. American statistics substantiate the fact that a large number of drug and alcohol abusers were sexual abuse victims during childhood. [Mistaken beliefs may be: 'I'm bad.' 'I don't count.' 'To be ugly (or fat) is to be safe.' 'I deserve to be hurt/punished.' 'I'm not important.']

**Low or over-emotional control**

Those people who have low emotional control are generally seen to over-react very quickly, easily bursting into tears, having outbursts of anger, pacing agitatedly, laughing loudly or inappropriately and generally appearing demanding and vulnerable. They make minor events into major crisis issues. They are often called 'dramatic or hysterical'. This behaviour may temporarily give them a sense of comfort from the attention received, but comfort is shortlived because the attention is usually negative. Surprisingly enough, the connection is seldom made by these people between their behaviour and the response people give them. Their inappropriate behaviour has become a second skin, and to them, it feels right. In their opinion, the other person is wrong.

Then there are those people who are extremely over-controlled emotionally, almost robot-like. They may be in a fairly consistent state of emotional and physical numbness, not much really 'gets' to them. Still others may have physical pain or numbness only associated with particular memories, emotions or situations. The most common denominator in over-controlled people is that they are terrified of their anger, believing that to show any strong emotion could cause them to lose control and give in to the violent rage they fear. For other people over-control stems from the mis-guided childhood belief that the less emotion displayed, the less chance of being noticed; a hope that this control will lessen the risk of further abuse.

Some children have learned that they have no rights to emotion, and they therefore find it difficult to laugh, cry, complain or even express an opinion. Parents or carers may well have crushed any sign of emotion from these children from an early age. As adults they often build an invisible wall around their feelings, promising themselves that no one will ever see the pain they have suffered, no one will be allowed in to hurt them again. [Mistaken beliefs may be: 'I don't count.' 'It's not safe to have feelings.' 'I can't be known.' 'No one can be trusted.' 'Hurt other people first.' 'People will always hurt me.' 'I'm bad.' 'I'm not important.']

**Panic attacks**
Panic attacks can include the following physical symptoms: difficulty with breathing, throat closing up, heart racing, vision changes, sweating, shaking, nausea, desire to run, feeling out of control, feeling trapped, a desire to scream, feeling as if they are going to pass out, feeling as if their body will explode and a fear that they are going crazy or will die. A full-blown panic attack is terribly frightening.

Panic attacks are triggered by some thought, smell, taste, sound, feeling or action reflecting the abuse suffered in childhood and most of the time the victim does not have a clue what that trigger might have been. Some people who have not yet remembered abuse suffer from panic attacks and are understandably very confused about the cause. Their panic attacks seem to come from nowhere, but there is always a trigger. [Mistaken beliefs may be: 'I have no control.' 'I will always be unsafe.' 'There is no safety.']

**Phobias**
Phobias can be a form of self-sabotage, self-punishment, an underlying feeling that 'I am not worthy to enjoy life, therefore if I cannot function properly then I will not enjoy life'. It can also take the form of a distraction. When a person has a serious phobia or illness to deal with then the fear of facing the deep emotional scarring of sexual abuse can be put off. [Mistaken beliefs may be: 'I deserve punishment.' 'I don't count.' 'I'm bad, dirty, contaminated, ruined.']

**Illness**
Emotional trauma that has never been settled can produce physical illnesses such as migraines, stomach disorders, asthma, skin disorders, bowel disorders, back problems and gynaecological problems. General aches and pains are the most common symptoms. [Mistaken beliefs may be: 'I'm bad, dirty, contaminated, ruined.' 'I deserve punishment.' 'I don't count.' 'My body is bad.']

**Self-mutilation**
Common examples are: biting or clawing limbs, cutting body with razor blades or knives, burning body with cigarettes, repeated bruising, injuries or banging head on the wall or with an object.

Self-mutilation is sometimes used by victims of abuse to control their experience of pain. It can also provide an intense feeling of relief and release that is often craved. It can be an attempt to control something in one's life, a type of self-punishment, a means of expressing anger or a way of having feelings. It can be manifested in both children and adults.

Sometimes the physical pain can be a distraction from the more feared emotional pain or it can be an attempt to indicate to others just how strong the emotional pain is. [Mistaken beliefs may be: 'I'm bad, dirty, contaminated, ruined.' 'I can't be angry.' 'I'm defective.' 'It's all my fault.' 'I deserve to be punished.' 'I can't let the pain out.']

**Sleep disturbances**
Recurring nightmares are the most common sleep disturbance. Insomnia is also a frequent experience, and some people may use excessive sleep as a form of escape, a method of coping. [Mistaken beliefs may be: 'I'm bad, dirty, ruined, contaminated.' 'It's all my fault.' 'I'll never have peace.' 'It's unsafe to be still.']

**Flashbacks**
Flashbacks can be in the form of quick visual pictures, like watching a film, or in the form of feelings (emotional or physical). These often take place during lovemaking, but can also accompany everyday activities (triggered by some connection with the abuse) or perhaps reading or hearing about other victims' abuse experience. Flashbacks are fragmented views of the abuse and can offer a 'way in' to a more complete memory. [Mistaken beliefs may be: 'I have no control.' 'I will never be safe.' 'There is no safety.' 'I'm trapped with the pain.']

**Inability to touch or be touched**
This problem can be triggered by feelings of dirtiness (a fear that the other person will somehow know of the abuse and be rejecting), fear of contaminating others (an irrational thought stemming from feeling dirty and bad), low self-esteem (not worthy, self-punishment) and the fear that in some way, by allowing physical contact, one is at risk of further abuse (loss of control, being at another's mercy). Touch may bring back memories of unwanted touch from childhood or touch which produced some pleasurable feeling but now brings shame and self-disgust, a fear of one's sexuality. [Mistaken beliefs may be: 'I am bad, dirty, ruined, contaminated.' 'I have no control.' 'My feelings are bad.' 'I don't count.' 'I deserve to be punished.']

**Depression**
People with abusive childhood backgrounds will experience depression because they believe they will never change, their environment or relatives will never change, they are so bad and dirty that they do not belong with 'nice' people, no one understands them, etc. If a person has no memory of abuse, depression will result because there is no logical reason for the symptoms he or she is experiencing. Having said that, many people do not associate the symptoms they have with the experience of abuse, even when they do remember it. Depression can also result from repressed anger. [Mistaken beliefs may be: 'I am bad, dirty, ruined, contaminated.' 'I am trapped with the pain.' 'There is no escape.' 'I will never be safe.']

**Suicide attempts**
People who have suffered abuse may see suicide as their only way out of the pain. Until recently there has been very little help offered to adults who were victims of childhood abuse in this country. Some of those who have displayed acute symptoms of abuse have been judged mentally ill and sent for psychiatric treatment. As a result of not being understood, little help was forthcoming and the client often left sessions (with ill-informed psychiatrists or therapists) feeling more suicidal than upon arrival.

Typical advice given (as reported by clients) were remarks such as: 'Well, that is all in the past. Do you feel that you will abuse? No? Well then, go home and concentrate on your partner and family, find yourself something else to think about. Take your mind off it and stop dwelling on it.' The inference taken was often, 'I think you are wasting my time, it is a lot of fuss about nothing.' With the person's last hope of finding someone to help and understand shattered, suicide may have seemed the only way left to stop the pain. This is particularly true for people who have struggled with symptoms for a long time and feel they are in a losing battle. [Mistaken beliefs may be: 'I can never escape.' 'I am bad, dirty, ruined, contaminated.' 'There is no way out.']

**High risk taking**
Some people find they almost have a compulsion for 'daring the fates', their work or social life can be a series of very high risk taking events. On the flip side of that, there will be other people who go in the opposite direction and find it impossible to take even the smallest risk. [Mistaken beliefs may be: 'I don't count.' 'I'm not important.' 'I can never be safe.' 'There is no safety.']

**Security seeking**
In stressful situations some people may actually hide or cower in a corner. They become nervous when they feel they are being watched and often report feeling watched when no one is actually around. There is usually a very strong startle response to surprise situations, which may be followed by anger or nervousness. Often there is a need to be invisible. [Mistaken beliefs may be: 'I have no control.' 'I cannot be safe.' 'There is no safety.' 'No one can be trusted.' 'I cannot trust myself.']

**Alienation from body**
Some people are not at home in their own bodies. They often fail to heed body signals (pain, fatigue) and they do not take care of their bodies in either fitness or health areas. They usually have a poor body image and there can be a manipulation of body size to avoid sexual attention. (This

may dovetail with the food/drug/alcohol abuse and low self-esteem listed above.) Often these people spend much of their time in a disassociated state, i.e. 'watching' their life happen rather than experiencing it. [Mistaken beliefs may be: 'I don't count.' 'I'm not important.' 'I'm bad, dirty, ruined, contaminated.' 'My body is bad, dirty, etc.' 'I am not safe.']

**Aversion to making noise**
This includes sex, crying, laughing or other body functions. These people are often soft spoken and may pause a lot while speaking as they monitor their words. [Mistaken beliefs may be: 'I don't count.' 'I'm not important.' 'I am not safe.' 'Feelings are unsafe.']

**Memory blanks**
People who have memory blanks of a year or several years during their childhood *and* have several of the above symptoms are typical examples of people who have repressed abuse memories. This usually happens when trauma experienced during childhood is so threatening that the child shuts off all memory of it as a coping mechanism.

May I also point out here, if someone has memory blanks but shows no symptoms of abuse, please don't feel obligated to search diligently for abuse or announce with the flair of Sherlock Holmes, 'Aha! Memory blanks, just as I suspected, childhood abuse!' If there are no symptoms, it is probably just a case of fairly uneventful experiences blurring into each other and appearing as a blank.

One common experience for those with repressed abuse memories is that they will have strong emotional reactions to information concerning anything they actually experienced. Often a client will hear about some horrible experience someone else has had and be moved and upset by it. That is natural. However, when clients have an over the top reaction (as though they are experiencing it) it is not natural—*unless they have experienced something similar, in some manner, at some time.*

There will sometimes be certain words they cannot say and have difficulty hearing—although they do not know why. There may also be certain behaviours they cannot do or watch (often sexual in nature, particularly if it was sexual abuse)—but do not know why. Sometimes there will be ordinary, everyday events that they cannot bear—but do not know why. All of these will more than likely be connected with the abuse experience they are blocking off.

A typical example of this is a client of mine named Priscilla, who could not bear her children to close the curtains on a sunny day. So, if the sun was shining on the television screen and the children got up to close the curtains, Priscilla would panic and have to open the curtains quickly. If the sun were not shining, she had no problem with the curtains being closed. This behaviour did not make sense to her and it quite regularly annoyed her children.

Priscilla had no memory at all of abuse happening to her, but she did have many symptoms of abuse. After we had built up her Adult aspect sufficiently to allow her to have the personal resources needed to 'know', we did a memory retrieval exercise (outlined later). What we discovered was that six year old Priscilla had been taken by her childminder to a house where two men lived. One man paid for the sexual use of Priscilla. He took her upstairs to the bedroom and as she stood against the wall terrified, he closed the curtains against the bright sunlight coming through. He then turned and walked towards Priscilla and subjected her to lengthy and severe sexual abuse. Up until that memory retrieval exercise all that Priscilla's subconscious had let her know was that when the curtains closed on a sunny day, it was time to panic and run. [Mistaken beliefs may be: 'I cannot be safe.' 'I can't tell.' 'I will die if I know.']

# 2   PICT Steps

Adults who were sexually/physically/emotionally abused during their childhood suffer from the effects of shame and guilt, which are demonstrated by common symptoms and self-sabotage (problems with health, relationships, personal achievement). It is the counsellor's job to create an atmosphere of safety and empathy to facilitate the disclosure of experiences involving shame and guilt. Facing, understanding and reframing these experiences, in conjunction with removing mistaken beliefs, will enable the client to curtail his or her self-sabotage behaviour.

People operate their lives according to their beliefs, therefore their lives will reflect those beliefs. People who experience childhood abuse develop limiting, mistaken beliefs about themselves and those beliefs are clearly demonstrated in their behaviour. The PICT steps are a simple and extremely effective way to identify and change mistaken beliefs, to reframe the traumatic experiences and consequently to empower the client to live without the former restrictions, i.e. unwanted and unhelpful symptoms and behaviours.

Many people have 'head' knowledge about their problems, but are still unable to change their behaviour. This happens because knowing or understanding something does not always change one's deep-seated beliefs. Of course, there are occasions when one can change a belief by simply hearing new information, but that does not work for the more deep-seated beliefs. This book will be discussing several ways of changing limiting beliefs. Some people need to do writing exercises to start with, while others are able to use visualisation work. For most clients, a combination of the two is the most effective method.

## MATCHING BELIEFS

It is useful to explain to your clients how the brain functions with regard to beliefs. The brain continually sorts through the information we take in and looks for the information that matches our beliefs or goals. Anything that does not match the already established belief or goal is discarded as unimportant or insignificant. In other words, all information or data coming in will be sifted, weighed and valued in a precise search for the material that gives emphasis or confirmation to our present beliefs. Information or events not containing that information will be ignored to a large degree or distorted.

Limiting/mistaken beliefs are nurtured and verified in this way. As a result life always seems to hand that person the short straw. Positive beliefs are processed in the same manner, with similar results—life seems to be handing the person 'good luck'. Life is doing nothing more than giving us what we believe; our beliefs are creating good or bad 'luck' by focusing solely on matching information and discounting the rest.

This helps explain the behaviour of people we see around us and also our own behaviour. For instance, people who believe, 'I'm not good enough', are always dissatisfied with their accomplishments. No matter how many people tell them how well they have done, the mistaken belief, 'I'm not good enough', rules.

When a person believes 'I'm not good enough' his or her brain sorts through daily information identifying and recording every mistake . . . criticism . . . helpful hint . . . failure to gain approval as confirmation of that belief. (It is almost as if it is saying, 'Ah, there's one, there's one, there's one'.) All the positive comments, praise, achievements and awards which should challenge the belief are disregarded. (As if the brain were now saying, 'No, that's not one, that's not one, that's not one'.) An example would be a football goalie who blocked nine goal attempts and missed one. He walked away from the game feeling down because he could only see the one he had missed. People observing such behaviour scratch their heads in bewilderment, wondering why the person does not recognise his own accomplishment.

The brain continues doing the same efficient job when the belief is a positive one, sorting through all incoming information looking for a match with the existing beliefs and discarding anything that does not match. All of us have witnessed or heard of someone who accomplished something against all odds, and when congratulated he or she is heard to say, 'I always knew I could do it'. The brain was simply doing its job, identifying information that matched the established belief, 'I can do X'.

## BELIEFS CAN BE CHANGED

The good news for your client to know is that we are not stuck with mistaken/limiting beliefs, they can be changed. Sometimes limiting beliefs are changed simply by gaining a missing bit of vital information. In those cases, we experience a profound understanding (the penny drops) and the limiting belief automatically changes. Many beliefs, however, cannot change in that manner, they need more specific assistance. Those are the beliefs that usually carry on throughout a person's life, causing mild to extreme disruption. Logic does not touch these beliefs and people are often very frustrated when trying to dislodge these beliefs solely with the application of logic or a reframe. Some of the tools in this book will identify and address beliefs directly and others will change the past experience which established the belief, therefore releasing the belief. Either way, clients will experience profound change.

## NEGATIVE FEELINGS

Most people think that their negative feelings are statements about reality, or facts, but feeling is not a statement of *fact*, only of *emotion*. Experiencing your emotions is not the same as accepting them as statements of fact about your own identity. Feelings express emotional reactions to beliefs. If one feels inadequate, for example, one can actively experience that feeling, realising that even though one feels inadequate this does not mean that one *is* inadequate. One can say, 'I feel inadequate', and at the same time understand that the feeling is not a statement of *fact*, only of *emotion*. What you feel is not who you are.

If feelings express emotional reactions to beliefs, we can then also give our attention to negative feelings to discover limiting beliefs. Looking at clients, you could ask yourself, 'What belief might match up with those feelings?' or 'What might this person believe about him or herself to generate such feelings?' You might even ask your client, 'What does that feeling say about you? or 'What meaning, about yourself, do you give that feeling?'

Negative feelings are signposts to limiting beliefs. Once limiting beliefs are discovered, you are in a position to remove them. Once limiting beliefs are removed, an individual is free to be who he or she really is; who she would have been if limiting beliefs had not been implanted and accepted during childhood. We were all meant to be free to explore and expand our own personal potentials.

## STARTING THERAPY

Below is the general procedure involved in beginning work with a client, but there are no hard and fast rules as to timing. Go as fast or slow as is appropriate to your client's needs.

Most people are very nervous about the first session. They may worry that they will be required to discuss abuse detail immediately. You can put them at ease by explaining, 'In case you may have been worried about having to go into detail about abuse experiences, please relax, that will not be happening. I am simply going to make general enquiries.'

If your client has had that worry, she will immediately feel understood and you will have helped to establish rapport. If she did not have that worry, you will have lost nothing by making the comment. The only way you could lose something by making such a comment would be if you had said, 'You *are* worried, etc.', for it is quite foolish to claim to 'know' anyone's feelings. Throughout therapy you can safely make generalised statements such as, 'Many people feel (think, worry, believe, etc.) . . . Some people feel . . . There are people who feel . . . I wonder if you feel (have ever felt) . . . Sometimes people feel . . .', without your client thinking that you are labelling her or attempting to read her mind. Any information you give in that manner is unobtrusive. Sometimes people will reply to generalised statements and other times will simply listen to the information you are sharing without comment.

At this point, I usually use a tool called The Well Formed Outcome, described in Chapter Five, which identifies whether the client is actually ready for change work. If not, I will need to refer the person on to someone else, so it is important for me to discover this information early on.


## GIVE INFORMATION

Giving general information about the kinds of feelings victims have assists in establishing rapport. When you are discussing issues usually attached to shame/blame feelings, generalised statements will spare your client the embarrassment of making personal detailed disclosures about similar issues. Always stress that it is *normal* for people to experience *whatever feelings they have felt* in response to childhood abuse.

It is also helpful in establishing rapport with your clients to match their general posture, energy level, voice tone and demeanour and continue to pace them for the first five or ten minutes of the interview. Then you can begin to relax again into your own posture and way of being. This is one more subtle way of helping your clients feel understood and accepted and also it will lead them into a more relaxed state. Students on the PICT Training Course have the opportunity to discuss, explore and practise these techniques.

A theme that will be repeated throughout therapy is that the **client did nothing to cause the abuse** and was not generally capable of stopping it. Children are at the mercy of adults and even the most assertive child cannot *enforce* his or her 'No' statements. Sadly, most children are not equipped to even consider saying 'No'. You will be repeating this information over and over again to your clients.

Clients and, unfortunately, some therapists, make the mistake of judging the 'child's' behaviour in the past from the κnowledge and ability the same person currently has as an adult. That is one reason you frequently hear clients claim that they can see that other victims were not guilty of causing childhood abuse but cannot see their own childhood innocence. They are observing other people as the children they were—powerless and innocent—while viewing their own childhood experience through their current adult knowledge and ability.

I must point out here that the same principle applies to people who went on into adult life continuing to be abused by the same abuser. Because the abuse is still happening, these people usually have a huge block in recognising their own innocence. It will be useful to point out that a child who has been programmed to accept abuse does not magically change into an assertive person just because he or she has turned 18. When the abuser is a parent, the person has an even more difficult time taking charge of his or her life and saying 'no' to the abuse. I often give the following example to explain this point.

### John

John was a 45-year-old managing director of a large company. He had no difficulties being the person in charge and he had the respect of his employees. At home, with his wife and three children, he had no difficulties in his role as husband and father—for here too, he was respected. John's problem was his mother.

On the telephone, or in person, John could not be assertive with his parent. He could not say 'no' when it was inconvenient to go for a visit or receive one, he could not stop his mother from telling him how to run his life, he could not even be himself around her and he certainly did not feel respected. He came to see me because he had developed a very uncomfortable rash whenever he spoke to his mother on the telephone or saw her in person. The relationship with his mother was literally 'getting under his skin'. He had a cream from his doctor, but it did not bring much relief and John could see that he needed to deal with the cause of the rash, not just the effect.

John was very self-punishing about his inability to be

assertive with his mother, especially when he could see that he was assertive in all the other areas of his life. John's mother had never sexually or physically abused him, but as John spoke about his childhood it was obvious she had been rather manipulative. In the name of 'his best interests' she was able to ignore his rights and ensure that he made the choices and decisions she wanted him to make, the choices that suited her or, in other words, were actually in 'her best interests'. Her manipulative behaviour was presented in a most gentle, caring manner and consequently John never recognised it as being manipulative.

Coming to that realisation was very helpful to John, but not enough to enable him totally. In the words he used to describe his feelings he said repeatedly, 'I can't let my mother down.' When I reflected this phrase back to him as a possible limiting belief, it had substantial impact. I then asked who was the 'I' that was unable to let mother down. As tears rolled down his face, he answered softly, 'The little me'.

I explained that sometimes parents can be doing something that they think is helpful for their child, but in actuality it is not. I 'wondered' if this might be that sort of situation. John nodded affirmatively. 'Perhaps it is time for the child to give this limiting belief back to mother. After all, it is *her* belief.' John agreed, and we did the mistaken belief visualisation, which changed the belief to 'I am a loving person'. Obviously, 'letting mother down' implied that the child would be unloving.

The main point of telling John's story is to assist your client to recognise that it is difficult for most people to stand up to their parents—even people who are assertive in other ways. I end the story of John with this question: If people who are male, well into maturity (45), understand and practise the principles of assertiveness in other areas of life, have powerful positions in life and have not experienced overt abuse, but *can still be controlled by their parents*, where does that leave the person who is younger, female (in particular), passive or aggressive, powerless and abused in many ways? If John had problems standing up to his mother, with all the things he had going for him, how in the world would someone without those attributes be able to stand up to her parent/abuser?

It is impossible to say 'no' when you have a limiting belief prohibiting you from doing so. It is impossible to say 'no' to parents, when all around us, in society, it is believed to be wrong to do so. We therefore become trapped in the behaviour we learned as a child—the behaviour of saying 'yes' to parents when we really mean 'no'.

## LIST TRAUMA MEMORIES

When you are using the PICT letter series, start by asking your client to list the most traumatic memories from her childhood. (It is preferable to do this as part of the session to avoid the possibility of your client becoming focused on a trauma while at home without your assistance.) Ask your client to just say the first ones that come to mind, without trying to evaluate them. There will be the obvious damaging memories, but this list may sometimes also contain what appear to be fairly ordinary events. This is not unusual, because the actual events are secondary to the traumatic feelings and consequent meaning the child gave to the events. Accept whatever comes forward from your client without either of you making evaluations, i.e. 'That doesn't sound that bad, maybe we should leave it off the list'.

Do not ask your client to tell you the whole memory, ask her just to give you a sentence that describes the experience clearly enough for her to identify it later, i.e. 'The time in the shed with Uncle Harry'. It is not useful to have your client go through a detailed account of several memories when you are not ready to engage in any change work. If your client wants to tell you the details, explain that until you know where to start on the memory list it is not appropriate to focus on any one memory.

Explain that when you begin work on the memories you will start by looking at the least traumatic memory to avoid your client feeling emotionally overwhelmed and perhaps then reluctant to go further, so therefore first you will need simply to list the memories, without discussing them, and then you will assess their severity together.

Sometimes your client may have a memory that is so difficult she cannot tell you about it, even in a sentence. In that
case, ask her to give you a key word that represents the
memory, i.e. 'kitchen'. When you finally get to the 'kitchen'
memory, your client will usually be ready to face it, but if
not, you can also use the Personal Resource Exercise
described in Chapter Five, which does not need the content
to be disclosed.

Some memories may be about specific events, others
about a common experience that happened frequently over
a period of time. For the second category it may be necessary, in some instances, to choose one experience to represent the rest. In that case, simply ask your client if there
is one experience that stands out from the rest or one that
seems to have all the common elements of the experience.
If your client cannot remember any specific instance because
the memories in that category seem to 'blur' together, it is
acceptable to piece a representation together from what she
does remember.

Generally speaking, this list will contain between four and
ten memories. Occasionally your client will produce 15, 20
or 30 memories. In that case, write them all down and then
try to group them into similar topics, i.e. separating memories involving physical, emotional or sexual abuse, separating abuse memories according to abuser (mother, father,
uncle), separating abuse experiences by place (school,
home, relative's home). Within each topic choose the worst
memory and use that one to represent the rest (i.e. the worst
one of the physical abuse by father) and put that one on the
final memory list.

Your task is to find the mistaken belief contained within
each memory. Since some of the memories will reflect the
same belief you will seldom need to work on every memory
on the list. As you complete work on successive memories,
check those remaining on the list with your client to find out
which ones can be ticked off.

To do this, simply ask your client to listen as you read
each memory sentence and then to tell you what emotional
response she experiences. (Even if the memory sentence is
one word it will still have the impact with your client.) Read

each one slowly and distinctly, then pause and let your client assess her reaction. Usually, if the memory needs to be worked on, it will still have emotional 'punch' and immediately you will see that in her physiological reactions. If, however, she seems nonplussed and is slowly searching to see if there is a reaction, you can rest assured that the mistaken belief in that memory has been disconnected. Your client will usually shrug and say something like: 'I don't know . . . it just doesn't seem that important now.' You can then cross that memory off the list. Go on to the next memory and read it in the same way, slowly, distinctly and then pause. If you were to read quickly through the list without pausing for a reaction between each one, your client would not have time to assess them separately and you would not get an accurate response.

One client who had a list of 17 memories, which we couldn't reduce down further, ended up only having to work on six. The mistaken beliefs in those six were also contained in the remaining memories and therefore disconnected the emotional punch formerly contained in the remaining 11.

## SHAME AND BLAME MEMORIES

After the client has finished giving the initial list, enquire further if there are any memories connected with shame or blame that are not already included. Shame memories are typically about times when the child was ridiculed or somehow stood out from the crowd in a way that was not acceptable. A shame memory in connection with sexual abuse may be one where the child felt physical pleasure and consequently responded to the abuser or felt special and important and therefore returned to the abuser.

A blame memory could be one where the child somehow felt responsible for a negative event. This could be an event that that she was directly responsible for, or had no connection with at all, except in her own perception, i.e. feeling responsible for someone's death because the child was angry with him and thought, 'I wish you were dead'. In the case of sexual or physical abuse, the child may have had a chance to tell someone she was being abused, but did not.

If there are any shame or blame memories, it is advisable to give immediate information to help the client understand those reactions and to avoid the possibility of her leaving the session feeling exposed or dirty. You can give that information without knowing the details of the memory. Ask your client to signify if the memory is shame or blame and then explain the following information using general terms, i.e. 'some people feel . . . sometimes shame (blame) memories cause people to feel . . . often people experience . . .'.

In the case of ridicule or standing out from the crowd, it would be useful to reframe the experience drawing your client's attention to whatever lack of information or lack of personal resources any child has, as being a natural state for children and a responsibility of parents to provide adequate information. Also point out that most people judge the child they were with the information and resources they now have as an adult, saying things like, 'I should have known better', totally forgetting that the child did not have the current information and knowledge and therefore did not 'know better'. It is important to take into consideration the child's particular circumstance and age group. Also draw her attention to the lack of information and personal resources of the other people involved in the situation. In doing this you are meant to be assisting your client to realise that the shame situation was something that happened *to* her, that it was *not something inherent in her* (not part of her identity), that it was something that could happen to *anyone* who was without the needed information or personal resources, that it was not a direct reflection on her identity.

Physical and emotional pleasure experienced during sexual abuse can leave a crippling guilt. The counsellor must impart the knowledge that the first is a normal bodily response and the second a result of the child's emotional needs being inadequately met. Offer the information that any child who responded physically to sexual abuse is simply a child whose genitals worked properly. It does not mean that the child is bad or dirty, nor does it mean she must have 'wanted' the abuse to happen. (These are two of the most common misconceptions of victims.) Any child's body can respond to a gentle touch, that is the way our bodies were designed to react. It only means that a child's body is normal, that his or her 'plumbing' works.

Children who felt special and important and returned to the abuser were simply children whose emotional needs were not being met properly. Explain that it is the parent's responsibility to meet children's emotional needs appropriately so that those children will not have to settle for abuse attention. I often give this example to explain children settling for abuse attention: 'I think I can safely assume that neither of us would relish eating out of a dustbin. (I have not had anyone disagree with that assumption as yet.) If I offered you a mouldy piece of bread, you would probably politely decline while you attempted to keep your stomach calm. However, if neither of us had eaten anything for one solid month, the contents of that dustbin would take on new meaning. You would not think twice about eagerly accepting that mouldy piece of bread—counting yourself lucky to have it. Your need would overpower your want. It is the same situation happening when parents do not meet the emotional needs of their children. You see, emotional needs are **just as important**, just as necessary for survival, as our need for food. All children need to have the experience of feeling special and important. If their parents are not able to meet that need in an appropriate way, children will eventually settle for whatever is on offer, from whatever source—their need becomes bigger than their want.'

## BLAME MEMORIES

When you are discussing blame memories, you will be exploring 'responsibility' issues, i.e. 'I should have known better, so it is all my fault'. It is vital for your client to know that certain information or personal resources would have been needed in the abusive situation in order to be responsible. Obviously, if the child did not have that information or those personal resources at the time of the event, the responsibility passes from her shoulders—perhaps onto the shoulders of her parents who had not given the needed information either before the event or after it so that the child could understand what had happened.

Blame feelings arising from not telling someone about sexual abuse do not indicate a 'bad' child. Most children sense that the adults around them do not want (or even know how) to talk about the subjects of bodies or sex, let alone the subject of sexual abuse within the family. Most children fear that if they disclosed sexual abuse, they themselves would be risking imprisonment, at the most, or becoming a social outcast, at the least. In addition, if the child is aware of any other child who disclosed abuse with traumatic results, this of itself would prevent most children from risking the same. A child who does not take the opportunity to tell, is simply a child trying to survive—a child trying to protect him- or herself the only way she knows how, by keeping the abuse secret.

## ASSESS SEVERITY OF MEMORIES

Add any shame or blame memories to the list and total the list, i.e. for example, six memories on entire list. Next ask your client which of the memories is the most traumatic and place the number of the total (six, as per example) next to that memory, for you will number these in reverse order. Then, out of the remaining memories enquire which is the next most traumatic and list it as number five (as per example). Complete the rest of the list in that way. Once you have determined the order of severity of the memories, you are ready to start with number one—the least traumatic memory on the list.

Do not determine the order of severity by starting with the least traumatic memory, for it will end depressingly with your client looking lastly at the worst memory. By starting with the worst memory and ending with the least traumatic she will feel the burden becoming lighter and more bearable.

We begin the letter series with the least traumatic memory because it is the easiest (although still difficult) for your client to face and she will have less problem with feeling overwhelmed as she starts this work. It is important to be aware that even the least traumatic memories will contain very powerful and controlling beliefs and often it happens that memory number one will be the most difficult one of the bunch. Of course, neither you nor your client will realise that until you have sorted through a few memories. However, if the first one on the list really is a whopper, do give your client the information, at that time, that minor-seeming memories can contain strong material. Otherwise she may think the others are going to be too much to face.

## WRITING EXERCISES

Now it is time to explain about the writing exercises and the fact that your client's Adult, Child and Parent are going to communicate initially through letters. Keep in mind, however, that the PICT letter series (or other letter exercises) will be used predominantly with some clients; will pave the way towards using visualisation exercises with others; and will only be used as back-up, or not at all, with the rest. It is most useful if counsellors have a full tool bag to use with clients, rather than one rigid way of working. PICT offers a variety of tools to use with the variety of clients you will encounter.

Most people experience the thought, 'I know I shouldn't feel this way, but I do!', in response to some feeling or behaviour that they want to change. Explain to your client that the writing exercises are one of the tools you will use to bridge that gap between logic and feelings. Writing exercises are an effective method for facilitating difficult change, a way of teaching the brain what to do in order to instigate change. For some clients, simply speaking or hearing statements, aloud or in their thoughts, does not always work to shift deep-seated beliefs. Writing is a slower way of working, but it is a thorough and powerful one.

Another positive aspect of the writing is that your clients do not consciously have to believe every word they are writing for it to work. They simply have to write the information correctly. Of course, you will have to re-assign letters until the altered belief is strong enough, but they do not have to believe it fully to engage initially in the writing exercise. Each time they write it, they will 'own' more of the information.

Overall, some clients will need to write more than others and some will write very little or nothing, because their change work will predominantly be done through counsellor-guided visualisation. Without some coaching or previous experience, most people find it difficult to guide themselves through visualisations of traumatic memories very effectively, particularly when they are feeling upset and confused. Writing is easiest to manage when working on your own (still difficult, however). For those reasons, writing exercises solely were used in the self-help guide, *Rescuing the 'Inner Child'*.

In this chapter we will cover the letters: how they should be written, what their effect is and when to re-assign. Sample letters from actual clients will be found in the following chapter. When clients bring an assigned letter to the session, simply ask if they would like to read it aloud or would rather you read it aloud or to yourself. Most often people choose to have the counsellor read it to him- or herself.

Make your first comment, 'Good', when you have read the letter, even if you notice evidence that suggests that it needs re-assigning. You should then ask, 'What was the most difficult part for you?' After that has been answered, ask 'What was the easiest part for you?' Those two questions ease the way into discussing the letter material and also give you useful information.

## FIRST PICT STEP—LETTER FROM:

You will ask your client to write a letter FROM the Child to the Adult about the first memory (the easiest memory) on the list he or she has made. A small paragraph from the Adult should head the letter, as in a supportive way the Adult asks the Child to write what she remembers and felt about the memory event. After leaving a small space on the paper, to separate the writings, the client must let the Child write about the memories and feelings. To begin with, the Adult may start the 'Child' writing from conscious memory, but soon the words should begin to flow spontaneously. (This information from the Child must be written in the first person, i.e. 'I went there', 'I said that', etc. rather than, 'She went there', 'She said that'.)

Once the Child has finished, again the Adult should write a small paragraph, this time thanking and praising the Child for his or her courage, and repeating that they are together in this—the Child is not alone.

The homework sheet you give the client should be written as follows: .

Letter FROM: Title of memory (i.e. Time in the shed with Uncle Harry).

1. Adult supportively asks Child to tell about her feelings and memory of the event.

2. Leaving a little space after the writing from Adult, Child writes about her feelings/memory in the first person, i.e. 'I said, I did'.

3. When Child finishes, Adult comes back (leaving space again between writings) and thanks, praises and gives support, i.e. 'Thank you for telling me what happened, it was very brave of you to face it all again. I am here for you now and I will do my best to help you feel safe and happy.'

The purpose of this letter is twofold: to give the Child the opportunity finally to tell someone (Adult) who cares and will help; and secondly, to identify the mistaken belief that the Child has developed as a result of the negative event.

When searching for the mistaken belief in the Letter FROM: it is often found within the last paragraph or the last few lines of the Child part. Sometimes it is obvious, other times it seems to defy the most determined sleuth. When it is difficult to determine, you can simply guess, as will be explained shortly. The sample letters further on will have the mistaken belief identified.

Mistaken beliefs are usually 'I' statements, but not always. You will normally have to explore to find them. You will have to make several statements to your client and observe the effect of those statements. The core mistaken belief will be the one with the most impact. Don't feel uncomfortable about doing this exploration, because no one knows what another person's response to any given situation will be, so it is literally impossible to 'know' what someone's mistaken belief might be. You might have a good guess and that is fine, but never assume your guess is correct. Always check it out with your client.

Some of the usual mistaken beliefs are:

I don't count.
My feelings don't count.
I'm not important.
It's all my fault.
I'm bad (dirty, ruined, contaminated or all of those).
I can never be safe.
No one can be trusted.
I will die if I know.
I can't tell.
I tell lies.
I make things up.
I cannot be safe.
Feelings are unsafe.
I'm not good enough.
My body is bad (dirty, ruined, etc.).
I have no control.
I cannot trust myself.
There is no safety.
There is no way out.
There is no escape.
I'm trapped with pain.
I deserve to be punished.
My feelings are bad.
I'll never have peace.
It's unsafe to be still.
I can't be angry.
I can't let the pain out.
People will always hurt me.
Hurt other people first.
I can't be known.
It's not safe to have feelings.
To be ugly (fat, smelly, etc.) is to be safe.

I'm defective.
I don't deserve happiness.
To feel is to be unsafe.
I can never be known.
I'll always be trapped with hurt, there is no way out.
I can't win.
I'll never win.
I ruin everything.

The list goes on and on. As you may notice, many beliefs sound alike, and to you one may be as good as another. This is not true. Your client's beliefs will have a certain wording and that wording is what holds the power. When you are reflecting belief suggestions to your client, you will notice when you are getting close and when it is just right her reaction will be totally congruent (i.e. her physiology and words will match).

Sometimes beliefs are double-barrelled: there will be two together; on some rare occasions there could be three (perhaps more, but three is the most I have found so far).

So, here you are reading your client's letter FROM: and wondering what in the world the mistaken belief could be. Take a guess. It does not matter where you start, even if you are 180 degrees out. Your client will tell you if it does not fit.

When you offer a belief suggestion to your client, it is most helpful to look away for a moment before you say it, pause and then ask, 'I wonder, does your belief seem like . . . [look away and pause] . . . I'm not important?' When you say the actual belief suggestion ('I'm not important'), look directly in your client's eyes and speak clearly.

If you are totally off target your client will frown, look away, shrug and say something like, 'I don't think so.' If you are near but not quite there, she will show brief recognition, then look around as though searching, make a concentration expression, look confused and say something like, 'Yes, that's sort of like it'.

When you have hit the target dead centre people will have a variety of reactions. Some will react as though they have been pushed (shoulders rearing backwards, head going back); some even start to cry; for others you will see the muscle tension in their face relax; people may go pale or red; you may notice their eyes widen and not be able to break your gaze or they will begin to look around very quickly; or they may simply look very positive about the statement, nodding their head, saying, 'Yes'. People may also say something like, 'Oh! That's it.' or 'Yes! That's just how it feels.'

You may find that you make a few suggestions and still do not get anywhere. In that case, ask your client what she thinks it might be. This is work you can do together, brainstorm until you find it. You might ask, 'What needs to be different?' 'How else could you word it?' 'What seems right to you?' 'How would you change it?' One word of advice: whatever you do—write it down once you have found it. After all that searching, later on when you are writing out the homework, you may forget what the mistaken belief was. That is very aggravating, not to mention embarrassing.

Identifying mistaken beliefs is usually difficult for people at first. However, soon you will find it easier and easier and eventually you will wonder what you used to find so difficult about it—so persevere. If you are feeling nervous about it, the first few mistaken beliefs that you uncover will probably be more exciting for you than they will be for the client. You may feel like jumping about shouting, 'I got it, I really got it!' I know I felt that way. Don't forget to say, 'Well done!' to yourself.

**Systems of Beliefs**
There are individual beliefs (one to three covering the same issue) and there are systems of beliefs. These will have some common thread that connects them (not always easily recognisable) and, on average, there may be three to six in the series. (Eleven is the highest number I have found so far.)

If there is a series of beliefs, your clients will have a different reaction to the MBV (Mistaken Belief Visualisation). They will feel some relief when you change the first belief, but not experience that totally congruent, 'Yes! That's right' feeling. You will usually become aware of this the following week when your client describes how the week has gone. If it is a system of beliefs, the person will use statements such as: 'I felt really good at first, and I haven't actually felt like I used to with the old belief, but still something stops me from really doing what I want. It's like I'm saying, "Yes, I don't have the mistaken belief, 'I don't count', any more, *but* I still can't stand up for myself."'

I usually then ask, 'So, what do you say to yourself instead of, "I don't count"?' Often the next belief in the system is right there where the old one was. The client may answer with, 'Oh, I think, "I'm just not good enough"'. At this point, explain to the person that some beliefs are part of a system and total relief will not come about until all of the beliefs are dealt with. Then tackle the next one, i.e. as in the sample, 'I'm just not good enough'.

Each belief you change will give partial relief, but when you come to the last one in the system your client will finally experience the totally congruent, 'Yes!' feeling.


SECOND PICT STEP—LETTER TO:

After discussing the letter FROM: the Child and ascertaining the mistaken belief, ask your client to do an 'Adult TO Child' letter. The two purposes of this letter are: (1) To give information, support and love, and (2) to correct the mistaken belief. The letter must contain the following five points in the following order, and the Mistaken Belief Visualisation (MBV) should be utilised by the client at point number four. The homework sheet for your client to take away should read as follows [my additional comments will be in square brackets]:

Letter TO: Name of memory (i.e. Time in the shed with Uncle Harry).

1. Acknowledge the Child's feelings as a normal reaction to the abusive situation (i.e. 'Of course, you felt frightened/angry/hurt, *any* child would feel that way. That is a normal reaction to that sort of situation.'). [You may write out an example as above or give your client a sample letter from

this book. Have your client list the actual feelings expressed in her Letter FROM:.]

2. Explain that the abuser/problem person's behaviour was wrong (i.e. 'It was wrong for Uncle Harry to touch you that way'). [Other types of examples might be: 'It was wrong for your mother to stand by and not intervene on your behalf.' 'Your brother and sister were wrong not to offer some form of comfort, instead of laughing (ignoring, blaming).' It is often very difficult for some clients to put into words that their parents were wrong. You might suggest they use the wording, 'It was not useful for your parents to . . .' or 'Your parents made a mistake'. Clients can write as much as they want about why it was wrong, but for the purpose of this letter it is only necessary to say in a sentence, 'Daddy (or whatever problem person) was wrong to . . .']

3. Describe what proper behaviour would have been like (i.e. 'Uncle Harry should have taken pleasure in showing you how his woodworking tools were used. Perhaps he should have given you a bit of wood to work on and praised your efforts and given you a proper hug. That is what an emotionally healthy person would do.') [The phrase 'emotionally healthy person' is a helpful one to suggest. You may also have to assist your client in deciding what would have been appropriate behaviour. Many people do not know what healthy parental or adult behaviour really is, others cannot think past what they imagine they deserved as a child. Explore this with them and make sure they understand the appropriate information to write before you send them off to do it.]

4. (a) Explain that as a result of this experience, and others that were similar, the Child has developed the mistaken belief of: (name the belief, e.g. 'I don't count.').

(b) Explain how that belief has affected the rest of the Child's life. [Have your clients give examples from adult life where the mistaken belief (m/b) has had a negative effect—perhaps in a work, social or relationship situation. It is best to discuss these during the session so that your clients are clear about it. It is vital to make this link between the childhood belief and present-day behaviour, because doing so assists your clients to identify that their problem behaviour is linked to the m/b and that the m/b has developed as a result of the abusive experience.]

(c) Explain how it benefited the abuser/problem person for the Child to keep the m/b. [The benefit will be similar in most letters—the problem person benefits because as long as the Child has a belief that allows her to accept poor treatment, the problem person does not have to make any changes to his own problem behaviour. If a problem person does not have the desire or ability to make change, it will be very beneficial if other family members play the game the problem person's way. So, children with mistaken beliefs (m/b) are essential in dysfunctional families for if the children had positive beliefs about themselves, they would be expecting proper treatment.

You may be asking yourself, 'Does the problem person even know that a child has a mistaken belief?' The answer is yes, but the label 'mistaken belief' will not be used. The parents or problem person will see the mistaken belief as poor or negative feelings or behaviour. Children's feelings and behaviour demonstrate their beliefs—positive or nega-. tive. If the adults in a child's life are emotionally healthy, they will want to know what is troubling a child who demonstrates negativity about self or negative behaviour. They will explore the matter with the child and get professional help if necessary. The emotionally inadequate person will find the child's negativity about self or negative behaviour a useful excuse for condemnation and blame while relieving him- or herself of personal responsibility.]

(d) Tell the Child that it is now time to give the mistaken belief back to the abuser/problem person for that is the person it really belongs to. Stop and do the visualisation. [Here your client should lay down the paper and pen and take up the Mistaken Belief Visualisation (MBV) sheet you have given her—see end of chapter for client's MBV sheet—and follow the visualisation. Explain that she should read step one, then stop and make the required images in her mind's eye. When that step is complete, she should continue with the remaining steps in the same way until the visualisation is finished.]

[Sample of how point four can be written: 'As a result of the time in the shed with Uncle Harry, and other similar times, you developed the mistaken belief that: "I don't count". This has affected the rest of your life by causing you to allow people to treat you poorly and never allowing yourself to achieve—all because you believed you didn't count, you were not as important as others. Remember how it has been during meetings at work? You always stand back and let others put forward their ideas, even when you have a very good idea, because you always think no one will want to know your idea. That is because of this mistaken belief, "I don't count". I also want you to know that it actually benefited Uncle Harry for you to have this m/b because then you would not complain or argue about his treatment of you or even think you should tell anyone else. He gave you the m/b and made sure you kept it, so that he would remain safe. But now, my sweet, it is time to give the m/b back to him for it is really his property.' At this point your client should stop and do the mistaken belief visualisation (MBV).]

5. Give support and love (i.e. 'I am here for you now and I will do my best to help you feel safe and happy. I love you.').

Writing out the homework sheet for the 'Letter TO:' takes a long time, so allow yourself extra time for this. To save time, you may want to have a printed copy of the basic format, with spaces left for writing in the specifics of each client. Also, make sure your client understands how to write the letter. Go over the steps one by one and ask if there are any questions.

**Rating the Belief**
When the letter comes back you will want to rate how much the information was believed by the Child part of your client. Sometimes a couple of letters may have to be written to the Child explaining the event before she thoroughly believes the information.

It is usually preferred for the counsellor to read the letters silently to him- or herself, but some clients will want to read their homework aloud to you or have you read it aloud to them. Ask your client for her preference. After reading and discussing the Letter TO:, ask your client, 'On a one to a hundred per cent basis, how much does the Child part believe the information?' To determine the Child's belief, a good rule of thumb is to ask how many 'Yes, but . . .' statements came to mind while your client was writing the letter, for 'Yes, but . . .' statements are usually coming from the Child. Clients are soon able to ascertain when their Adult 'logic' may have believed the information, but their Child 'feelings' did not.

If the Child's belief is below 80 per cent, re-assign the letter. However, first go over the letter asking your client on which part(s) she registered 'Yes, but . . .' statements. Discuss them again and give more information about those parts. The re-assigned letter need only cover the part(s) that was (were) not believed. However, still use the five-point format to address that part—the mistaken belief being addressed/changed will be the same one identified for the first Letter TO: on this memory event.

## USING THE MISTAKEN BELIEF VISUALISATION (MBV)

Now we will take a look at the Mistaken Belief Visualisation. When you are using the PICT letter series, this will be a part of the clients' 'Letter TO:', something they do on their own in conjunction with writing. However, it is also a useful and efficient tool for use on its own, without a 'Letter TO:', by either the client or counsellor.

I would recommend that the counsellor use the visualisation in session with the client for the first memory in order that the client's future sole use of it be made easier and more beneficial. In that instance, the client should write the 'Letter TO:' up to the point of the mistaken belief visualisation and then stop. During the next session the counsellor should use the visualisation and afterwards the client can write the last few sentences of point number five in the 'Letter TO:'.

When used by the client, she should read the first step and then visualise that, read the second step and then visualise that and so on. When used by the counsellor, he or she will simply talk the client through it as a visualisation (process described at the end of this chapter), discussing the content afterwards. Whether used by client or counsellor, the Mistaken Belief Visualisation (MBV) is a very powerful tool.

We will first go through the MBV step by step. As mentioned before you will find the separate counsellor and client versions (the wording is different for each) at the end of this chapter. Copy the counsellor's version and keep it handy for use with clients. Copy the client's version and give it as a handout for use with the 'Letter TO:'.

**MBV Point One**
*Imagine an unknown, isolated, but pleasant outside place. Now imagine yourself in your most resourceful Adult state, standing in this place. Be sure to imagine yourself associated (that means being in yourself looking out of your eyes, as opposed to looking at yourself in the scene from a distance).*

The first point involves visualising an unknown, isolated, but pleasant outside place. It needs to be outside and in an unknown, isolated place to diminish familiar associations being made or to prevent possible distractions from other people. Placing the scene in a busy town centre would not be particularly useful. Occasionally, your client may choose a place that is known, but if it does not seem to have interfered with the rest of the process, let it be. However, it would be useful to suggest to your client that the next MBV be done according to the suggested form to avoid any possible difficulties.

The resourceful Adult should be imagined in this place. Be sure that your client is associated (in the Adult) rather than looking at the adult from a distance.

**MBV Point Two**
*Imagine the problem person standing about 15 to 20 feet away.*

Point number two requires the problem person to be added to the picture and placed 15 to 20 feet away from the Adult. If your client has a very strong fear of this person, it will be helpful to have the problem person confined in a jail cell or employ 'George' [see Rescue Scene on p. 76 for an explanation of 'George'] to help out by holding the person. If the problem person cannot be imagined, it may be due to fear of that person or it may be the wrong problem person. If it is fear, and the jail cell is not enough, perhaps you can add a sack over his head, have him facing the opposite direction or perhaps place a see-through wall between them. You might simply ask your client, 'What can we do to the problem person to help you feel safe?' and offer a few of the above suggestions to indicate what you mean.

Sometimes clients find it difficult to place parents in the problem person position because their parents are now old, frail and vulnerable. 'I can't be angry or face the strong feelings I have when I look at mother/father now.' If that is the case, please remind your clients that you are asking them to address their parents as they were in the past—not as they are now. So, your clients should be making images of how their parents looked in the past, during the client's childhood years, not making images of how the parents are today.

If your clients still cannot get the problem person to appear in the picture, ask, 'Why do you think he or she is not appearing, is there any possibility it may be the wrong problem person?' If your client is sure about the identity, is not afraid of the person, is not using current images of parents, but still cannot get a picture, perhaps it is a case of difficulty with imaging. In that situation, tell your client simply to pretend to see the problem person, it will work just as well. Just pretending you can see whatever a visualisation calls for works as effectively as being able to see clear pictures. You can use the 'just pretend' tool in any visualisation context.

**MBV Point Three**
*Adult notices the Child is approaching from a different direction from the problem person, wearing a filthy, ill-fitting garment that belongs to the problem person. (There may be more than one garment if there is more than one problem person.) Imagine a banner across the garment bearing the words of*

*the mistaken belief. The Child walks up and stands next to
the Adult.*

The Adult notices the Child approaching, wearing a filthy,
ill-fitting garment (**always** use the word 'garment' for the
mistaken belief and the word 'outfit' for the new belief) that
belongs to the problem person, and has the words of the
mistaken belief on a banner across the garment. The Child
approaches and stands next to the Adult.

If a garment does not appear (although the child is there),
it may be an indication that the m/b is incorrect. Sometimes
m/bs are in layers, one attached to the next, perhaps there
is a stronger one beneath the one you have. In that case you
will need to explore further with your client to find a statement that has even more impact than the one you had. You
may find that perhaps two or more mistaken beliefs need to
be on the banner together.

The degree of grubbiness of the garment does vary greatly,
usually being an indication of the strength of the belief's
influence. The actual garment varies from things clients
remember the problem person owning to things they have
never seen before. It may be one item or several. Often the
garment is symbolic of the m/b, i.e. a very large, hooded
overcoat for the m/b 'I don't know who I am'. It could be
something as simple as a belt. It may be something shapeless,
like a filthy sheet. The words of the m/b may appear directly
on the garment, or in the shape of a banner—either way is
equally effective.

If there is more than one problem person, your client may
have a garment for each or may simply turn one garment
into several when it is thrown over to the problem people.
Either way is fine.

On one occasion when relating what happened while
doing the MBV at home, my client said that the Child would
not show up for the visualisation. This was the first time any
client had experienced this particular difficulty and I was
wondering what it meant. She had done these exercises
before, and had not found them a problem, so she was as
surprised as I was at this development. When I enquired
what exactly had happened, she said that the Adult was
there, the problem person was there, but no matter how

hard she tried the Child would not appear. She did not have a session with me scheduled for a few weeks so she made several more tries over a few days, but eventually she gave up.

When I saw her next, I could not think what her experience meant either, so I went back to the beginning of her Letter TO: and went through it, paragraph by paragraph, with her. I read the first paragraph aloud and asked, 'How did the Child feel about what was written here, were there any "Yes, buts"?' The first paragraph was fine, no problems with belief. I asked the same question with each paragraph. It went smoothly until we got to point number four in the Letter TO:, the mistaken belief. Here she said something was wrong but she couldn't tell exactly what. I said, 'Tell me what part feels wrong, even if you don't understand why.' She decided it was the actual mistaken belief, it didn't seem right. She then quickly added that she did *know* it *was* right. 'What seems wrong about it?' I asked. 'I'm not sure . . .' she replied, furrowing her brows in concentration. I then said, 'Perhaps the Child part can tell you. Just go inside yourself and ask the Child part what needs to be different.' She did this and within seconds tears started to flow and soon she said, 'It was because of me.'

It turned out that we had the m/b incomplete. It had originally been: 'People will let me down.' It needed to be changed to: 'People will let me down, because of *me*.' It needed the focus point to be that it was the Child's fault that people let her down, believing it was because of something she did or did not do. Apparently, the Child part would not cooperate until the m/b was worded accurately. I never cease to be impressed with the accuracy of the information available from the unconscious mind, if we simply make the effort to communicate with it.

During that session, I had my client rewrite the m/b on her 'Letter TO:' and rewrite the section of how the m/b affected the rest of her life. I would have guided her through the MBV but she preferred to do it at home on her own. I assigned the MBV and the Rescue Scene for homework. When she returned for the next session she reported that she sailed through the MBV, with no problems at all.

**MBV Point Four**
*The Adult now removes the garment from the Child, screws it up and throws it at the problem person. The problem person is compelled to put the garment on (m/b banner attached), the Adult and Child watch and see that it fits the problem person perfectly. Notice whatever reaction the problem person may have.*

Now the Adult has removed the grubby garment, screwed it up and thrown it over to the problem person (with assistance from the Child if desired). This is the most likely point for people to have difficulties. Sometimes they cannot get the garment off the Child, or if they do, another one appears. Often they cannot throw the garment, it will not leave their hand or it falls very short of the problem person.

This is usually an indication that more needs to be written or explained (reframed) concerning the fact that the m/b belongs to the problem person; or there may be a second m/b that was not noticed. Discuss these points and give more information. You may want to assign the 'Letter TO:' which solely focuses on the fact that the m/b really belongs to the problem person; or verbally explore to discover a second m/b. Once the difficulties are solved, you can finish the MBV with your client during the session or, if she prefers, she can do it at home.

If the problem person does not put the garment on, it usually indicates that again more work needs to be done on the fact that the m/b really belongs to him or her. Discuss it, give more information until your client is congruent (physiology and words match—more explanation in Chapter Five), or if necessary, re-assign another 'Letter TO:' covering that point to obtain congruency.

The reaction of the problem person after putting the garment on will vary and generally fit in with the client's understanding of the person. You can reflect this back to the client—this information is generally not noticed by the client and her or she normally finds it helpful to know.

## MBV Point Five

*The Adult asks the Child if there is anything he or she needs to say to the problem person, reassuring him or her that it can be shouted if needed (i.e. 'You are wrong!' 'NO!' 'Take it back!')*

Not everyone's Child will need to say anything to the problem person, but sometimes there will be a message the Child needs to impart. Sometimes the Adult may want to first assure the Child that he or she will keep the Child safe from the problem person as the Child says or shouts whatever needs to be said. When you are running the MBV during the session, you may find that some clients want to say the message aloud. Please respect that.

## MBV Point Six

*After the filthy garment is removed, the Adult and Child notice that the Child's skin and hair are now glowingly clean and the Child's hair is combed just the way he or she likes.*

Frequently, this step is overlooked by clients when they do the MBV on their own. 'Oh, I missed that one somehow!' they exclaim in surprise. Again, if the rest of the points run smoothly, let it be. However, when this point is completed by the client, she experiences a strong sense of well-being. This is not absolutely necessary, but it is nice to have—more icing.

## MBV Point Seven

*The Adult now produces an outfit that is just the Child's size, in the Child's favourite colour and favourite style. The Adult puts the outfit on the Child, then steps back to take a moment to determine if anything else needs to be added to the outfit and if so, adds it. Next imagine a banner across the Child's new outfit and then watch the words of the new positive belief appear on the banner. This new belief needs to be positively stated and in the first person, i.e. 'I am innocent', instead of 'It's not her fault'.*

The new outfit represents the new positive belief about self. Only use the word 'outfit' for the new belief. It does not matter how many times you repeat the word 'outfit', but it would make a negative difference if you used the word 'garment' for the new belief.

Clients usually see the words identifying the new belief appear on the banner, but on rare occasions they become aware of them later on. That does not stop the new belief from being evidenced in their life.

The inability to produce an outfit or put it on the Child usually means your client has not been able to imagine him- or herself without the old m/b. Discuss how she will be without the m/b, until she seems congruent with the information, i.e. 'What do you see yourself doing when the m/b is gone?' 'What do you hear yourself saying?' 'What will you feel like?'

The more elaborate and accessorised the new outfit is, the more this usually indicates that the new positive belief has taken hold.

If your client's new belief is negatively stated, i.e. 'It's not my fault', ask him or her to reword it in a positive statement. To help in this effort you might ask, 'If it is not your fault, what does that make you?' The likely answer would be, 'I'm innocent'; have your client then change the new belief to, 'I'm innocent.'

If your client's new belief is worded in the third person, i.e. 'She's innocent', ask her to change it to a first person statement, i.e. 'I'm innocent'.

**MBV Point Eight**
*Now take a few moments for the Adult and Child to celebrate the new belief properly, in whatever way seems best. Remember that the new outfit is magical and will remain clean, so any rolling about in grass, dirt or splashing about in water is completely acceptable. Make this celebration as free and expressive as desired.*

Now it is time for the celebration. Adult and Child may take hands and skip about, jump around individually while whooping and shouting, or they may simply hug each other and laugh. The more expressive they are is sometimes an indication of the strength of the Adult/Child bond or may also be an example of congruency concerning the new belief.

**MBV Point Nine**
*After the celebration, Adult and Child take hands and walk in the opposite direction from wherever the problem person was standing—walking down a path towards the sunshine. Take a moment to observe the path and surroundings, notice what you see, what you hear and what you feel. This path represents your future.*

After the celebration, the Adult and Child take hands and walk down a path. This path is symbolic of the future with the new belief. Some people will see winding, difficult paths, others will see wide beautiful ones—this often reflects how they evaluate their personal inner resources.

**MBV Point Ten**
*Pause for a moment on the path, and observe a large screen that has appeared before you. Adult and Child watch the screen as three scenes from likely future events unfold, revealing successful interactions available from today onwards with the new positive belief in place. These future events may be work, social or relationship situations. Adult and Child watch these three positive events with excitement and happiness.*

If your client has a problem seeing the large screen where future events take place showing the new belief in action, it probably means the new belief needs a bit of reinforcing. You may ask, 'What has to be true (or what has to happen) for you to be able to see the new belief in action?' It may also mean the new belief could use a better wording. Whatever information your client gives you, act on it and fix the block so your client can see the results on the large screen.

**MBV Point Eleven**
*Have a photograph taken, in vivid colour, of the Adult and Child happily watching the successful future interactions. Give the photograph to the Child. Adult and Child hug lovingly and the Child merges into the Adult—into his or her safe place. Remember that any time you have an occasion to wait (doctor's surgery, bus stop, etc.), you can access the photograph and again experience that special occasion.*

Now the photograph is taken. This is simply a lovely

memento of this event. It is an opportunity for your client to have something beautiful from that experience to treasure. It is a magical photograph, one that has all the feelings, sights and sounds of the original experience. It is a useful tool when stuck waiting somewhere with nothing to do. The Child is given the photograph. Adult and Child hug and the Child then merges with the Adult, into his or her safe place. Any merging difficulty is usually a bonding difficulty. The exercise can still be a success even if this happens. Explain to your client that with some people the bonding takes longer than with others.


## MISTAKEN BELIEF VISUALISATION SAMPLE

Alice chose to write out her Mistaken Belief Visualisation. It was so delightful that I felt it needed to be included here. You will notice that Alice deviated from the format of the Mistaken Belief Visualisation, although she kept the main pieces there. As a result, I have incorporated some of those changes into the way we did the visualisation at that time. As we experimented with the MBV to see just what effects are possible, I have added even more changes. The PICT method is simply a model and I encourage counsellors to fine tune it according to their client's needs and according to their own intuition.

You will also notice that Alice uses lower case letters when writing the abuser's name (uncle jimmy). As that breaks the rule of punctuation we were taught in school, 'Capitals for all proper names', it becomes a nice little tool to diminish the power/status of the abuser. It is a play on words to say that the abuser has not behaved in a proper manner and therefore his or her name does not deserve a capital letter. It is simple, but nonetheless powerful.

### Alice's Mistaken Belief Visualisation

I went off to the place where I had to meet Little Alice. It was a big, white place, stretching as far as the eye could see, with some large objects in it. I had my magic basket.

The first object I came to looked like a large sack. As I got closer, I could see that it was made of old clothes

... no, it wasn't! It was someone wearing a huge, huge straitjacket with the sleeves strapped across his chest, a pair of shoes far too big for him and a trapper hat.

The hat was huge and came over the person's ears. The peak rested on the bridge of his nose. I gently took the peak of the hat between my thumb and forefinger and lifted it up. Two brown, frightened eyes looked back at me, blinking in the sudden onrush of light.

'Hello', I said.

'Pleh, pleh', said the person.

I didn't understand.

I looked at the rest of the body. The shoes were far too big and the person was not wearing socks. His ankles were red and chafed where the shoes had rubbed.

I lifted the peak of the cap again and said, 'Who are you?' I looked into the eyes and suddenly recognised the person.

'You're Little Alice, aren't you?'

'Sey, sey. Pleh, pleh. Yppahnu os m'i. Em pleh esaelp.'

I realised what was happening.

Little Alice indicated with an elbow something away to her right. I turned and saw a nasty, tall, skinny, greasy man holding up a hand with a finger raised in warning. I turned back to Little Alice and she looked at me pleadingly. 'Em pleh. Em deppart s'eh. Ytsan s'eh. Pleh.'

I took her hat off. I unbuckled the straitjacket. I pulled off the too big shoes.

I threw the shoes at the man and hit him squarely on the head. I threw the straitjacket at him and it landed on him, smothering him and knocking him over. I spun the cap round on my finger and it landed on the man as well.

The straitjacket was not trying to smother him. It was trying to get on him, so it could be worn by him. It was as if the jacket were trying to put the man on, more than the man putting the jacket on. The shoes and the cap were doing the same. They all succeeded. They fitted perfectly. Tailor-made. Obviously really his.

Meanwhile, Little Alice was shivering in her vest and knickers. I looked in my basket and found:

A pink satin petticoat with lace and bows,
white lace tights,
a red tartan dress with smocking, lace collar and red sash,
black, patent leather shoes,
a red hair ribbon and
a bottle of Gardenia perfume.

I dressed her and dabbed some perfume behind her ears. She looked at me and then smothered me in a hug. 'It was me all the time,' she said. 'Yes, I soon realised,' I said.

'No one could understand me,' she said.

'No,' I said, 'You were talking backwards. That was so that even if you did try to tell, no one would be able to know what you were saying.' She caught my hand and said, 'There's something else that isn't right,' and set off at a run, pulling me after her.

We came to some words carved out of big blocks of stone. One set was beside the man with the straitjacket. They read, 'YOU MUST NOT TELL'. They were about eight foot tall and one foot wide.

Reaching into my basket, I got out some Semtex explosive, a fuse and a detonator box with a plunge handle. I ran to the back of the words and placed the explosive, set the fire and brought the detonator box back. I counted 'One, two, three . . . GO!' and Little Alice plunged the handle and the words blew up and rained down in 60,000,000 pieces, burying the straitjacket man as they did so. 'Hurrah!' yelled Little Alice, jumping up and down and clapping her hands.

Then, she grabbed my hand and pulled me away again. 'There's some more,' she said. The next set read, 'ALICE TELLS LIES', and leaning against one end were mummy, daddy, nana and mandy, all drinking cups of tea. They looked down their noses at Alice. Nana just raised one eyebrow and sniffed, 'Hmmmmm!'

'Right,' I said, 'We'll sort this one out too.' I took ⌐
some more Semtex and fuses and another detonato⌐
up the explosive and Little Alice pushed t⌐
again. (She counted the 'one, two, three'⌐
words exploded and so did mum⌐
nana. Bits of stone and chi⌐
made of) came clatte⌐

Little Alice whooped ⌐
excited. Dancing around she wa⌐
and jumped. She took both my hands and we skipped
around in a circle and jumped about until all the thrill and
exhilaration had been celebrated properly. Then we sat
down and I looked in the basket and found a nice picnic.

While we ate and drank, I explained that the too big
clothes had really belonged to the straitjacket man who
was uncle jimmy. He had made her believe that silence
was safety and to tell was wrong. He had even made extra
sure that she couldn't tell by making her talk backwards
so that she couldn't make people understand even if she
did try.

The stone words were what uncle jimmy and the family
wanted to believe and had forced Little Alice to believe
too. However, we knew better. We believed the truth and
knew that it was safe to tell. We were strong and powerful
and could destroy their stupid beliefs.

Little Alice was fresh, free and smelling deliciously of
gardenias. She could tell whatever she chose now, knowing that she would be believed and be safe.

THE END
Or is it the Beginning?

## THIRD PICT STEP—RESCUE SCENE

This time your client will be asked to write a Rescue Scene.
Your client, as an Adult, will powerfully enter the memory
scene, stop the abuse and tell off the problem person. He
or she will comfort the Child using words, touching, smiling
or all three. He will then take the Child to a safe and happy
place, which must be described.

The purpose of the Rescue Scene is to provide a buffer for the original painful memory and consequently desensitise the memory. Your clients will never forget what originally happened, but the Rescue Scene will act as a buffer, because after writing the Rescue they will never remember the original event without automatically bringing forward the Rescue Scene as well. The Rescue will have feelings of victory and accomplishment attached to it and will therefore desensitise the original memory.

The Rescue Scene homework sheet should be written as follows:

Rescue Scene: Name the event (i.e. Time in the shed with Uncle Harry).

1. The Adult steps back into that situation as the most powerful person in the scene, stops the abuse, comforts the child and tells off the abuser/problem person. [Clients usually kick in the door, slam the door open and have sometimes crashed through walls—whatever the choice, the Adult needs to present as a super-hero might. Stopping the abuse is usually done by shouting something or pushing/hitting the abuser/problem person. It is most useful if the Adult hugs, holds or comfortingly touches the Child to comfort her/him.]

2. The Child must see that the Adult is there just for her/him. [This is important to ensure that this letter is about someone finally coming for the Child and does not become a letter that is primarily about punishing the abuser/problem person—anger letters are the best format for doing that. Therefore, the Adult's focus must be on rescuing and comforting the Child. Although words or actions are displayed to the abuser/problem person, it must not be to the degree that the Child is left as an afterthought. The Child needs to recognise that the Adult is there especially for her/him and receives verbal or physical exchange of affection.]

3. The Adult takes the Child to a safe and happy place and describes that place. [Give some suggestions to clients of the safe and happy place: 'A park, a fun fair, a pond or lake, a country walk or perhaps your house—not the house

you live in now or perhaps have ever lived in, but "your house".' How your client and the Child get to this place is irrelevant, explain that they can just suddenly 'be there'. The description of the safe and happy place is usually a lovely symbolic description of the person's inner resources. The PICT Training Course explains how generally to decipher the symbolic language used and therefore be able to reflect that information back to the client. Reflecting back that information is not needed for your client's recovery, it is just a bit more icing on the cake.]

## POINTS TO REMEMBER

Each memory's Rescue Scene is carried out afresh, as though no other Rescue Scenes have been written. Occasionally, your client may have quite a bit of retaliation written into the Rescue. As long as she is keeping the Child close to her, in a comforting role, while she doles out punishment to the problem person you do not need to re-assign the exercise. The Child benefits from seeing the Adult standing up for her against the problem person. However, if the Adult has left the Child off in the corner while she spends masses of time 'punishing' the problem person, then you will need to re-assign the Rescue Scene. It would be best for your client to use an anger letter to punish, not the Rescue Scene.

## CHILD FANTASY ESCAPE

When assigning the Rescue Scene, in some cases, you may also want to assign a visualisation where the Child escapes from the memory scene solely on his or her own. In these escapes the Child may use 'magic' to assist (otherwise your client may not be able to figure out a way for the Child to liberate herself). This magic may take the form of toys that come to life to help the Child, adults who become 'frozen' and unable to move, or the Child may suddenly have 'super powers'.

This exercise gives the Child part an opportunity to experience a feeling of power over the memory and therefore it is important that the Child (not others) wield whatever magical power there is. This exercise may be assigned at the same time as the Adult Rescue, and is suggested for use particularly with those clients who have a greater need to experience personal power.

Magic is not usually used in the Adult Rescue because we are trying to establish a bond and trust between the Adult and Child part, not trust between the Child and magic. Magic can be used with the Child Fantasy Escape because the Child is in command of the magic, using her own power of command, rather than magical things just happening arbitrarily.


## 'GEORGE'

On occasion your client may be so afraid of the problem person that the Adult cannot even imagine coming powerfully in at the door, stopping the abuse or telling off the problem person. When this happens, introduce 'George'.

George is a six foot gorilla. He represents your client's personal power. He cannot speak and he cannot take any action without instruction from the Adult. Therefore, responsibility for all action and words stays with your client. She or he must tell George, for instance, to kick in the door and restrain the abuser, for George cannot take any action without instruction. All 'telling off' must also be the client's job, because George cannot speak. George's function is simply to exercise physical force (at the command of the Adult, not of his own volition) to enable the Adult to carry out the Rescue.

When the scene to be entered involves a group of people who are all very terrifying to the client, for instance, ritualistic abuse, I suggest the client use 'George and his friends'—in other words, a group of gorillas. The same rules apply—none of the gorillas can speak or act on their own initiative.

If for any reason your client has a problem with gorillas, simply ask what powerful animal (not person) would be most suitable, and use that animal in George's place. If there is a problem with the name 'George', ask what name would be suitable.

## NEW MEMORIES

It is not unusual for new memories, of which your client was not previously aware, to surface during therapy. These memories are often more traumatic than the others (that is why they were repressed). On some occasions your client will want, and need, to deal with the new memories immediately, but when possible, add them to the end of the list.

## SIBLING ABUSERS

Sibling abuse is just as damaging and hurtful as abuse at the hands of adults. Most juveniles who abuse have already been abused themselves. That may mean someone in the immediate family has abused them, but it could just as easily be someone outside the family. In most cases, the sibling abuser is able to continue with his or her abusing because the immediate family is dysfunctional. Therefore, when doing the letters, or simply giving information, the parents should be shown to share responsibility for the abuse. Anger and responsibility will be given to the sibling, but it also needs to be given to the parents for not creating an atmosphere for the child to 'tell' and to receive support.

### Parents Share Responsibility

Often clients believe that their parents could not help or take time to listen because they were so burdened down with problems, had to work, had too many children, were ill, etc. In other words, they believe their parents had no choice. It is important to point out that many parents have that same list of problems and still make time to help and listen. It is not the list of problems in the way, it is the parents' *ability* to help or listen. It is important for clients to realise that parents do have a choice about finding help to improve their lives; it is children who do not have choices.

Explain to clients that whether parents have useful parenting abilities or not, they still have to take the responsibility for mistakes they make. They may have problems because of their own experiences during childhood, but that does not remove responsibility for their actions in adulthood. It may seem unfair, but once we turn 18 we automatically become responsible for our actions.

During my own childhood I was emotionally, physically and sexually abused. As a result, I had many emotional problems. I was not responsible for what was done to me before 18, and I had no choices or real power to make changes in my life. I was not responsible for the problems I had, it was not my fault. However, when the magical age of 18 arrived, suddenly the responsibility shifted onto me. I still was not responsible for what happened to me in the past, but I was now responsible for doing something about it. I was responsible for changing whatever behaviour problems I had as a result of the childhood experiences. I was also responsible for any future actions, even if they were the result of the damage from my childhood.

When my own children arrived, I still had not been able to make enough changes to enable me to be a healthy parent. Therefore, I was unable to keep an even emotional balance and would behave violently and abusively towards them. I must take responsibility for those abusive actions, even though they were a result of the damage I had received during childhood. It was important for me to say I was *wrong* and I was *sorry*.

Most people have never heard their parents say, 'I was wrong' or 'I am sorry'. That is unfortunate because those two statements would go a long way towards repairing some very deep rifts in families. Parents can explain why they have the unwanted behaviour (a result of childhood experiences), but they cannot use it as an excuse to remove responsibility.

When my daughters were about ten and 12 years old, I explained to them about my childhood experience and explained how I felt and behaved as a result of it. I went on to tell them that I still had some of those poor behaviours and was working to be rid of them. I also said that those behaviours were *wrong* for parents to have and that I was *wrong* to behave in those ways. I told them I was *sorry* that they were suffering because of my problems. I explained that how I behaved was not their fault, it was mine—they

were not responsible for my abusive behaviour. I went on
to explain the situation in a metaphor:

> When people are born, they have an inner garden.
> Some people's garden is full of flowers, some full of weeds
> and others a little bit of both. Each of us inherits our inner
> garden from our parents and then it is our responsibility
> to make what we will of it. No one can do our gardening
> for us, we each have to do our own.
>
> When grandma was born her garden had a lot of weeds.
> Unfortunately, grandma was not too good at tidying her
> garden and so when I was born there were still a number
> of weeds for me to inherit. I worked on those weeds and
> removed some of them and also planted a few strong
> flowers, but I was not fast enough to get all the weeds
> removed before you were born.
>
> Now you have inherited those remaining weeds and it
> is your responsibility to do some inner garden tidying.
> You have a few strong flowers to encourage and cheer
> you and you may be able to pull out all the weeds before
> you have children. However, if you do not, the weeds that
> remain will be passed on to your children and it will then
> be their responsibility to finish the job.
>
> I hope you too will add a few more strong flowers to
> give encouragement and cheer. I am sorry I was not able
> to do more effective gardening so that you would have a
> better inheritance, but I am happy that I can at least
> explain the gardening task before you, and I will always
> be happy to give any information you need. Perhaps in a
> few generations our family will be able to produce children
> whose inheritance will be lovely flower-filled inner
> gardens.

When I say that parents need to say 'Sorry', I am not
suggesting that 'Sorry' makes the abuse okay. 'Sorry' does
not wipe out responsibility, nor does it take any pain away.
However, parents need to express regret about their abusive
actions and their children (young or grown) need to hear it.
When parents offer 'Sorry', it should be with the intention
of expressing regret. **It is not for the purpose of hearing their**

**offspring offer forgiveness.** This is not an exercise for the victim of abuse to sooth the guilt problems of an abuser, it is an exercise for the abuser to admit guilt and remorse.

Working with sibling abuse will mean sharing the responsibility with sibling abuser and parents. Examples of sibling work will be found in the following chapter in 'Sally's' letters.

## SPACING OF THE LETTERS

When you assign any of the letters, take time to be sure your client understands the directions for carrying out the assignment. Write down the instructions and check that the person can read your writing. If you do not have time to do this, leave the assignment until the next session.

**Letter FROM:**
When the assignment is given, the client will go home to do it. If it is the Letter FROM:, tell your client to wait until the last day before the next session before writing the assignment. This letter's focus is the abusive experience and that brings up the associated negative feelings; it is not very comfortable for your client to carry those around for a long time. Doing the homework just before seeing you will cut down on that carrying time.

When your client comes back with the Letter FROM:, you will need to read through it to find the mistaken belief. When you have found it, you will be ready to assign the Letter TO:. Without knowing the mistaken belief, the Child's expressed feelings, and the abuser/problem person's behaviour, as described in the Letter FROM:, you would have very little accurate information correctly to assign the Letter TO:. For this reason, it would not be wise to assign the letter series all in one lump or even two together.

**Letter TO:**
When you receive the Letter TO: you will need to assess how much the letter was believed by the Child part. If that degree of belief is not high enough, you will need to re-assign the letter. You can see that if you had assigned the letter

series as a whole, you would not have completed the work properly because your client would not 'own' the information.

If there were any hiccups on the Mistaken Belief Visualisation, you will need to discuss them, give further information and re-assign the Letter TO: covering that information. If, however, you had assigned the letter series as a whole, your client would not have disconnected the mistaken belief and you would be moving on to the next memory without properly completing the work. Therefore, do not assign the next step in the letter series until you are sure that you have appropriately completed the letter at hand.

The Letter TO: can be done by the client the day after receiving the assignment, if desired, because it gives the much needed information, support and love *and* disconnects the mistaken belief. Your client will feel good after completing it. However, having said that, most clients tend to wait until the last moment to do any of the assignments.

**Rescue Scene**

After you have made sure that the mistaken belief is changed and the Child belief is high enough, you are ready to go on to the Rescue Scene. The Rescue Scene can also be done by clients immediately after being assigned if desired, because it gives a lot of pleasure and clients are left feeling good. However, do not assign the Letter FROM: for the next memory on the client's list to be done with the Rescue Scene, because you do not yet know if the Rescue may need to be re-assigned.

You should allow three sessions, minimum, to run the PICT letter series, but of course, if anything needs to be re-assigned then that time slot will be lengthened.

Whenever you assign written homework, please explain to clients that you are not interested in their spelling or grammatical abilities. Also explain that there is no way they can fail with the homework, because whatever is done will give you useful and important information and that is what you are looking for. Explain that you will learn something important even if they cannot actually do the homework at all, because whatever stopped them from writing the homework will be useful information for you. Most people go back to negative school experiences when you use the word 'homework', so please take time to redefine the word in this manner.

**Never correct spelling** or make comments on sentence structure. If you cannot read the person's writing at all, ask them to read it to you. If you cannot work out a few words, simply ask your client to tell you what those words are. It is not appropriate to play 'teacher' games with your clients.

## PICT STEPS REVIEW

Below are listed basic points to remember about the three PICT steps, the Child Fantasy Escape and the use of 'George'.

### Step One—Letter FROM:
— Adult asks Child to tell about specific memory (from the list).
— Child then writes (in first person) about his or her feelings/memory.
— Adult thanks and praises child for telling, promising support.
— A space should be left on the paper between Adult and Child writings.
— This letter gives the Child a chance to tell someone who really cares and will believe her about the traumatic event/memory—something every child who has faced frightening events needs to do. This letter contains the mistaken belief.

### Step Two—Letter TO:
— Adult writes to Child explaining the following five points.

1. The Child's feelings (regardless of content) are a normal reaction to the abusive situation.
2. The abuser's behaviour was wrong and the abuse was not the Child's fault.
3. What the proper behaviour from the abuser should have been like.
4. How this event (and perhaps others like it) created a

specific mistaken belief about self, how the mistaken belief has affected adult life, that the mistaken belief actually belongs to the problem person and how it benefited him for Child to 'own' the belief—also include Mistaken Belief Visualisation at the end of explanation.

5. Adult gives support and love.

— This letter helps change the Child's mistaken beliefs about him- or herself and consequently stops self-sabotaging behaviour. Every child who has experienced confusing situations wants and needs correct information to be given in a supportive and loving manner.

**Step Three—Rescue Scene**
— Adult must be most powerful person in scene.
— Adult may use 'George', the six foot gorilla, when his or her own personal power is developing, but only as directed.
— Adult steps powerfully into the scene before (or just as) the 'bad' thing happens—stops abuse, tells off abuser, comforts Child.
— Child must see that the Adult is there just for his or her rescue (not to engage in lengthy disputes with abuser, an anger letter should be used for that purpose).
— Include some affectionate interaction between Adult and Child (words, gestures, smiles).
— Adult takes Child to safe and happy place and describes this.
— This letter gives the Child the feeling that someone is finally on his or her side, someone has finally come for her or him. This is something that every child in trouble wants to happen. The combination of the three letters desensitises the traumatic memory.

**Child Fantasy Escape**
— In addition to the written Adult Rescue, sometimes it is helpful to assign a visualisation fantasy escape solely achieved by the Child (Adult is not present). This is particularly useful for clients who have very little personal power.

— Child may use the assistance of magic (i.e., people 'glued to floor', magic wands to stop people, lightning bolts to stop people, powerful beams from eyes to influence people, super powers, etc.) to escape the abuser in a memory scene.
— This exercise gives a sense of empowerment.

### 'George'
— A six foot gorilla representing the client's personal power.
— George cannot take action of his own volition, Adult must give commands.
— George cannot speak, Adult must do all the speaking.
— George can only perform physical tasks, i.e. break down doors, restrain people, silence people, kill people, etc.
— Several George gorillas may be used if there are several problem people.

## MISTAKEN BELIEF VISUALISATION FOR CLIENT'S USE

The following wording is designed for the client to use on his or her own. The client's work with a counsellor will disconnect the major limiting beliefs, but there will no doubt be less significant mistaken beliefs surfacing as time goes on, which the client can then deal with personally. I therefore give clients this copy to use with the 'Letter TO:', and to keep for use on their own, should they wish, whenever they think they have recognised a mistaken belief. The copy begins with a paragraph to remind them of the importance of the m/b being worded properly and reminds them that the problem person's identity is not essential.

### Mistaken Belief Visualisation
You must have the correct wording for the mistaken belief (m/b) before you begin this exercise; remember it will be the phrase that has the most emotional impact. (Sample: 'I'm not important.') Then ask yourself, 'Who did I *first* learn this from?' That person will be the problem person in the exercise (there may be more than one person). If

you cannot access the identity of the person, simply use a shadowy form of a genderless person. Sometimes the identity or gender will manifest while doing the exercise, but if not, it does not diminish the effectiveness of the exercise if you do not know from whom you first learned the m/b.

1. Imagine an unknown, isolated, but pleasant outside place. (Unknown, so that you will avoid making associations to other events; isolated, so that you will not have unwanted distractions; pleasant, so that you will connect 'change' with 'pleasant'.) Now imagine yourself, in your most resourceful Adult state, standing in this place. Be associated in the Adult (looking out of your own eyes as opposed to seeing yourself from a distance).

2. Imagine the problem person standing about 15 to 20 feet away. See this person as he was when you were a child, **not** as he is now. (*Note*: If there is a strong fear of the problem person then imagine him confined in a jail cell or use 'George' for protection.)

3. Next the Adult notices the Child approaching (from a different direction than the location of the problem person) wearing a filthy, ill-fitting garment that belongs to the problem person. There can be more than one garment if there is more than one problem person, or just one garment, for this garment represents the mistaken belief. The garment may be something remembered that actually belonged to the problem person or not. Do not struggle with this, just let a garment appear. Next, imagine a banner across the garment bearing the words of the m/b (i.e. 'I'm not important'. If appropriate, the words can be written on the garment rather than on a separate banner). Wearing the garment the Child walks up and stands next to the Adult.

4. The Adult now removes the garment from the Child, screws it up and throws it at the problem person (both Adult and Child may throw the garment together if desired). The problem person is compelled to put the garment on, the Adult and Child watch and see that the garment (with the m/b banner) fits the problem person

perfectly. Notice whatever reaction the problem person may have to the garment.

5. Adult asks Child if there is anything he or she needs to say to the problem person, i.e. 'You are wrong!' 'Take it back!' 'NO!' Adult also asks the Child if this message needs to be shouted. Then allow the Child to shout or say whatever message is important. (This can be done totally within the visualisation or you may let the Child use your voice to say it aloud.)

6. After the filthy garment is removed, the Adult and Child notice that the Child's skin and hair are now glowingly clean and the Child's hair is combed just the way he or she likes.

7. The Adult now produces an outfit that is just the Child's size, in the Child's favourite colour and favourite style. The Adult puts the outfit on the Child, then steps back to take a moment to determine if anything else needs to be added and, if so, adds it. Next imagine a banner across the Child's new outfit and then watch the words of the new *positive* belief appear.

When you have completed step seven, take a moment and jot down the words of the new belief. (Occasionally, the banner will remain blank and the words will come to mind later. If that is the case, just accept it, for either way is equally effective, because the conscious mind does not have to know the new belief for results to happen.)

8. Now take a few moments for the Adult and Child to *celebrate* the new belief properly, in whatever way seems best. Remember that the new outfit is magical and will remain clean, so any rolling about in grass, dirt or splashing about in water is completely acceptable. Make this celebration as free and expressive as desired; utilise laughter, whooping and shouting, dancing about, fireworks, or whatever you choose.

9. After the celebration, Adult and Child take hands and walk in the opposite direction from the problem person—down a lovely path towards the sunshine. Take a moment to observe the path and surroundings, notice what you see, notice what you hear and notice what you feel—this path represents your future.

10. Pause for a moment on the path, and observe as a large screen appears before you. Adult and Child watch the screen as a few scenes from likely future events unfold (perhaps from social, work or relationship situations) revealing successful interactions available, from today onwards, with the new positive belief in place. Adult and Child are happy and excited to see the upcoming successes.

11. Take a photograph, in vivid colour, of the Adult and Child happily watching the successful future interactions. Give the photograph to the Child. Then both embrace and while doing so allow the Child to merge into the Adult, stepping inside to his or her safe place.

Remember, as you come back to the present, whenever you have an occasion to wait (doctor's surgery, bus stop, etc.) you can access the photograph and again see the Adult and Child happily observing the results of changing to the new belief. You can again experience that occasion—seeing what you saw, hearing what you heard and feeling what you felt.

## MISTAKEN BELIEF VISUALISATION FOR COUNSELLOR'S USE

Follow this outline until you know it by heart, do not try using the MBV in a haphazard way or you will get poor results. It does not put clients off for you to hold a piece of paper for reference as you work, unless you behave in an embarrassed or unprofessional manner.

Eyes can be closed or open, whichever suits the person. Your voice needs to be relaxed; speak clearly and at a slower pace. Do **not** speak in a monotone or very soft voice, put appropriate expression in your voice—use your voice as the important tool it is.

1. 'Imagine an unknown, isolated, but pleasant outside place and let me know when you have that image.' [Wait for client's response] 'Good. Now imagine yourself in your most resourceful Adult state, standing in this place. Be associated, in other words, be in your body looking out of

your eyes, as opposed to watching yourself from a distance
. . . Let me know when you are there.' [Wait for response]
'Good.'

2. 'Now imagine the problem person [name this person
i.e. your father] standing about 15 to 20 feet away. See this
person [your father] as he was when you were a child, **not**
as he is now.' [If client indicates fear of problem person, give
further information about using 'George' or placing problem
person in a jail cell.] 'Let me know when you have that
image . . .' [Wait for nod] . . . 'Good.'

3. 'Now, looking in a different direction from the problem
person, you notice the younger you approaching. You see
that he or she is wearing a filthy, ill-fitting garment that
belongs to the problem person [your father]. You are aware
that this garment represents the mistaken belief, in fact, you
can see the words of the mistaken belief [quote belief, i.e.
'I'm not good enough'] on a banner across the Child's chest.
Let me know when you have that image' . . . 'Good.'

4. 'As the Child comes up to you, remove the garment,
screw it up and toss it over to the problem person [your
father]. You and the Child observe as the problem person
puts it on and you both notice that it fits him or her perfectly.
Let me know when that is complete' . . . 'Good.'

5. 'Ask the Child if there is anything he or she needs to
say, any message s/he needs to give to the problem person
[your father]. If there is, allow the Child to do so, assuring
him or her that the message can be shouted if he or she
wants to, for you are there to support him or her. Let me
know when that is complete' . . . 'Good.'

6. 'Now, turning your back on the problem person [your
father], you and the Child notice that the Child's skin and
hair are now glowingly clean. In fact, his or her hair is
combed/styled just the way he or she likes it best.' [As you
go along you may not need to continue to ask clients to
indicate when the picture is complete, for they usually indicate it to you spontaneously. Of course, if at any point they
seem to have forgotten to indicate, simply say, 'Let me know
when you've done that'.]

7. 'You now produce an outfit that is just the Child's size,
in his or her favourite colour and favourite style. Put this

new outfit on the Child.' [Wait for a nod] 'Now stand back a few steps and see if there is anything else that needs to be added. If there is, please do so and let me know when you've done that' . . . 'Good.'

'Now, place a new, clean banner across the Child's chest, and then stand back and watch the words of the new, positive belief appear—let me know when you see the words' . . . 'Good. What are the words?' 'Very good.' [*Write down the words of the new belief.* **Note**: If your client has a negatively stated sentence, i.e. 'I'm not bad.', ask her or him to state it in the positive. 'If you are not bad, what are you?' The response may be, 'I'm good'. When you have a positively stated new belief ask her or him to see the positive belief on the new banner. If your client has a belief stated in the third person, i.e. 'She is good.', ask him or her to state it in the first person, i.e. 'I am good.', and then see that statement on the new banner.]

8. 'Now it is time for you and the Child to properly celebrate the new belief, [state the words, i.e. 'I am good']. Remember that if the celebration requires rolling about or splashing in water, the new outfit is magical and will brush right off—so make this celebration as free and expressive as you desire. Let me know when the celebration is complete' . . . 'Good.'

9. 'You and the Child take hands and walk in the opposite direction to wherever the problem person [ your father] was standing, noticing a path open up before you. As you take a moment to notice the path and its surroundings, you are aware that this path represents your future. Just be aware of the path . . . what you see . . . what you hear . . . and what you feel . . . let me know when you have done that' . . . 'Good.'

10. 'As you and the Child begin to walk down the path, you are delighted to see a large cinema screen appear before you. You both watch the screen in curious anticipation as three likely future events featuring you, the Adult, unfold on the screen. These events may be social, work or relationship situations, but each one reveals the successful interactions available, from today onwards, with the new positive belief in place. Just observe these three events and let me know

when they are complete' . . . [Wait for nod] . . . 'Good.'

11. 'It is time to have a photograph taken of you and the Child happily watching the upcoming successes on the screen.' [Wait for nod] 'Now give that photograph to the Child.' [Wait for nod] 'Good . . . now you and the Child lovingly embrace, and as you do so, just allow the Child to merge with you. Allow the Child to rest in his or her safe place inside.' [Wait for nod] 'As you come back to now, remember that whenever you like you can take out the photograph and relive the happiness and success of those events . . . So now, when you are ready . . . you can open your eyes and come back to this room.'

## Discussing the MBV

You are now ready to discuss what your client has just experienced. YOU DO NOT ASK YOUR CLIENT WHAT IS HAPPENING DURING THE VISUALISATION, except for the words of the new belief. Of course, if your client runs into difficulty you will have to discuss the bit that they are hung up on, but all things being equal, do not discuss the pictures they are making until the MBV is completed.

To keep the discussion brief and within a reasonable time scale, I suggest that you ask the following questions one at a time.

'What was the outdoor place like?'
'Where was the problem person standing in relation to you, the Adult?'
'Which direction did the Child approach from?'
'Tell me about the garment the Child was wearing.'
'How was it, throwing the garment over to the problem person?'
'What was the problem person's reaction to wearing the garment?'
'What, if anything, did the Child want to say to the problem person?'
'What was the new outfit like?'
'What, if anything, did you add to the new outfit?'
'What colour were the words of the new belief?'

'Tell me about the celebration.'
'Tell me about the path which represented the future.'
'Tell me about the three events you saw on the screen.'
'What was the photograph like?'
'Tell me about the merging?'

## IDENTIFYING MISTAKEN BELIEFS WITHOUT LETTERS

As previously stated, the 'Letter FROM:' is used to allow the Child finally to 'tell someone who will help' and to ascertain the mistaken belief developed as a result of an abusive event. However, mistaken beliefs can also be developed by less traumatic events which your client may not even recall. Obviously, the use of a 'Letter FROM:' to identify the mistaken belief would be pointless in such a situation.

You will recognise that a mistaken belief is in place by the fact that your client has an unwanted problem behaviour which he or she is unable to stop, i.e. 'I know I shouldn't be/feel/behave this way, but I do!' The original event (which created the mistaken belief) may be out of consciousness, but the unwanted behaviour developed as a result of the mistaken belief will remain. You can use this unwanted behaviour to identify the mistaken belief.

Any problem behaviour will be 'operated' by a mistaken belief (m/b). To explore for the unknown m/b attached to an unwanted behaviour, tell your client that you are going to ask some questions that might normally be cast aside by logic. Explain that you would like the first answer/sentence that comes to mind, even if it sounds illogical. Explain that you are not trying to find a logical answer, you are looking for a mistaken belief. Therefore you would like your client to just let the answers/sentences flow, even if a part is saying, 'That's not right.' You might say to your client, 'I would like you not to assess or evaluate your answers, just say the first sentence that comes to mind.'

Begin the questions by asking, 'What is the first negative thought you have about yourself concerning (name the unwanted behaviour)?' When your client gives an answer, note his or her response and continue with: 'Good . . . and what further negative thought about yourself does that lead you to?'

Continue to ask that same question to each answer given. While you watch for the one which has the strongest impact. In doing this you may go past the strongest one, but when you notice that the overall impact is diminishing, just stop and go back to the statement that seemed to be the strongest one. Explain that you are now going to repeat what appeared to you to be the strongest statement and ask if he or she would verify if it also seems the strongest to him or her. Please ask for input from your client to ascertain if the wording of the m/b needs adjusting, just as you would do with the m/b found in the Letter FROM:.

Next ask who your client first learned this m/b from or from whom it seems most likely to have originated—that will be the problem person. If, however, your client cannot ascertain who it might be, just use an unknown figure for the problem person. You now have the mistaken belief and the problem person, so you are ready to use the Mistaken Belief Visualisation.

Of course, once you get used to listening for mistaken beliefs you can recognise them in your client's conversation. In that case, you can explore a bit to determine if the wording used is the most powerful form for your client, discuss who he or she first learned the statement from (or who he or she connects the statement to) and then use the MBV.

The PICT Training Course includes practice in identifying mistaken beliefs and using the MBV.

# 3 Samples

## HANDWRITING SAMPLE

On pp. 94-6 is a sample of how handwriting sometimes changes when your client is writing the Letter FROM:. This happens frequently with some people, occasionally with others and never for the rest. When it does happen, it is simply an indication that the access link with the Child part is very strong. It is not an indicator of 'success' with the method or of lack of 'success', it is just how that person's link with the Child is demonstrated. It does not mean that the person has a stronger 'bond' with the Child part either.

This sample is from Peggy. As usual, the Adult starts and finishes the letter, but, in addition, cuts in to comfort the Child when the Child becomes more and more distressed. The Child's writing finally becomes an unreadable scrawl, but notice how the writing from the Adult part stays uniform. Sometimes the Adult part interrupts to comfort the Child. At other times Peggy first hugs and rocks her Teddy, giving comfort in that way to the Child before carrying on with the writing. [If you cannot comprehend the child's scrawl, look ahead to Chapter Eight, 'Sexuality', where you will find the entire letter series—Peggy's Letter Series—Sleeping, p. 228.]

## Peggy's handwriting sample

Hello again my precious love. How are you feeling now? A little bit rested I hope, come, sit with me darling I want to talk with you again. You have been such a very brave girl to tell me some of the scary things about your daddy. Do you remember when we were at Nicks house and you helped me to talk to Penny? Well honey I would like for you to tell me some more about the time when you were 7 and you were all curled up in bed pretending to be asleep and daddy came in. It's okay - love you will be safe, you are here with me and I will keep my arms around you loving and protecting you while you talk. Go ahead sweetheart I'm here for you now Listening with love ...

That's right darling you are 7 years old and you're in your room curled up on your side in your bed, what happens now love?

Daddy ... daddy's coming I can hear him up the stairs - He's big and they make a noise. It's all dark in my room except where the landing light comes through the top of my door. There is a special glass part for it high up. I am in my bed behind the door and I am curled up like the nurse showed me when I went to have my tonsils at, I can do it on my own now without her fingers in me to twist me up. Daddy creeps in the door quietly and I am all curled up to be asleep but he is leaning the edge of my bed goes down and I hold tight to the cover in my fist and screw up my eyes tight I am asleep really I am but he is leaning I look asleep I don't even breath but he is on the

bed and it goes down more his hand is
on my face stroking my hair and touching
my cheeks. Go away please please don't
go away I am asleep please go away ...
I am a good girl please go away
I am a very good girl I am I am
daddy daddy please I am I am
a good girl I didn't do anything please
don't

---

Oh honey it's okay my lovely one I am here and you
are safe. There now, there now ... I am here
with you. It hurts you so, I know that baby
just take your time let me hold you darling I
love you so very much Peg, it cannot happen
again, it is a memory this time love, just a bad
memory, I promise it is not real now, I will
not let him do that again. Try my love, try to
tell me the rest, it's okay you are safe ...

---

Daddy is pushing the covers up into a heap
on me and it feels cold on my back and
my bottom I want to be asleep but I
can't because he's still there Oh please don't
daddy I am a good girl mummy will hate
me I am a good girl mummy will be
horrid I am a I am
Daddy is pushing me he is pushing my
nightie up it is pretty pink with white lace
neck and a pink daisy and daisy buttons
My neck is slithery wet and hot breathy
go away please go away where's my
mummy she will hate me I am a good
girl daddy please love me I am good girl

Oh no daddy please don't pushing his
finger ... my legs and wetting on
my neck and cheek and hurting
me underneath and pushing my legs
over one up and tickling and
my bottom out don't don't go away
please don't

I am a dirty girl a bad bad dirty
girl mummy has tried me before I am
a bad girl I should set an example
I am a bad girl and I know better
he's pushing in at my bottom go away
please go away big finger my
bottom I want to be asleep I am
good I love my daddy don't don't
I love my daddy go away I hate
you wet and slobbery and
hot breath and horrid and horrid
grunt grunt piggy grunt Crabby me
grabbing my bottom like squeak piggy
squeak a game like squeak piggy
squeak and I am blind and it
is him I love daddy I hate him he
is doing it.
Ow no no no no ow ouch ow
no please no no I curl up like the
nurse showed me no no I curl in
tight and he spits and makes the noise
my bottom sore and cold and I have
gone stiff and dead. He is gone and he
covers are tidy I am dead I am gone.

Peg, my beautiful little girl you are ...... so very

## SAMPLE LETTER SERIES

The following is an example of the three PICT steps in the letter series format. This is from Sally, who was sexually abused by her brother.

### Sally's Letter Series

*Letter FROM: Stopping the abuse*

*Dear Sally,*
*I want you to tell me about the time that you stopped Marvin [brother] abusing you. I know that will be hard for you and frightening, but remember I am here with you and you can stop if you are too upset.*

It was after school. We were both at home and Mum had gone to see her aunty. It was always then that he started because he knew we were on our own. It was always the same, only now it was too much. It was bad before but I knew about periods now and I was scared I'd get pregnant. I wasn't having periods yet but I was still scared, and I'd had enough.

I always felt so bad, so dirty, so different. Everyone else around me had boyfriends and friends and fun and all I got was him and how he hurt me. I didn't want to be hurt no more. I didn't want to be all those bad things and I didn't want to grow up and I just wanted him to stop or me to stop being me.

So I used to plan how I really could die—just like he wanted. [A frequent remark made by Sally's brother was: 'Everyone would be better off if you were dead!'] I thought and planned it over and over—wondering how I could do it. I couldn't shoot me because I didn't have a gun, and pills can get washed out, and I didn't want to drown.

When he got in and started to go on at me I couldn't take it no more. I just wanted it to be over and it didn't matter how, just as long as he stopped. So I ran upstairs into the bathroom and I shut the door, bolted it and shut him out.

He kept knocking and pleading and I thought he'd get mad and get in and do it. So I put the plug in and I turned on the tap and I watched the water fill up the bowl. He was shouting at me, wanting to know what I was doing and to let him in.

I wanted to and I didn't want to—I didn't know what to do. I was scared I'd give in, but I opened the bathroom cabinet and I took it out. A razor blade. It was so horrid, all rusty and old and sharp. I put my arm in the bowl and I put the razor on my wrist and I began to press the edge down on my skin and I watched the vein bit stand out and I began to cry.

'I'm going to do it Marvin, I am, I am. I will kill myself and bleed and bleed and you can't stop me. I'll die and they'll find me and they'll know it was you who made me. They'll hate you then, they'll know. I hate you. I hate you and I will die. You touch me again and I'll die, I don't care. I don't matter and I hate you. You made me. You made me. All I am is bad and you made me. I hate you. I will die and you can't stop me.'

All the time he's out there. I can hear him, pleading, telling me he'll stop now, but it's all lies and lies and lies. He mustn't get in or he'll stop me, but I don't want to do this, I'm scared. I want to be safe not here trying to die. I want you to hold me, I want you to love me. Please love me, I'm sorry, I'm sorry, I'm sorry. [Addressed to Adult]

Why won't they come and help me? I'm so scared and alone and he's out there and I can't get away. I've locked the door and I'm in here and he's out there and all I can do is cut across my wrist and die. I can't let him win, but I'm frightened and tired and cold and I don't want this. I just want everything to go away.

He's saying he won't touch me again—just as long as I come out. But I'll wait till Mum comes home. And I have to be ready always, in case he's lying and he does try. But I don't want to fight. I want someone to help me. I'm scared of dying. Why can't someone look after me, love me. Why have I got to do this. It's the only way I've got to stop him, but I don't want to. *I don't want to be on my own.* [Mistaken belief was, 'I will always be on my own'.]

*Sally, love, it's okay. You're not on your own. I'm here.
I love you. I won't leave you. You've been so brave and
strong to tell me all that. It's over now and he's not here.
I am. I'll keep you safe always, I promise.*

### Sally's Letter TO: Stopping the abuse
### 90 per cent

Dear Sally,

You were so brave to tell me all about the time you
stopped your brother abusing you. The feelings you had
were so strong and so painful for you. I want so much to
reassure you that the way you were feeling was not wrong.
Anyone in your situation would want to get away from
everything that was hurting them. No one wants to carry
on being hurt and humiliated, abused in the way you were.

Of course, you wanted it all to go away and because
you thought the situation could not change, you wanted
to stop being you. As a child that was the only way you
could see to stop things—you wanted for you no longer
to be the child being abused. But you knew you had to
go on being you and that you needed someone to come
along and rescue you—but who?

Marvin had always lied to get his own way so you could
not trust his word. All the escape routes were dead ends
for you except to stop living. And no little girl with a
whole life to grow up into and explore the world in wants
to have to end that life. But you could see no other way
so that's where you were driven. It wasn't wrong or stupid
or bad. It was the only way you could see, no matter how
scared you were.

You were forced to feel that dying was the only way
open to you, because of the terrible way your brother
behaved. It was him that forced you to think that you had
to die to escape. It was the abuse of your body, your mind,
your innocence and your childhood that caused it all.

And then, despite all that, maybe you could have had
an alternative if your mother had not failed to meet her
role—she did not see your problems, she did not step

in, she failed to 'rescue' you, even before you were so
desperate. She should have been there for you. It was her
role as your mother to be someone you could go to and
to talk with. She should have been aware of that dreadful
despair long ago and given you comfort and support. She
was the adult and it was up to her.

Marvin should have been a person who loved you. If
he had told you the truth, let you draw on him as a support
in life, cared for you, treated you with respect, then you
would not have had to suffer. That is how an emotionally
healthy brother would have behaved.

When they both failed to be there in normal, natural
mother and brother roles in your life, when they failed to
support and protect you, but instead abused and aban-
doned you, what else could you believe other than you
were alone? They made you alone without anyone to lean
on or support you, until you could only see yourself as
someone who had to be alone, made to be alone for the
rest of her life. That was the mistaken belief they left you
with.

Just think what that has done to your life. You have
never looked towards a time when you could have a partner—you discounted it as impossible. You have always
coped because you never looked for support—you
believed it not to be there so you did not find it. Any help
you saw as temporary, not given freely.

Not everyone in life has a partner relationship, but
everyone can have it if that is what they choose. Until
now that was not possible for you—because you were sure
you had to be alone. That is not true. It has never been
true and it never will be true. There is nothing anywhere
that demands you be alone—except a mistaken belief that
Marvin and your mum forced you to accept as fact. It has
no truth. It is not fact—it can't be proved.

They had to let you believe it in order to protect themselves. Marvin was quite safe while you had to handle all
the abuse alone—that way you would never tell. And
because you believed it, then you didn't tell—and so your
mum was safe too. Safe from having to face the truth
because she did not have the courage or ability to cope.

They forced you to cope alone because they were too weak to face responsibility, and they have denied you for too long the chance to look towards a future with security, support and someone special. Don't let them deny you this, Sally. You don't deserve it. Let them have the lies—you have the right to the truth. You can be loved and you will be loved, if that is what you choose, one day in the future. That is the truth. Take that now and leave the rest for them.

[Mistaken belief visualisation is done here.]

Oh Sally, it's over now. I'm here with you and you are safe and warm. No one can hurt you here with me. I love you so much and now we are together. I won't let anyone take that away. You're safe. It's all right now.

### Sally's Rescue Scene—Stopping the abuse

As I ran up the stairs I could hear their voices; Marvin's pleading and begging, Sally's full of despair. I could sense the terrible loneliness, feel her closeness to the edge. I stopped as I reached the landing and saw him by the door. Him and the door between me and Sally.

'Get away from there, now.' I spoke softly and yet he knew I could make him. As he turned to look at me, I could see the fear in his eyes, fear of discovery, of the guilt about to land on his shoulders.

'Please', he begged, 'please help me. Stop her. Don't let her.'

'Help you? No way. Save you from the truth? Why should I? Oh, just get out of the way and let me go to her.'

The hatred and scorn I felt for him burned into him, but then, he was irrelevant. He didn't matter—whether he was there or not, whether he lived or died, didn't matter. I just had to go to Sally.

I walked calmly towards her into the bathroom, through Marvin and through the door. Sally didn't move, her wrist in the water, the razor pressing into her skin.

'No, Sally, no.' My voice reached out to her, soothing and gentle. 'That's not the way. You don't need to do that. You're not alone now. I'm here. I'm here for you. I won't leave you.'

She turned her head slowly, turned towards me and gazed with lost, disbelieving eyes. Gently, so as not to frighten her, I reached out my hand. 'Come on. I'm here now. Let go. You don't need all that. Just let go and take my hand. Trust me, Sally. I do love you.'

She let the razor drop down into the water, and halt-ingly, then joyfully she stretched out her hand, a warm glow starting in her eyes. Then it spread as she finally and trustingly put her hand into mine. Tears welled in our eyes as our fingers met. Gently I led her through the door. Marvin was gone and all her fears with him.

In front of us stretched a carpet of green, soft new blades of grass, scented with freshness. Above lay the never-ending blue of the sky and both went on forever until our eyes could see them meet and blend. This was bathed in a brilliant golden haze, spreading out from the central white sphere of the sun. It was all so perfect, so much more beautiful than any grass or sky or sun we had ever seen.

We stood dazed, clinging to each other, almost unbe-lieving of what we could see. It was as if we could reach up and touch the sky and it would be soft and smooth. Our senses strained to take in the vision before us, every scent, every sound, every touch.

It was without interruption; nothing to mar the endless colour, to break the smooth lines of earth and sky. We were there in the centre, walking into that light. As we went forward, it was as if we could paint on to the back-ground whatever we wanted, but always the purity of that background remained. We could change the foreground, could add gardens, buildings, people, places, anything— and all the time the same strong clear sky, grass and sun, the same natural warmth remained.

And we were there together.

## METAPHOR EXAMPLE

Sandra wrote a beautiful metaphor Letter TO:. I felt it was a lovely example so I am including it here. Sandra started out unable to really care for her inner Child at all. The damaged Parent part was in extremely strong control of the inner opinions of the Child, which were all bad. Consequently, Sandra was one of those clients who 'hate' the inner Child, making frequent blaming comments, i.e. 'I hate the Child, it's all her fault. She should have stopped it. She is revolting, there is nothing good about her. I don't want to get close to her. I want her out! She doesn't belong here. I hate her!'

I need to point out that at times Sandra was able to write nice-sounding letters to her Child, but she could not feel anything she wrote. It is all right when this happens. Your client does not have to start out believing everything she writes, she just has to write it correctly—Sandra did so. After a period of time, feeling started creeping into the letters and finally Sandra was able to write and *feel* letters such as the following. This letter was one Sandra did on her own; it was not assigned. It was also simply a Letter TO: on its own. In other words, it did not include the Letter FROM: or Rescue Scene—which is one of the ways to vary the PICT method.

### *Sandra's Letter TO:*

Dear Little One,

I'd like you to come and sit with me so we can have a chat, a special story. Remember, I am your special person, here to listen and help you. Would you like a cuddle?

That's it, snuggle in, I'll wrap you up in a blanket, you hold on to your bunny. It's okay, you cry, you are safe with me, I'm not going to harm you. Crying helps to get the pain out. I can feel you are hurting inside and I want to help you to stop hurting, so you can be a fun-filled little person, enjoying life, playing freely, doing things you enjoy and feeling cozy and at ease inside.

That is how you would have been if you had a childhood of love and care, where you were special, treasured and valued. Children need to be acknowledged, cherished, played with, accepted for who they are—a beautiful person, so lovely to know and be with. I want to help you to feel this inside of you. To take away the turmoil that is all that hurting and aching inside of you. All the tears and screaming need to be set free to come out, leaving more and more space for the love and fun to be inside you.

It's like a doll's house full up with rubbish—tins that could cut you and make you hurt and bleed, old jagged wood that could give you splinters (they are small but they hurt). Rotted smelly food that has mould on it that could make you sick if you touched it, if you ate it. So the doll's house would be full of things that could hurt you, make you cry and scream.

Rats may crawl amongst the rubbish, suddenly appearing, making you jump, scaring you. You might not know how many there are, some may be hiding or you may hear munching and rustling and not know what it is, this may frighten you. A rat may bite you and you may have to go to the doctor to make it better.

All these things in the doll's house wouldn't feel very nice, they would feel horrible and you would not be able to see the pretty wallpaper or feel the soft carpet in the doll's house, because of all the horrid, messy rubbish in the way, all filled up inside the doll's house.

So here you are with this lovely looking doll's house all filled up with horrible rubbish and someone comes along and gives you some beautiful doll's house furniture. A little bed with soft pretty covers on it and cozy little pillows. A wardrobe to put pretty clothes in, a dressing table with a mirror so all the beauty can be seen and admired. Tables and chairs and pots and pans to cook with and sit at and eat yummy food. A cozy sofa to curl up in, all safe and warm in front of the fire. A rocking horse to play on, a toy box full of treasures.

Lots of things to be curious about, have fun with, and lots to make. Dressing up clothes to be spontaneous in, trying out being somebody you know or would like to be—seeing what it could feel like. Lots of gorgeous dollies to try all this out on, what fun, how happy that playing would be. So many wonderful things to do, lovely games to make up and play.

So now you have a beautiful doll's house, full of horrible rubbish on the inside and all these lovely, gorgeous new gifts and nowhere to put them. They cannot fit inside the doll's house and be displayed for all to see and share, with space to be free to be played with and have fun. So how can we fit the new gifts, the dolls and furniture into the doll's house? What do we need to do?

Yes, what a good idea, I think that is very clever of you. We need to take out the horrible rubbish, clean it up so that it smells nicely, the stains are removed and we can see the pretty wallpaper, feel the soft carpets and put all these lovely gifts inside, displaying them how we choose. That would be so lovely, wouldn't it?

I can see you like that story with its happy ending. It didn't start off very nice did it? With all that horrible rubbish that could hurt us and rats that may frighten us. It looked horrible and felt painful too. Though we had to clean out the horrid rubbish and the rats, this didn't feel nice to do. Some rubbish may hurt us, felt horrid to touch, smelt disgusting and we didn't know what we would find next in amongst the rubbish inside the doll's house.

When we had fully cleaned it out we had a wonderful, wonderful special place to be, all that space to play in and have fun, it felt so good. It looked so pretty, we could put all the gifts and treasures inside, all special. My, I can see it sparkling and shiny inside that doll's house, all the dollies are so smiley, happily playing and chatting, all cozy. What a lovely special doll's house to live in. What do you think? You like it too, you would like a doll's house like that. So would I.

Now this story is a special story, very special for you and I, because inside you feel like you are full up with rubbish—horrible hurting rubbish like the doll's house. I have got some lovely treasures, special gifts for you but I want them to go inside you, like the doll's house, so you can feel all warm and cozy inside. So you have space to be free, have fun and play. Space to feel smiley and happy like the dollies. Space for you to sparkle and shine, for you and others to see and feel the glow.

Like the doll's house's horrible rubbish, which we had to take out to put the lovely treasures in, so we need to take out the horrible hurting, crying, screaming—all that pain and fear inside you. Then you too can be free, clean, warm and glowing inside. You can be sparkling inside. You can be sparkling on the outside just how a child would be who didn't have all this horrid rubbish causing them to feel ill and hurting inside.

You and I need to take all the rubbish out, not leave anything behind. Sometimes this may not feel very nice, but we shall be doing it together, not you on your own. As the rubbish comes out, all that hurt and crying comes out, so the special treasures and fun will have space to go in. You will feel warm and loved, cherished and valued, safe and clean.

This story of the special doll's house shows us how we can help get the treasures, fun and love inside us by removing, taking out, the pain, tears and fear. I know it will work, I believe it will work and I promise it will work. Penny will help us to be able to do this. Penny and I are with you in emptying out all this hurt and replacing it— putting in all the goodness, love and specialness, so you can be free to have fun and sparkle—glow.

That's it, Little One, you have a sleep, all safe in my arms. You listened very well, it's very tiring. Sleep well, Little One.

## LETTER TO INNER PARENT

Another way to vary the PICT method is to write to the inner Parent part. This is not always necessary because the Parent part usually learns new parenting skills by listening to the letters written to the Child by the Adult. However, on occasions when your client's Parent part is in strong control, then a letter (or few letters) can be written *from the adult* directly to the inner Parent part. I used to assign those letters to be addressed to the 'Damaged Parent', but now they are simply addressed to 'Parent'.

Although the damaged Parent communication is destructive and negative, as learned from the actual parents or parent figures, the Parent part does have a positive intention. That intention is to do its job—teaching, monitoring and acknowledgement. Unfortunately, the role models used to learn its job were less than helpful, which is the information you want to give the Parent part when assigning Parent letters.

The following letters are two examples of a letter to the Parent. The first follows our present format and the second our former format (addressed to Damaged Parent). The first is from Sandra, as she wrote to her very controlling damaged Parent part. The second is from Priscilla, also addressing a similarly very controlling damaged Parent part.

### Sandra's Letter to Parent

Dear Parent,

The way you are responding to the child is normal, given the feelings you have which have stemmed from the model of the birth mother. It is therefore understandable that you feel and behave the way that you do, although the way you are reacting is unfortunately having a negative, unhelpful effect on the parent/child relationship. By behaving in the way that you are, although understandable, it is causing a spiral of pain and disharmony which is not useful to reaching what we would like—peace and inner harmony of living and being together. Not useful in working in a positive way, growing and being free.

This negative spiralling takes a lot of your time and effort. Now if this amount of time and effort was put into a positive, constructive rippling out, think for a moment how much better that would be for us. All the gains we could have, all the achievements, freedom from restrictions. How enabling it would be for us, how liberating. How much happier we would feel, free to do what we choose and to enjoy doing it. To be able to feel good in ourselves.

To enable this to take place you will need to concentrate on responding to the child in a loving, caring way. Being aware of the tone of voice you use and what words you say. Hurriedly said or 'snapped at' words do not feel the same to the giver or receiver as words that come from the heart—words that are lovingly given, truthfully felt. Start gradually and in time you will find it gets easier and then becomes a way of life.

To help you to say things in a useful, constructive way, you will need to be responding to the child by showing her respect, being concerned about her, being interested in her and what she is saying and doing, through wanting what is best for her. Show her this in encouragement, listening carefully, attentively to her, giving her space and time to be with you and allowing her freedom of expression. You could be listening in a non-judgmental way and saying positive things to her.

You could make suggestions of things she could try and mention various ways of doing things. You could take great pride in enabling the child to learn and to feel secure. You would be sharing in this, how lovely that would feel for us. You could remind the child in a gentle way of things she may have forgotten or not noticed, showing your loving support and that you are with her, proud of her, that you value her.

Through doing the things I have suggested you will enable the linking of the parts [Adult/Parent/Child] and a wholeness of harmony, which in turn will ripple out so that we, as a powerful unit, can be free to live the life we choose. We can be free to do the things we want to, and enjoy them. Free to be the positive, caring, loving being that underneath all this we are. It would enable us to sparkle through, to grow. It would be very useful to have this put into action starting today, then we can reap the benefits sooner.

### Priscilla's Letter to Damaged Parent Part

Dear damaged parent,
For most of my life you have been in charge of me and for a large part of that time I accepted you without ques-

tion. Now I realise that you have been very wrong and damaging to me because you are damaged yourself. I am no longer prepared to accept and believe all you try to put on me with your constant blaming, bullying, criticising and accusing.

I have felt for some time that I cannot always be wrong—I have seen myself doing good things, right things, but have listened to your criticism and jeering. I will no longer accept your opinions—you are no longer in charge—I may hear you but I may choose to ignore you.

Now about this issue of being sick. I know that most people can be sick without feeling anything other than unwell and that in most cases being sick brings relief. You have always made me feel how dirty, disgusting, uncontrolled—how BAD—it is to be sick, whatever the reason. This has kept you in a powerful position because you have always threatened me with it in almost any situation.

I am now challenging your right to this power. From now on I will choose whether or not I use being sick as a reason for actions. If I am physically ill it may help me to be sick and I will choose—I will still have power over it. If it should help me I will be strong enough to survive it. I will no longer link it to situations where it is inappropriate—you will not use it as a means of keeping me down.

## VARIATIONS OF PICT

People who have come from dysfunctional families have usually experienced parents who have not expressed their love, support or approval. Those are things every person needs to receive from their parents. Those things are as important as food, clothes and shelter. The negative after-effects are life-limiting decisions and mistaken beliefs. These problems are made even worse if the parents made a public pretence of caring, but were actually cold and indifferent behind closed doors or if they supplied plenty of food, clothing and shelter, but relatively little in the way of love, support or approval.

Funnily enough, as adults, we often wait and wait and wait for a magical day when our parents turn to us and lovingly say, 'I am so proud of you! I love you.' (Of course, we may not admit that to others or sometimes not even to ourselves.) We may continue to 'be good' throughout our lives by performing charitable acts, courageous acts, superior acts, talented acts or responsible acts, hoping at last to receive some positive recognition from our parents. We may excel in academic fields, or gain the admiration and respect of the general public in some manner, all to no avail; for we could gain the entire world's love and respect and still not feel fulfilled *if our intent had been to gain those magic words from our parents*.

The problem with parents from a dysfunctional family is that often they simply cannot, do not know how to, or will not, verbalise love, support or approval. Therefore it is usually a futile and painful wait. A wait we are often willing to make as we hang on to a thin thread of hope . . . maybe someday . . .

Priscilla was one of those waiting for someday, hoping that somehow she could gain a few crumbs of approval and love. Then her father had a stroke and was lying in the hospital not expected to live. He was conscious, had some movement, and could still manage to speak. Priscilla went daily to see him. She stood by the side of his bed desperately willing him to say something loving to her. It wouldn't have to be a lot, she would be satisfied if even with his last few gasps of breath he could manage, 'I love you. . . .'

However, not only did Priscilla's father not say those few words, he would not say anything—even though he could speak. He would not speak to her or her mother. Nor would he allow them to hold his hand, not that holding hands was something they normally did as a family, but under these circumstances Priscilla thought surely he would do it. He simply shut them out, but for five days Priscilla stood by his bed enduring his silence and withdrawal, hoping he would change his mind, hoping he would finally give her what he had never yet given her—that simple phrase. It never happened. After his death Priscilla slid into a deep and isolating depression; it had been the ultimate rejection. Her thin thread of hope was gone.

Even though it is a thin thread of hope, when it is

wrenched from our grip the result is devastating. It is all the more confusing for those people who professed to 'hate' or care nothing about the parent, when they find themselves deeply grieving. In those cases, the truth is that the little child part inside knew it was still waiting for the magic phrase, even if the adult part had pushed that information to some obscure shelf in the back of the mind. Therefore, when the parent dies and the thin thread of hope is gone forever, a searing, and sometimes confusing, grief engulfs us. Mind you, we may not call it grief and we may become rather angry if someone else suggests it might be grief, but grief it is, just the same.

Priscilla had insomnia, loss of appetite, mood swings and obsessive thoughts and behaviour. She was often troubled in the middle of the night by irrational thoughts, such as thinking that her father was still alive and trying to get out of the coffin and that she should rush down to the cemetery and start digging him up. Like any sane person, she was reluctant to tell anyone about these thoughts for fear they would think she was crazy. (In comparison, someone not in the balance of their mind usually finds irrational thoughts very normal and has no qualms about sharing them with others.) She was very relieved to hear that irrational thoughts are a common experience of grief.

To assist Priscilla in dealing with her feelings about her father, I used a variation on the letter writing. This time I asked Priscilla to write a letter to herself (Adult) *from* her father. However, this was not to be a letter from her father as he had been, instead it was to be a letter from her father as he was meant to be. In other words, the person he would have been if he had not been limited by the mistaken beliefs that ruled his life. The person he would have been if he had all the emotional resources he needed to cope with life. That resourceful father was to write a letter to Priscilla giving her the information, support and love that she needed.

During the session I asked Priscilla to close her eyes and make an image of her father as she thought he would look as the resourceful person he should have been, asking a few questions to assist her picture to have as much detail and clarity as possible. The image established, she was now ready to go home and write the letter from her resourceful father. She was to make the image clear in her mind and then just listen to what the resourceful father had to say and write it down. Priscilla was rather sceptical about her ability to do this (who wouldn't be?), but set off to give it a go. The following is her result:

### Priscilla's Letter from Father

Dear Priscilla,

I was very fond of you and your Mum—it may surprise you as I was never able to tell either of you, particularly you, how much I felt for you. I was proud of you, what you did for yourself and what you did as a wife and mum, but somehow I was never able to show you. I was very frightened of feelings and did exactly what you have done until recently, show how much caring there is with actions—practical things such as gifts, little jobs done to please. I wanted you to know, but always backed off when feelings came too near the surface.

I found the responsibilities of being a husband and father too much. I made you too special. I set my standards too high for myself and everyone else around me. I wasn't able to be satisfied with myself and I am sorry that this overflowed to you.

I couldn't tell you I was afraid and I was so relieved at the end, as I lay in hospital, that the responsibility was at last over and that I didn't have to talk to you and maintain a position—that is why I decided to say nothing. I am sorry that I couldn't show you by holding your hand, letting you touch me, but it was too late, I couldn't face the tears.

I really was not that wonderful, strong, good, right person you thought me. I could never say, I love you.

Priscilla was quite surprised that she was actually able to write such a letter and surprised that she felt so different after having written the letter. She felt that something was settled for her, something was now at rest, she could now get on with the rest of her life.

**Messages From Parents**

Your client's parents do not have to be deceased to use the above letter format. It works as well when the parents are still alive. I tend to use it whenever I notice symptoms of grief towards parents (whether parents are dead or alive) or when my client makes numerous 'if only' statements or 'I wish' statements concerning his or her parents.

The most difficult part will be explaining that you want them to create an image of how their parent was meant to be (as described in the preceding example to Priscilla) rather than how they are. It usually takes a person a good few minutes to develop an image of their parent as resourceful. Please have the person develop the image during the session, then use that image at home while writing the letter. People often say, 'I'll have to make a whole new picture of them!' and you can reply, 'Yes, that is exactly what you will need to do.'

It is helpful to ask your client to describe to you what she is visualising in the image in order to assist in fully developing it. 'What do you notice that is different? . . . How is his posture? . . . What is he wearing? . . . What facial expression does he have? . . . How is his voice different? . . . How does your resourceful parent feel? . . . How do you feel towards him? . . . What else do you see (hear, feel)? . . . What do you like best about him?' etc.

## RE-ASSIGNING PICT LETTERS

When evaluating any of the letter series (FROM:, TO: or Rescue Scene), simply compare what is written to the format you have asked them to follow. If it does not match up, just 'wonder' what stopped them from including that point, give whatever appropriate information is needed—then re-assign the letter or ask them to make amendments during the session. Of course, with the Letter TO: you will also be monitoring the belief level (1—100 per cent) and the Mistaken Belief Visualisation (see Chapter Two for directions).

There are a few points to keep in mind when assessing the PICT letter series:

a. *Adult and Parent role must be separate.*  The Adult should never refer to him or herself as 'mummy' or 'daddy'. The Adult can describe him or herself as the Child's special person or simply say, 'I am who you will be when you grow up and I am here now to help you feel safe and happy.' If the Damaged Parent messages surface during a Letter TO: you will notice the tone changes to an accusing, blaming tone. Identify this for your client and strike out those words or, if there are too many, re-assign the letter.

b. *Child must communicate with Adult only (unless you have specifically assigned a letter addressing the problem person or someone else).*  Sometimes in the Letter FROM: (which is written from the Child to the Adult about what happened in the past), the Child starts to address blame to the Adult, i.e. 'You treated me badly'. This must be identified and changed. Hand the letter back and have your client change 'you' to the name of the problem person or re-assign the letter. The Letter FROM: is only meant to be written to the Adult, not to the Parent or problem person—the Child should be talking *about* them not *to* them. Keep alert for any statements that turn from 'they/he did' to 'you did'.

c. *Adult must provide realistic information to the Child.* On some occasions, clients will write extravagant promises to the Child, i.e. 'From now on you will always be happy. No one will ever dislike you again. You will always get what you want.' Re-assign these letters to something more realistic, i.e. 'I am here for you now. I will do my best to help you feel safe and happy. When you are unhappy, you can come to me for comfort. When you are disappointed or sad, I am always here and on your side.'

d. *Adult never takes the blame for past events in Child's life.*  At times clients will write a Letter FROM: that blames the Adult for the past events, 'You weren't there for me, it's all your fault'. These statements need to be crossed out or re-assigned. The Adult was not present in the past and therefore cannot shoulder any blame.

e. *Child is never accused or blamed.*  Should this happen it indicates that the Damaged Parent has surfaced. It usually happens in the Letter TO: i.e. 'You should have done . . .' or 'You should not have done . . .' Either have your client cross out these statements or re-assign the letter if there are too many.

f. *Letter TO: continues until Adult logic matches Child feelings—belief percentage 80 per cent or above, or MBV runs without hiccups.* Re-assign this letter until the belief percentage is high and the MBV runs smoothly. The percentage rate should be 80 per cent or above, but I have accepted as low as 70 per cent if the MBV runs very smoothly and my client is congruent, because some people rate themselves lower than others. If you are using some of the other tools (Chapter Five) in addition to the PICT letter series, you can also leave the belief rate lower and finish it off with another tool.

## LETTER FROM:—ERROR

In the Letter FROM: you will be expecting to see: Adult asking Child to tell about his or her feelings and memory of a specific event; Child writing to Adult (*not parent*) in the first person; Adult thanking, praising and giving support and love.

Below we have an example of a Letter FROM: that did not follow the format and needed to be re-assigned. As you read, notice that it is written entirely by the Adult *about* the Child. Although the Adult appropriately asks the Child to tell about the event, the Adult instead goes on to write in the third person about the Child, (*She* said, did, etc.), rather than the Child writing in the first person, (*I* said, did, etc.), telling her own story.

You will also notice that what is supposed to be the 'Child' writing, is actually full of adult words and phrases—nothing like what a four or five year old (as she was in the event) would actually say. It is an accurate account of the event, but not from the Child's point of view, the Adult part is writing it.

You will also notice that at the end, the Adult part does not come in to give love and support (not surprising, since the Child did not have a part in this). When the Child has written it, this is an important part of the Letter FROM: because it is a much needed acknowledgement and acceptance. Just think about it for a moment. If you were to tell a good friend a very difficult and embarrassing piece of information and your friend just sat there looking at you without comment, you might begin to feel very uncomfortable. However, if your friend acknowledged what you had just said by thanking you for trusting her, praising your courage for facing it and told you she still loved you just the same—you would feel it was worth the pain of disclosure. The inner Child will feel the same.

If your client does not write the Adult beginning or end bit, have him or her add it on during the session, rather than re-assign the whole letter. Only re-assign if the Child part is incorrect.

After reading Nikki's Letter FROM:, I praised her for facing an obviously distressing memory. I explained that it appeared that she had found it difficult and therefore she had dissociated to write it. In other words she had remembered the scene as happening away from her, while she looked on, rather than being in the scene, experiencing everything as the child she once was.

Nikki was surprised and told me that was exactly her experience while writing the letter. I then explained that it was going to be more useful for her to experience the event as the Child so we could get a clearer understanding of the Child's feelings (as opposed to an Adult understanding of the sequence of events) because we needed to find the Child's mistaken belief.

We went over the steps for writing the letter again and I re-assigned it. The next effort was quite successful and, in addition, Nikki gained a greater understanding of the letter's effect by comparing her experiences writing the letter both ways.


### Nikki's Letter FROM: Chinese food

Dear Nikki,
    Please tell me about the time your daddy was angry because you spat the Chinese food into your napkin.

She looked very sad and began to tell me what had happened. It seems that she was four or five years old at the time and they lived in a small caravan. The table was one that dropped down from the wall to fit between two long bench-type seats. She sat on the inside, her mother on the outside and her father on the opposite side.

On this particular evening her mother had prepared Chinese food which the child hated. She was not allowed to 'hate' food and always had to eat whatever was put before her. She was not allowed to argue about it either.

The child began to chew very slowly and try to pick through the food and find bits that were not so bad tasting. This was difficult as most of it was repugnant to her. She then got a bright idea and began to very carefully spit the food from her mouth into her napkin each time she wiped her face. She was very clever though and kept on pretending to chew after she spat the food out.

Before long her father figured out what she was doing and demanded to see her napkin. Of course, when he opened it there was all the chewed food and her heart sank because she knew she was in big trouble.

Her father was most angry because she had tried to 'trick' him. His face turned red and he was swearing and calling her all kinds of horrible words. He got up from his side of the table and reached over her mother and grabbed the child's arm. He then yanked her right out of her seat, knocking things over on the table.

He was at the bed in a couple of steps and whipped his belt off and turned her over his knees. He began to beat her with the belt over and over. Her mother tried to ask him to stop but he just told her mother to shut up and she did. He kept hitting the child and saying, 'I'll teach you to lie. I'll teach you to try to trick me!' Each word was accompanied by a hard blow.

The child was crying so hard she could not breathe properly, then she started to choke and was horrified to find herself vomiting. It went on her father's leg and shoe and he was not very happy about that. You would think that she did it on purpose.

He finally got tired or something and just shoved her

to the floor, like she was some kind of dirty piece of clothing. 'You can sit in your mess!' he shouted, 'And stop
that god damn crying before I give you something to cry
about!' She didn't dare want to think what that could be.

## LETTER TO:—ERROR

You should make sure that all five points are included in
the Letter TO: and check with your client that the Mistaken
Belief Visualisation (MBV) was completed. If any of the
points were left out, ask, 'What stopped you?' You can
either ask the client to write out the missing part during the
session or to take it home to do so. If the client did not do the
MBV, again ask, 'What stopped you?' and give appropriate
information. You can also take him or her through it during
the session or, if needed, assign it to be done at home.

Next we look at an excerpt from a Letter TO: the Child,
written by Priscilla. It was meant to explain that Priscilla's
mother could not meet the Child's needs because of her own
problems and that the Adult would now take over that role.
However, Priscilla at that point still had a damaged Parent
part that 'hated' the Child and that part caused her to reject
the Child. Priscilla vacillated from there, alternating
between being Child and Parent.

In the second attempt, you hear a much more Adult letter
and you learn about the constant stream of damaged Parent
messages that Priscilla struggles with. With that list of
insults, no wonder Priscilla found it difficult to function in
a positive manner.

*Priscilla's Letter to Child*
*Error*

Dear Prissy,
    . . . I have to tell you that mum will always be the
same—she does care but somehow that caring doesn't
show as you would like it. She can't be any different
because she has her own problems which she has never
been able to face. Nobody really listened to her needs,

her worries, her unhappiness so she never learnt how to do that for you.

She was very good at providing your material needs but I think she knows that emotionally she has very little to give. Now you have realised that there is more than just material needs, you will have to accept that mum can't give you them, she doesn't know how.

I am supposed to say that I will help you and be there for you, but I can't. I don't like you and I've always wanted to hurt you.

Yesterday [present time] mum came with me to the dentist. Prissy was frightened, she held the nurse's hand. I came round and was immediately concerned not to be a nuisance. I made you stay quiet. Mum took me home and I said I would like to be alone and then you cried with no one to hear except me, and I can't comfort you.

I suppose I will learn and I will try to help you and be with you and eventually like you.

### *Priscilla's (Second Try) Letter to Child*

Dear Prissy,

Last time I wrote to you I became confused. I want to try to explain that all I can do is give you information for you to take in and act upon in your own way. I will not judge you. I will try to encourage you and praise your good efforts and will be here to comfort you when things get you down.

It is the parent who judges, who criticises, who scorns and ridicules, who is impatient with questions and the inability to understand and act immediately. It is the parent who gets angry, who punishes, who hurts, who walks away from you to leave you alone and frightened. It is the parent who calls you 'stupid', 'clumsy', 'careless', 'rude', 'ugly', 'awkward', 'unlady-like', 'big', 'noisy', 'vulgar' and 'bad'.

You are not bad, how can you be? You are still learning and that means that you imitate those around you. If you are all those things, then you must have copied that from—the parent. The parent cannot be changed by you but you can change yourself.

If you find that certain reactions and actions bring a response which you don't like, see whether it is really your fault. If so, then see what alternative there is. If you find the old patterns of behaviour creeping in again, don't be hard on yourself, you are a child, you are learning.

I will be gentle, encouraging, so that you needn't feel disheartened. If I hear the parent coming in with judgments, I will tell her to go away, sit down and be quiet! I can do that, and hopefully, soon you will be able to also. Perhaps the parent would be glad to get rid of the responsibility so that she could settle down to being content.

This last sample was some time later after Priscilla had a break from counselling. She began to re-establish contact with the Child part by writing the following letter. The main point to give your attention to is where Priscilla is able to recognise a damaged Parent message and defuse it.

*Priscilla's Letter to Child (Stopping parent voice)*

Dear Prissy,

It's a long time since I last wrote to you. I have been busy and you don't seem to be around. I think that is a good sign. My feeling is that we have lost contact and that makes it difficult to remember where we have got to, but I have found it much easier to get on with the day-to-day tasks. I want to leave it like that, it's a long time since I enjoyed the present as much but I suppose I have to accept that you still are capable of butting in and demanding attention. (That sounds more like the parent—go away damaged Parent!)

You were remembering how you felt guilty and bad and used to punish yourself by going without or deliberately choosing the least attractive item, activity or whatever. You used to make yourself do things you did not want to, in an attempt to please even though, more often than not, these sacrifices went unnoticed.

There was no need for any of it—you were only little and any mistakes were made while you were learning. People always make mistakes when learning something new and you have always found this difficult, if not impossible, to accept. You were not bad, you were not guilty, you were just little, inexperienced and ready to learn.

You should not feel so uncomfortable when learning new skills—should not feel such embarrassment at making a mistake—should not feel defeated and unable to go on—but you do. Someone must have made you feel these things, they do not come naturally from inside a child. Who criticised, took away all will to succeed, surrounded you with such restrictions that at times you can't function?

You feel guilty by failing but you also feel guilty if you succeed. There is nothing wrong with failing and you can feel proud of success. You must risk repeating things. If you have failed, try again. If you have succeeded, repeat the success and enjoy it. Whatever the result, let go of the experience and go on to the next.

I hope you will come back because it would be easier to go on and look to the future if the past would settle.

## RESCUE SCENE ERRORS

In the Rescue Scene you will be looking for errors such as: the Adult does not take charge of the situation (is not the most powerful person); the Adult does not tell off the problem person; there is no affectionate or comforting exchange between Adult and Child; or the Adult does not take the Child away to a safe and happy place.

One example of the Adult not taking charge was a letter in which the Adult climbed up a ladder to the Child's bedroom and quietly slipped her out of the window. Although she rescued the Child, the Child will still see the problem person as more powerful and therefore still able to influence her. I re-assigned the letter with the addition of 'George'.

When 'George' is used, the Adult still looks powerful because she is the one in charge of this large, menacing

Gorilla; she is the one telling the Gorilla what to do (the Gorilla simply acts as the flunky to 'Mr Big'/Adult).

If for any reason (for instance, experiences of ritualistic abuse) your client cannot use a Gorilla, just ask your client what could be used that would feel comfortable. Of course, make sure that whatever is chosen does not speak or make any action without instruction.

**Rescuing Siblings**
On some occasions your client may rescue brothers and sisters, as well as her own inner Child. The first time, don't re-assign, but explain that it is important for the inner Child to have his or her own special time, that it is important that the focus of rescue is towards your client's inner Child. Suggest that instead of rescuing brothers or sisters, your client write the brother's or sister's own 'Resourceful Adult' into the scene to take the corresponding sibling away, leaving your client's focus on rescuing his or her own inner Child.

**Error Sample**
Our sample of error is from Marian, who had the landowners step in and perform the power work. On the second attempt, she wrote the letter to the Child rather than simply writing about the event. I did not re-assign again, but I did explain that in the next one it would be most useful to write about the event as though to a third party.

### Marian's Rescue Scene With Pony—Error

I'm finding it very difficult to write a 'rescue' tale for fifteen-year-old Marian. Below I have listed her rescue as I imagine it could have happened.

She has arrived in the farm yard and is being confronted by her furious father and mother.
Suddenly Mr & Mrs G arrive by car. They sum up the situation very quickly. They know of my father's ill temper (he is a tenant farmer of Mr G. Therefore we all live in house that belongs to Mr G, plus the farm).

My father and mother change from anger to being servile and try to explain that 'I only worked for the Gs and should not be treated in any way as an equal, so should not have been given the pony, etc.'

The other couple listen and then Mr G says if my father does not behave in a kinder way to me (Mr G knows of beatings, but not the sexual side of my life) then he will report my father to the right authority, but that in the meantime I can go home with the Gs and the pony and when I leave school I can go and work for the family in Suffolk and Berkshire.

My parents are taken aback and shocked since they know Mr G could one day throw them out of the farm. I suddenly feel protected against my tyrant father. I feel triumphant and vindictive towards them. I think them vicious and stupid. I feel no pity.

I'm aware I need help in this rescue so the above is a bit fanciful, but would have been an interesting event had it happened!


### Marian's Second Try Rescue Scene

I remember that dreadful summer evening so well, Marian. I knew your delight in taking the pony home with you. I also knew your father in particular would be very angry. I knew your mother would like the pony really but would not stand up for you if necessary.

I followed you home. You didn't notice. You were happy talking to the pony and patting it. When you reached the farm gate, I hid behind the hedge on the other side of the road. Then your father started shouting at you, then hitting you. You began to sob. The pony was frightened and I was furious.

I picked up a thick stick which was lying on the grass. I ran out to join you. Your father and mother were dumbstruck. I yelled at you to get on the pony's back— you did. I turned to your father and told him I was going to take you away, away to safety, but first I was going to report him to the police and NSPCC. I was going to tell

Mr & Mrs G whom I hoped would evict him from the farm.

While he, still shocked by my appearance, stood very still, I took the pony by the bridle while you held its mane and we left that farm forever—I with one hand on the pony and other around you. We will rise above all this trouble one day, you and I.

# 4 Anger

Anger is a much maligned emotion. Many people want to be rid of it, or at the least, are loath to admit to it. When raising a family parents seldom tell children it is okay to be angry. Instead, parents generally display a great deal of anger to tell their child it is not okay to display anger.

Anger is a very useful and natural emotion. In fact, children would still be slaving away in 'sweat shops' if someone had not become angry. When that one person shared his message and more people became angry, they were able to make a big enough noise to change the law and deliver children from the 'sweat shops'. Therefore we can see that anger is a very motivating emotion. It can motivate people to do or say things that would be too difficult for them otherwise— it can motivate people to positive action.

A good example of that is found in the Bible, in the New Testament, John 2:13–17. 'And the Jews' Passover was at hand, and Jesus went up to Jerusalem, and found in the temple those that sold oxen and sheep and doves, and the changers of money, sitting: And when he had made a scourge of small cords, he drove them all out of the temple, and the sheep, and the oxen; and poured out the changers' money, and overthrew the tables; and said unto them that sold doves, "Take these things hence; make not my Father's house an house of merchandise." And his disciples remembered that it was written, "The zeal of thine house hath eaten me up".'

Sometimes clients who are Christians are reluctant to write an anger letter or to do a physical anger exercise, because they feel that to display anger deliberately would be against their faith. I usually show this scripture passage

to them, pointing out a few things one might overlook at
first reading.

1. Jesus first stopped and made a scourge of small cords.
That looks as if he had a plan, rather than being overwhelmed by blind rage. If a person were overwhelmed and
out of control, I find it hard to picture them searching around
for several small cords and painstakingly tying them together
into a scourge. So Jesus was preparing to display deliberate
anger, rather than blind rage.
2. Next we see a very strong image of Jesus driving the
people and the animals out of the temple—even throwing
over the tables. That scene suggests to me a bit of noise;
oxen and sheep running about, closely followed by their
keepers, closely followed by their tables. I see a scene with
lots of dust and dirt flying (even with stone flooring it could
not have been too clean with that lot in there), oxen
bellowing and sheep bleating, doves making whatever noise
they make when frightened and people crying out in surprise
and shouting after their animals.
3. It also says Jesus threw the tables over, not that he
gently and carefully placed them on their side while he spoke
quietly to the people saying, 'Take these things hence; make
not my Father's house an house of merchandise'. No, I get
a picture of Jesus throwing the tables over, creating more
noise and confusion, and then having to shout his message
over the din.
4. The final point is the disciples remembering that in
Psalms 69:9 it was written (an Old Testament prophecy
about Christ), 'The zeal of thine house hath eaten me up'.
Perhaps that is where we got the phrase, 'Eaten up with
anger'. It certainly does not paint a picture of saccharine
sweetness, but rather a picture of righteous anger in full
display.
While I am pointing these things out to my client, I am
usually throwing myself about the room acting it out. First
the quiet passive Jesus, kindly and softly asking people to
leave the temple, painstakingly shooing the oxen and sheep,
carefully and gently placing the tables on their side—all the
time keeping the gentle, passive persona. My client is usually

laughing at the end of that pitiful and obviously impossible scenario.

I then act out a scene the only way it could have happened—in an active, straightforward way. Throwing tables over, hitting the oxen on the backside with the scourge, shouting 'Ha!' or whatever sort of word people use when trying to get large animals to run. (Since I am not expert on handling large animals, I make up the words as I go along— trying to remember what I've heard John Wayne say to cattle in Western films.) It soon becomes obvious that a lot of noise was generated and that Jesus had to shout his message to be heard.

So we end up with a picture of Jesus displaying deliberate anger—by acting the scene out, the message becomes quite unchallengeable. I then sit down, wait a moment, and say in a quiet voice, 'Jesus' actions make it clear that anger is an appropriate emotion, he was the role model. I wonder if a person could really now say, "Oh, that is okay for Him, but *I* could never do that!", without sounding as though they lived to a higher standard than Christ.' With that sensible reframe, I have never yet had someone decline the anger work.

Healthy anger has a few identifiable points:

- It is focused or targeted at the person who triggered it off.
- It is physically expressed without hurting self or others.
- It is in proportion.
- It is expressed when it arises or as soon as possible thereafter.

## REPRESSED ANGER

However, when anger is repressed, it becomes destructive and out of proportion. Repressed anger is simply anger that was originally triggered off in the past, but was not expressed at that time. The repression of anger often happens during childhood because typically it is not safe (or we are not allowed) to express it. Unfortunately, what we are encouraged to do with anger is to deny it ('It isn't nice to be angry, tell brother/sister you are sorry!'), and bottle it up ('Go and play nicely now'). Of course, if our anger is towards a parent rather than a sibling, we are convinced it is even more unacceptable and therefore we are more likely to repress it.

Seldom are we told that it is okay to be angry or how to safely and appropriately express that anger. Therefore, early on we begin our storehouse of anger, finding places inside to tuck it away and hide it. After a while it changes form and expresses itself in other ways, ways that do not resemble the original form, such as: illness, depression, self-harm, negativity, pessimism, etc.

Repressed anger reminds me of a leftover food item which gets pushed to the back of the refrigerator. It is fine for a few days perhaps, but then it starts to go off. After a period of time, when the telltale odour finally draws our attention to it, we are often unable to identify its original form. We sometimes gaze at the disgusting, mouldy, green lump and wonder what it started out as—just as we gaze at illness or behaviour problems and wonder what started them off.

## HELPING CHILDREN DEAL WITH ANGER

If parents felt comfortable with their own anger and had information about how to express anger safely and appropriately, they could help their children. It is important first to acknowledge children's feelings, ('You are very angry.' 'I can see you are upset.'); secondly to acknowledge the intensity of their feelings, ('You wish you never had to see Billy again.' 'You wish Carl would have something bad happen to him'); then to intervene with a safe alternative ('Why not punch the bed and picture Carl's face where you are hitting? Really hit him hard and tell him off if you want'). Anger disperses much more quickly if you assist children to defuse it. Once it is defused, children come up with their own logical solutions ('I guess I'll just go and tell Carl that I don't like what he did and that he'd better say sorry if he wants me to keep being his friend'). Unfortunately, parents and adults often try to force a logical solution onto children before their anger has been defused. It seldom works.

Telling children they should not be angry does not work

either, but you can often hear parents or adults pushing that theory at children ('It's not nice to be angry, just tell Carl you are sorry and play nicely together.' 'Of course, you don't hate Carl, don't talk like that—you know you are friends. Now shake hands and make up'). I find it rather amazing that some parents pull their two fighting children apart and exclaim, 'Now pull yourselves together, right now!' Do they really expect to see the children suddenly shake their heads, look about in glazed amazement, experience a total state transformation and say in level, civilised tones, 'Oh, thank you. Yes, I feel much better now'? Yet parents continue to give meaningless commands of that nature.

What would happen if the parent separated the two children, saying, 'Sorry, people aren't for hitting', then steered them to a bedroom and said to the one who seems most physical, 'Okay, John, make a picture of Carl's face on the bed and really hit it. Carl will have to watch just what you would do to him. Tell the picture of him off too. Carl will be here listening to whatever you are saying.' When John was finished, then it would be Carl's turn to do the same to an image of John. All the anger and words get out, but no one is hurt. Usually kids start laughing midway through and their anger naturally disperses.

## FOCUSING ANGER

When we have a backlog of anger we tend to over-react to present-day situations, we 'blow-up' over nothing or we may direct the past anger towards other, less threatening targets. Sometimes those other targets are similar to the original situation or have a familiar feel that links them with the original situation. The problem with those sorts of targets is that they are not satisfying—our anger does not find relief— we are still 'wound up' after we over-react or take out our feelings on a different target.

Relief comes when we can focus our anger towards the person who triggered it off in the first place. In fact, it is vital to focus the anger towards the person it really belongs to, the person it originated with. Most often those people are either our parents or other significant adults to whom we were not able to express anger. Children often find it very difficult to 'own' their anger towards parents, or other close relatives, because it is threatening to be against the people on whom you are dependent—it is much safer to bury the anger, blame yourself, give the anger to someone else or express it through another sort of destructive behaviour.

## IDENTIFYING THE PERSON ANGER WAS MEANT FOR

Some clients will know exactly who their anger belongs to and just need to know how finally to face it, express and resolve it, or how to give themselves permission to express it. Others will believe that their anger only belongs to someone in the present. In order to determine if that last belief is accurate, there are several points to check out.

   a. Is this a recurring anger (similar feelings towards other individuals)?
   b. Is the intensity of the anger out of proportion to the event/s?
   c. Does your client make comparisons? i.e. 'He acts just like my mother and that really makes me angry!'
   d. Does your client feel frozen by anger, unable to react?
   e. Is your client frightened to express anger or even to acknowledge anger?

If any one of these points is present, it is most likely that your client's anger has a different source or origin from the person it is presently aimed at. The last two are clear representations of childlike reactions and strongly suggest that the Child part is reacting to a familiar scenario. That being the case, it will relate to an event that happened when your client was a child.

A few questions that are useful in determining where the anger originated are: 'What person do you remember having similar feelings towards when you were a child?' 'To whom, from your childhood, do you think this anger belongs?' Or you could ask your client to give his or her attention to the anger feelings, perhaps by remembering the last time they were experienced. When you see by their physiology that this is happening, say, 'Now, just let your unconscious mind follow these feelings back, perhaps to the first time you felt them, . . . let me know when your unconscious mind gives you a sound, a picture or a feeling to indicate you are accessing that first experience.'

From there you could either simply collect information and assign anger work or perhaps use the Personal Resource Exercise found in Chapter Five. Some anger needs to be expressed and some simply needs to be acknowledged. The client should be made aware of his or her own personal resources. You could use the Personal Resource Exercise first and if that does not clear things sufficiently, go on to the anger work.

## GETTING RID OF ANGER

Expressing anger to the problem person is done through Anger Letters and Physical Anger Exercises. These letters are **not to be posted**, they are to be brought to the session and assessed to determine if they could be even stronger. Personally confronting the abuser/problem person with past anger may open up a can of worms that your client is not prepared to deal with. The ramifications can be quite extensive, affecting the entire family, often resulting in the person who was wronged in the first place (your client) being sacrificed again. It is best that your clients work through their personal material and regain their own strength before confrontations of any sort are considered. If that time comes, the confrontation and its ramifications must be thought through and a course of action prepared for each possible response before action is taken. However, in most cases, once your clients have worked through their anger, they choose not personally to confront the problem person.

## FEELINGS TOWARDS ABUSER OR
## COLLUDING PARENT

You will observe some of the following reactions towards abusers or colluding parents:

a. *Extreme anger or lack of anger.* Your clients may be crackling with anger and ready for anger work before anything else is done or they may not be expressing any anger at all. If that is the case, you will usually be faced with someone who is rather robot-like and unable to express any feelings very well. You cannot turn off one feeling without dampening the others as well. This client will need to work through his or her material for a while before engaging in anger work. Some of the suggestions for dealing with repressed anger will be helpful for this person.

b. *Betrayal of role of protector/nurturer/rescuer.* It is accurate when clients feel the abuser or colluding parent has betrayed the role of protector, nurturer or rescuer, but clients will usually feel very guilty for feeling betrayed. Verify to your clients that their parents did betray their role of protector/nurturer/rescuer if they abused, colluded or did not establish communication lines about bodies or sexual issues with their child. Even when parents were not involved in the child's abuse, they let the child down if they did not create open communication about bodies or sexual issues. For without those communication lines the child had no way of disclosing the abuse.

c. *Inability to trust.* Some clients cannot trust specific genders and others cannot trust people in general. It is not surprising when you consider that they were badly let down when they were first learning about trust. Tell your clients that the inability to trust is a normal reaction to their childhood experiences, but that they now have the opportunity to learn how and whom to trust.

d. *Does not feel loved.* The most common feeling for victims of abuse is that the abuse happened because they were not loved. Children are too inexperienced to understand that the adults around them are emotionally inadequate, so when those adults behave in hurtful and damaging ways, children believe it must be because the adult does not love them. It is important to explain to clients that the adults' behaviour was about their own limitations, and *not a reflection of their feelings towards the child*. In many cases, the adults do love the child, but have no useful way of demonstrating it. In other cases, the adults have no conception of the term 'love' and are merely acting out their own emotional pain and damage.

e. *Desires or loathes emotional link.*   Some clients will sacrifice anything (particularly their own self-esteem) to gain an emotional link with their abuser or colluding parent. This is a normal reaction to their past experiences. The Child part is still trying to get the love and attention that was never there for her or him. Unfortunately, the abuser or colluding parent is probably in no better position to give those things now than he or she was at the time. It is only possible now to receive those things from the Adult part, so it is useful for you to explain to your client that it is time to let go of the false hope of the past and grasp onto the real hope of the present.

Other clients will loathe any suggestion of an emotional link with the abuser or colluding parent. That is also a normal reaction to the past experiences. Sometimes clients feel guilty because they have such strong feelings, and think they should 'respect' their parents. In that case it would be helpful for you to explain how respect works.

Respect can only be earned, it is impossible to give respect to anyone who has not behaved in a way that has merited it. Just as it is impossible not to respect a person who has done something to deserve it, even when we do not like other aspects of that person. Therefore, if people do not respect their parents, for instance, it is a result of the parents' behaviour—a natural consequence—not a deficiency in the parents' child. If parents want respect from their children, it is important for them to behave in a manner that warrants respect.

f. *Abuser/colluding parent responsible for loss of childhood.*   Often clients will feel a profound sense of yearning for a lost natural, carefree childhood. Abusing or colluding parents have to accept the responsibility for their personal actions which damaged or restricted their children. Using the PICT letter series or some of the other tools, clients can take the learnings from their past and create the person they would have been if abuse had never happened. Doing this restores the person the child was meant to be. The Personal Resource Exercise (p. 161) creates a new childhood experience of 'naturalness', giving back part of the lost childhood.

The Happy Memory Retrieval Exercise (p. 184) expands and intensifies any happy times experienced during childhood.

g. *'I made them do it!'*   This is a very common reaction experienced by children, prompted by the mistaken belief, 'It's all my fault' or 'I asked for it'. (This is often encouraged by parental comments such as: 'Look what you made me do now!' 'You ask for trouble!' 'You get what you asked for!' 'You brought this on yourself!') Many people think they are responsible for the abuse experienced during childhood. However, it is always the adults who are responsible for whatever abusive behaviour they have demonstrated. It is the adults who had the choice of what behaviour they could use in any given situation. It is the adults who also had the choice to ask for help if they thought their behaviour was out of control.

## ANGER LETTERS

Anger letters can be written by the Child ('I hate you! You are bad and horrible! I don't like you touching me and I wish you were dead!') as direct statements of the feelings she was never able to express at the time of abuse or they can be written by the Adult on behalf of the Child ('You disgusting, evil bastard! How dare you do those things to a loving, innocent child. You are lower than the lowest form of life. Even comparing you to a stone would be an insult to the stone, you are in a class of your own—you and people like Hitler. You deserve to die, you are a waste of a human body. You can never harm her again, she is out of your clutches now, she is with me and I will protect and love her. We laugh in your face because we are safe and happy and you are alone, hated and despised—you are an insignificant piece of shit!').

I usually suggest that people think of how it would be writing their anger letter from both the Child and Adult, and then use the one that seems to give fullest expression to their feelings. Sometimes it is helpful to write an anger letter from both aspects—let your client choose.

## Love/Like on the Shelf

Most of the time your clients will be writing anger letters to the people that they are angry with but also love or like. Because the love and like can stop an effective anger letter from being written or a physical anger exercise from ever starting, ask your clients to take out the parts of the person that are loved or liked and put those parts on an imaginary shelf. Using both hands, make a scooping motion as though moving something from waist height in front of you and placing it on a shelf that is up and to your right. Now that those loved or liked parts are safely on the shelf, all that is left is the part they hate and despise. Gesture again to the place in front of you, as if distastefully referring to the bulk of the body of the person—'all that is left'. Remind your client to put the problem person's parts back together after the exercise.

## No Censoring

Since we have been conditioned from childhood never to give anger a place in our lives, it becomes difficult to launch right into the anger letters. Your clients may have to write a few before they get the freedom of expression they need. One way that you can assist in this is to encourage them from the first not to censor the letters.

Censoring simply refers to thinking of something to write, i.e. 'I wish you had a slow moving, painful cancer, so you would suffer like you made me suffer', but immediately thinking, 'Oh, what a terrible thing to say, I could never write that!' and instead writing, 'If you ever get a painful illness, you will know how I suffered.' Remind your client that wishing people physically ill (or dead) does not make the person physically ill (or dead).

An important aspect of anger letters is for the person to say the 'unsayable', whatever that means to the individual. Often it includes wishing people dead, or more directly, killing them. If clients bring letters where they have tortured and killed the abuser/problem person, please praise them for doing so. They will probably be worried that such a letter means they are a closet killer or that in writing the letter they have unleashed a killer force from within some hidden recess of themselves. Explain that *the intensity of the anger letter is simply a reflection of the intensity of the anger and rage the Child felt*, and consequently carried throughout life. Praise them for finally and safely venting such a force, because doing so actually allows that anger to disperse. Therefore, they have accomplished the relieving of any 'killer' potential rather than the creation of it.

## Swear Words

Tell your client to use swear words if they come to mind. This is the time to say what you were never allowed to say. Reassure your client that you will not be offended reading whatever he or she writes. I may joke and say the only way clients can offend me is if they write a 'nice' letter. I sometimes give clients a personal example of the importance of using words you were never allowed to use in the following way:

When I was six, I started school. Occasionally, an older child would write the F word on a wall. This action would get that child into big trouble for that was the worst word in the world. When some kid eventually told me what the F word actually meant, my world fell apart, because the F word was happening to me! The worst word in the world was happening to me, so I must be very bad.

That was a Friday. It took me until Sunday to get enough courage together, when my stepfather was out, to tell my mother about what had always been happening to me. Although it was very difficult to talk to my mother, I felt I had to tell her because I now knew it was so very bad. The immediate problem was that I did not know what words to use because I was not allowed to use the F word. Which is rather ironic when you think about it— I was not allowed to say fuck, but I was certainly allowed to do it.

In a very nervous state, I began to cry, then I began to sob. It seemed a rather sudden behaviour change to my mother and she even put me on her lap to ask what was wrong. Sobbing so hard that I was hiccuping, the sentence I blurted out was, 'Daddy puts his thing in my thing'.

When you think about it, it is quite pathetic that my

mother had not even given me a proper word for my own genitals. Yet again, I could see, touch and experience genitals, but I was not allowed to know their real name, not even my own.

Unfortunately for me, mother was not keen to know about daddy's thing and my thing, so she called me a liar. She shoved me off her lap and shook me, shouting, 'You're lying, aren't you, aren't you! You dirty, little troublemaker, you're lying aren't you!', until I finally agreed I was a liar. (I started off by saying 'no', but it soon became painfully obvious that 'yes, I'm a liar' was the only acceptable answer.)

Two weeks later, daddy reminded me that he had warned me no one would believe me and told me he had to 'really talk hard' to keep me from being sent to prison. Restating my same words he said, 'It wasn't very nice for you to tell mummy that I put my thing in your thing, was it?'

I followed the obvious script (what I was expected to say) and replied, 'no'.

Now, let's move ahead to my adult life, to where I am acknowledging my anger towards my mother. I dare say you will understand why, in my anger letter, I had my mother crawl towards me on hands and knees, crying and begging for my forgiveness, while I stood back coldly. Cutting in on what she was saying, and finally using the F word, I shouted, 'FUCK OFF, YOU FUCKING BITCH!' Boy, was that a relief!

When the strongest swear word is what needs to be said, say it. It is more important for your client to be free from crippling anger than to worry about some hypocritical rules about swearing.

Whatever your client writes, praise his or her effort. When assessing the letter's content ask, 'Is there anything you have censored? Anything you thought was too much to say?' If the answer is affirmative, discuss the censored bit, approve of it and re-assign the anger letter. Include the censored statement, and suggest she adds some more statements like it. I encourage clients to go over the top, lightheartedly saying, 'You can blame the problem person for the spots you had in adolescence if you like.' Remember, you cannot say too much in the anger letter, but you can say too little.

Your client will be finished with anger letters when she cannot conjure up any more anger, when the feelings have lost their impact, when your client makes statements such as, 'It doesn't seem that important any more, I just see him (problem person) as pathetic.'

**Focus on Problem Person**
I want to state again that it is vitally important for your client to focus his or her anger towards the person who triggered it. It is no good writing an anger letter about anger or about all the people in general who have wronged you. Writing letters in that way simply winds you up. What is most useful is to focus the anger onto one person at a time, giving that person the full force of your anger—that will bring relief. So, watch for diversions in your clients' letters, for instance where they include other family members when they are meant to be writing to mother. Explain about focusing on one person again and re-assign the letter (unless the reference was brief). You are looking for undiluted anger, as well as uncensored anger.

The letters can be started with the person's name, but without the polite 'Dear' that we learnt to use in school— unless it is used facetiously, i.e. 'Dear mother, which is exactly what you aren't to me!' Also, do not use capital letters. Keep the problem person's name in lower case letters; it is another way of diminishing his or her power. Some people start the letters with a colourful, descriptive word, such as, 'You bastard!' One letter I enjoyed reading started, 'Hello, you disgusting little worm!'

## PHYSICAL ANGER EXERCISES

Physical anger exercises can come in many forms, but a good starting point is pillow bashing. Ask your clients to go to their bedroom, place their pillow on the side of the bed, kneel down, picture the problem person's face on the pillow, remove the bits they like or love and then raise their hands (clenched in a united fist) and bring them down hard onto the face of the problem person. While doing this, it is helpful for them to say aloud, 'I hate you!' or 'No!' If your clients are not alone in the house and are not able to shout out, tell them that a 'stage whisper' voice is sufficient—give a demonstration of the clenched fists and 'stage whisper'.

Explain that everyone feels wooden and silly doing this exercise, but ask them to persevere for the rewards are worth it. They can do this exercise as the Child or the Adult, whichever seems appropriate for the issue at hand. They can try one role and then switch over to the other if it seems more effective. It is also permissible to use a badminton racket or tennis racket in place of their fists, but I suggest that, whichever is chosen, it needs to be a firm object rather than something soft and flexible.

When clients are doing a physical anger exercise, the 'focus' aspect is accomplished by simply imaging the problem person's face as the recipient of the physical blow. For instance, seeing the face where their fists hit the pillow, where their foot hits the ground (running), under the cloth while cleaning, under the hoover while vacuuming. Clients will know when they are finished with a specific anger exer-. cise, because they will feel spent.

Almost any physical task can be converted to a physical anger exercise. Some people have used Katie's idea (see *Rescuing the 'Inner Child'*) of imagining the problem person tied to the back of their exercise bicycle (or a real bicycle); as they pedal faster the problem person is bashed against the ground harder. Although the main aim is to place the problem person's face where the physical point of contact is, the bicycle example works because the force applied to the pedals determines the degree that the problem person bounces on the ground, so the harder you pedal, the harder he or she bounces.

## ANGER LETTER VS. PHYSICAL EXERCISE

When words are going round and round in a person's head and he or she wishes there was an 'off' button, that indicates that an anger letter will work best. However, if the person is feeling agitated, unable to sit still and finds him- or herself pacing, a physical exercise will be in order. Sometimes a person needs to do both.

I generally start clients off with written exercises, because most people have some words stored up that could use an airing. However, if a new client shows overt physical agitation and displays anger in other ways, I will start with physical anger exercises or a combination of both.

Explain to your clients how to determine which anger exercise to use, because these are tools they will be able to use for themselves for the rest of their lives—not because the abuse from childhood will be around, but because we are often faced with situations where it is not helpful to express our anger the moment it is triggered. For instance, the client may find a bit of a problem arising if she blows off steam to her supervisor or boss. Often people are faced with a job situation where the behaviour of those people in charge is stress-making, but are unable to change jobs. Anger exercises are wonderful tools to use to enable them to keep their cool at work and unload frustration and anger safely.

Clients may feel strong anger towards a partner but do not feel it is appropriate to deliver it full blast. This is a good opportunity to use an anger letter to defuse anger to a level that is more manageable. Using the anger letters gives the writer more control to choose an action rather than be the puppet of a reaction. Once your client has defused the strong anger, she will be in a better position to discuss the problem area and negotiate a solution. Going into a discussion like that with strong, undefused anger is unproductive. Sometimes an anger letter will need to be followed by a physical anger exercise before your client is ready for discussion.

When anger letters are not brought to a counsellor for assessment, there is a very useful way to destroy them. Advise your client to tear them up and keep tearing them into very, very small pieces. Take those very small pieces and put them into the toilet, sit down and do whatever comes naturally. It makes a wonderful exclamation point to an anger letter. Some people find more satisfaction burning the small letter pieces.

**Variations**

Sometimes it is useful to add sound to your anger exercise. One way of doing this is to scream into a cushion. At first, your client may be worried that the screams may be heard by the neighbours. Assure her that a scream muffled by a cushion is about the same level as a speaking voice, but encourage her to test it out at home using a cassette recorder, if she likes.

In some cases, it may be useful for your client to bite the cushion as she screams. I found it was particularly helpful to throw myself full length on the bed, scream into and bite the cushion, while kicking and rolling about. While lying face down, I could press my face down into the cushion and scream and pound the bed with my fists.

Another thing one can do with a cushion is strangle it. Small square cushions are best for this exercise. They are narrow enough to get your hands around, but thick enough to simulate a neck. It is good to shout directly into the problem person's 'face' as you strangle. Once I even spat in the problem person's 'face'. It was definitely worth the trouble of having to wash the cushion later. The 'heads' can be bashed on things too. Suggest that your client vary what she does until she finds the most satisfying expression of anger.

**Samples of Anger Letters**

Give your clients information early on to explain the use of anger letters and how to do them, then encourage them to use the letters when necessary. You should be assigning anger letters but also encouraging clients to write anger letters for themselves.

The first sample letter was done by Peggy while she was in the middle of a letter series. It was a spontaneous effort.

*Peggy's Anger Letter to Father*

Who the hell do you think you are? You are a worthless piece of shit. How dare you behave so monstrously. How bloody well dare you! You are despicable, you are nothing. There is nothing in this universe so vile and disgusting as you. You are worse than anything I can think of. I'm not surprised you hate to vomit, you might see it and notice that you are worse and even more vile smelling. You ARE, you know—worse than a pile of rotting, stinking vomit, even maggots wouldn't touch you. YOU ARE POISON AND I HATE YOU.

That was me, that frightened little girl you hurt, who only wanted her daddy to love her. This is me now, STRONG, CLEVER, POWERFUL AND OUT TO GET YOU!

Do you like it? It's what you created. You made this hate inside me. You put it there and now I'm ready to give it back. Ah, yes, you see, you know and you are afraid. Too late, too late. Go ahead, grovel, beg. My hate has no ears to hear with. There is only blind, black rage here now. Nothing else left for you, you destroyed it. Now I will destroy you. Get up on your feet, GET UP!

He's quivering now, consumed by fear and I have him. I advance and he tries to run but his frightened legs can't move. They've frozen into jelly like mine were, AND I HATE HIM. 'OPEN YOUR MOUTH. DO IT. NOW.'

He does, crocodile tears leak from his face and my hands big and powerful grip his sides. Ever so slowly I squeeze and out of his mouth his essence pours. The reality of him forced out by me before his eyes. His body is surrounded, covered and splattered by the stench and vileness he spews forth. He is drowning now, in the vomit that is himself.

'YOU DID THIS,' I yell, 'YOU ARE THIS.' 'Now you are covered and drowning in it and I am free. I have the power. Now you are really lost.' Choking and gagging on himself he dies and is consumed by the acid stench he is. Loathesome git.

**DOROTHY**

Dorothy was a victim of ritualistic abuse. When her memories finally started to surface, so did anger that she was scared to express. The following two letters are a sample of Dorothy's experience of dealing with terrifying anger. As you read it will not be difficult to recognise that the first is written by the Adult and the second by the Child.

The first anger letter is the completion of a prior attempt which was blocked by her fear of retribution, even though she was now living in another country. Her words were, 'If I express my anger they will somehow know and I will be punished'. So, we first did a Mistaken Belief Visualisation to delete that block.

When she was able to complete the anger letter, she discovered that the result was actually a strong sense of relief. Dorothy found that pushing past the fear gave her freedom rather than the bondage threatened by the 'retribution' belief. Pushing past the fear revealed the truth of her own power and removed the façade of 'their' power. In fact, her anger letter takes the form of retribution. Therefore she is able to direct what she fears *from* the perpetrators back *to* the perpetrators and in so doing has a powerful experience of the freedom from fear.

Notice how Dorothy reflects back to the abusers accurate descriptions of what they inflicted upon her. She literally gives the pain back to them. This is a very good sign that your client is getting full benefit from the anger letter and it is therefore something you need to look for in clients' anger letters.

Please be aware that your clients will not consciously be working out what they are doing. It is just happening spontaneously. They are writing quickly and are full of feeling and many times will be surprised when they read back what they have written. My comments in square brackets are guidelines for you to follow what is happening subconsciously with the client.

### Dorothy's Adult Anger Letter

Big Dorothy returns to where she and Little Dorothy left the group. The group is still bolted in place, still being tormented by the electricity. She can tell by the glimmer of hope and anticipation in their eyes when they see her that they suspect their torture will end soon. [*Reflecting back.*]

They are willing to bargain, say anything and promise anything to be released from their hell. But they are liars and Big Dorothy knows this. Nothing they can say or do will diminish or erase what they have done to Little Dorothy and others. Big Dorothy knows they are the embodiment of evil and hate. Given any moment 'out' they will hurt, maim, torture, harass, humiliate, shame, degrade, debase, terrorise, brainwash, defile, destroy, deceive and manipulate again. [*Reflecting back exactly what she had received.*]

They are vicious, cruel and inhuman. They are dangerous freaks capable of unspeakable and inhumane crimes and violations against humanity. They cannot remain, nothing about them can remain. The earth vomited them forth and that is where they should return. The earth agrees.

The ground begins to tremor and violently quake. Giant cracks in the ground start to appear. The group looks to Big Dorothy for any sign or acknowledgement that she will relent. [*Evidence that she is wielding the power.*] As they see the resolute stare in her eyes they are filled with the darkest terror. The kind which only their victims have known. [*More reflecting back.*]

Their still electrified bodies begin to retch. They vomit in excruciating fear and horror over what they now realise is their fate. They try desperately to scream and cry out for help. Their voices are still paralysed. All they can do is still vomit their terror all over themselves. [*More reflecting.*]

They smother, choke and gag. They are utterly and hopelessly trapped—wrenched into that spot from which there is no escape. They suffer totally and completely for all the terror and pain of their. pasts. THEY NOW KNOW. [*More reflecting back.*]

The crack in the earth becomes bigger and deeper. In an instant, the earth eats them alive. They are sucked into the darkest abyss. The giant chasm slowly closes. That is all. It is over. They are gone—trapped forever in their own hell.

My comment upon reading this letter was, '*Well done! Excellent!*'

### Dorothy's Child Anger Letter

[*This one starts out from the Adult, but begins moving into the Child at about the second paragraph. Notice the shift as she starts talking* **to** *them rather than* **about** *them. Notice as more childish wording is used, until it becomes totally childlike.*]

I don't like doing this now. I hate this shit. I hate how it makes me feel. I hate that it happened. I hate that I have to release this anger and hate. I hate the need to dredge up this poison, this hideousness, this terror, this horror. I want to go numb now. I want to get drunk. I want to escape. I want out of this. I want that it never happened. I hate that it happened. I hate all those people who fucked up my life. They fucked up my head. They fucked up my body.

They wouldn't leave me alone. They hurt me. They hurt others. They hurt my animal friends. Why? Why? Why? Who are you? What did you want? Why did you want me? Why did you hate me so? Why wouldn't you leave me alone? Why did you fuck, fuck, fuck up me? What could I give you? What did I have?

I was so little. I just wanted to play. I didn't want to be hurt. I didn't want to be scared. I just wanted to be little. I just wanted to play. I just wanted to be loved. You didn't love me. You fucked up me. You hurt me. I was too little to be hurt. Why me?

[*Now she's moving into present tense defining what she experiences—feelings, surroundings, behaviours.*] I hate being scared. I hate the terror. I hate the fear. I hate the snakes. I hate the screams. I hate the upside down. I hate being trapped. I hate you for fucking up me. I hate you for hurting me. I hate you for sticking me. I hate being hurt. I hate being tricked. I hate being fucked with. I hate the screams—I could never scream.

I hate your nastiness. I hate your scariness, I hate your trickery. I hate your stupidity. I hate your smell. I hate your tongues. I hate your red eyes. I hate your bloodiness. I hate your hatchets. I hate your ropes. I hate your sounds. I hate your skin. I hate your breathing. I hate your cold touch. I hate the warm blood. I hate the twisting. I hate the touching. I hate the squirming. I hate the sounds. I hate the chanting.

I hate the moaning. I hate the twisting. I hate the choking. I hate the vomit. I hate the spit. I hate the burning. I hate the flesh. I hate the sickness. I hate the hair. I hate the cutting. I hate the slapping. I hate the dangling. I hate the wetness. I hate the stickiness. I hate the sliminess. I hate the dead eyes. I hate the sores. I hate the holes. I hate the dead eyes. I hate the burning. I hate the white flesh. I hate the slipperiness. I hate the stink. I hate the slime. I hate the deadness. I hate the hanging.

I hate my legs apart. I hate things inside me. I hate that I'll explode. I hate being laid open. I hate ugly things in me. I hate stuff over my face. I hate being crushed. I hate being tied up. I hate holding my breath. I hate not being able to move. I hate being held down. I hate being twisted. I hate things touching me. I hate being licked. I hate tongues on me. I hate being gouged. I hate being poked. I hate your noses. I hate your bony hands.

I hate dead animals. I hate animal screams. I hate bloody fur. I hate being little. I hate wanting to cry. I hate being laughed at. I hate being ridiculed. I hate being smirked at. I hate slobbery kisses. I hate drooling. I hate being grabbed in the groin. I hate being tickled.

I hate all you fuckers. I hate what you did. I hate your nastiness. I hate your dirtiness. I hate your filthiness. I hate your roughness. I hate your coldness. I hate your hairiness. I hate your sweat. I hate between your legs. I hate that thing on you. I hate seeing you hold that thing. I hate seeing you touch yourself. I hate seeing you raise up those robes and all that pinkish, white flesh.

[*Now she moves into retribution—giving back to them what they inflicted upon her.*] I want to kill you. I want to hurt you. I want to slap and beat you. I want your skin to sting. I want the snakes to bite bloody holes in your faces. I want you to choke on your own vomit, in terror. I want you to feel like you're drowning. I want you to feel like you're choking to death. I want you to feel like someone is strangling you. I want you to feel like you're being eaten alive. I want you to scream 'til your throat burns and is full of blood. I want you not to be able to close your eyes. You have to see everything. You have to be eaten and bitten. Things have to crawl all over you. You're smothered under dead things. Snakes slither all over you. They look in your eyes. The snakes want in your mouth. The snakes want in your ears. They crawl between your legs. They bite up inside you. They won't let you alone.

The warm blood smothers your face. It drips on you. You have to put your hands inside all the bloody warm things. You can't get away. You're trapped. You're strapped down. You have to be naked. You have to be cold. You have to be on your back. You have to have your legs pulled apart. You have to ache. You have to scream. You have to beg, beg, beg. You have to be laughed at. You have to watch. You have to keep your eyes open. You can't hide. You can't escape. You have to stay alive while you die.

## ALTERNATIVES TO ANGER LETTERS

When your client is so frightened of his or her anger that the idea of writing an anger letter is enough to cause him or her to consider giving up therapy, there is another technique you can use. Very often these people are convinced that the results of consciously getting in touch with their anger would be totally to lose control and perhaps wreak havoc on the room or other people, or would cause them to 'go crazy' or have a breakdown. Understandably, these people are resistant to writing anger letters or doing physical anger exercises.

There is a Neuro-Linguistic Programming (NLP) technique used for phobias that I have altered somewhat for use with 'untouchable' anger. This technique allows clients to express their anger without having to 'see' it or feel it and yet still achieve the end result—relief. As you use this technique, ask clients to nod when they have the picture you have just suggested (pausing where indicated). **Do not go further until your client has nodded**. Do not ask your client to disclose the content of this visualisation. On some occasions he or she may choose to offer content information, but do not ask for it.

## Anger Visualisation

'Imagine you are walking down the street of an unfamiliar town . . . Notice the shops around you . . . Soon you come to a cinema . . . You buy a ticket and go in . . . Standing in the foyer you slowly observe your surroundings . . .

You see the door to the main cinema area and the sign marked 'Entrance' . . . You enter the cinema area and pause while your eyes adjust to the dim light . . . You are the only person in the cinema, this will be your own private viewing . . . You choose a centrally located seat and sit down . . . The curtains open and you see the wide screen before you . . . Across the screen is a colour, stationary picture of you doing something mundane and ordinary— maybe doing the washing up or reading a book . . .

While that still picture of you stays on the screen, you float up, leaving that 'you' in the seat, and go to the back of the room . . . Standing at the back of the room you observe yourself sitting in the centrally located seat, watching the screen . . . Now you float up, leaving that 'you' standing at the back of the room, and go up to the projection room . . .

Looking back down the stairs, you observe that 'you' standing at the back of the room, who in turn is observing that 'you' sitting in the centrally located seat, who is watching the screen . . .

Look around the projection room, particularly noticing the small viewing window with small holes to let in the sound . . . Touch the small holes on the viewing window . . . Notice the reel of film ready to be shown and the levers marked 'Start' and 'Stop' . . . You read the label of the film and see that it is in black and white, and is about you, expressing your anger/rage to the person you are most angry with . . . Make a note of the title . . .

You now pull the lever marked 'Start' and the film begins . . . You are only watching the 'you' standing at the back of the room, who is watching 'you' in the centrally located seat, who is watching the black and white film . . . That 'you' in the centrally located seat is watching the demonstration of your strongest anger . . . That 'you' standing at the back of the room is watching the reaction of 'you' in the seat . . . You in the projection room are observing the reaction of the 'you' standing at the back of the room . . . Observe the 'you' at the back of the room until the film has completed . . .

Now pull the lever marked 'Stop' . . . The screen again holds the colour, still picture of you doing something ordinary . . . It is time to walk back down the stairs and step into the 'you' standing at the back of the room . . .

Now walk to, and step into, the 'you' sitting in the centrally located seat . . . Sitting there you now watch as the screen goes blank and the curtains close . . . You leave your seat and return to the foyer of the cinema . . . Your eyes readjust to the light and you step out into the warmth of the sunshine . . .

Perhaps now, as you open your eyes and come back to this room, you would like to stretch and notice how relaxed you feel.'

After your client has reorientated and collected his or her thoughts, you may enquire, 'How was that for you?' [Notice this question does not ask for content, it merely enquires about the overall experience.] Give clients some relaxed time to check out how they feel and to answer your question, for it will no doubt be a very different experience. Classically, people who have shut off anger automatically shut off many other feelings and therefore may not be used to having feelings.

Once they begin to release anger and have access to their feelings, feelings may become a new, and sometimes scary, world. You will find yourself defining what emotions feel like. An example of that comes from a client of Pamela's who was explaining a very puzzling experience to Pamela. She was driving her car, thinking about a positive experience, when she began to have a feeling well up inside her. It was not scary, she did not feel bad, but it was very strong. It welled up from her tummy, into her chest and even filled her head and she noticed her ears tingled and she found she could not stop smiling. It lasted several minutes.

'What happened to me?' she asked. 'It sounds like you were experiencing the feelings of joy,' Pamela responded. 'Oh . . . ' the woman said in wonderment, 'so, that's what joy feels like.' For those of you who have always had access to your feelings, that example may sound very strange to you, but for those clients who have lived many years with feelings shut off, it will sound very normal. Please treat those clients with gentle understanding, just as you would if someone who had experienced severe leg injuries was relearning the use of his legs.

Approaching anger from the visualisation direction usually assists clients to realise they can face anger without dying or going off the deep end. After perhaps even a couple of these visualisations, you can move them on to another easier step—just writing individual words.

**Writing Words**
Sometimes clients may find writing a whole anger letter too daunting; putting all those scary sentences and complete thoughts down on paper may seem too much to face at first. You might suggest that they simply take one piece of paper, focus the problem person's face on the paper and write any one-word description of feelings or anger all over the face. One young woman wrote words like, bitch, hate, stupid, cow, cunt, whore, kill, spit. She said the words started slowly and then began to pick up momentum. Some words were written several times, others just a couple of times. After she filled the page once, she then wrote a second layer of words on top of the first. Some clients write several layers

of words. It makes a good starting point that can then be extended to writing whole letters.

## USEFUL BOOK ON ANGER

*Managing Anger*, Gael Lindenfield (Thorsons)
Written in her usual easy-to-read style and containing practical and enlightening information.

# 5 Tools

The PICT letter series, including the Mistaken Belief Visualisation, is the basic tool for working with clients who have experienced abuse. In this chapter we will look at additional tools which follow the basic formula of the letter series (child disclosures, new information given, old event changed).

People's needs vary and it is important for you, the counsellor, to have several tools available to meet those varied needs. For instance, some people need to work very slowly to know they are going somewhere. If this is the case, you will often hear them tell you that, 'I know it is going to take a long time for me to get over what has happened. I've got to understand why those things happened to me.' The letter series will suit these clients well. They will have the opportunity to experience everything step-by-step and will also have a wealth of information about themselves.

Other people will need to move more quickly and will not need to have much detailed information. You will notice statements such as: 'I just want to come to terms with everything now! I want to get on with my life and leave all that childhood stuff in the past.' For these people you can utilise some, or all, of the tools listed in this chapter as well as the Mistaken Belief Visualisation on its own.

For still others you may find a combination of the two (PICT letter series and additional tools) the best way forward. This is particularly true when you come to an area where the quick tools are not enough and the problem still persists. This is usually an indication that your client needs more detailed information for this area before he or she can continue forward. Stop and do a letter series or perhaps just a Letter TO:. No matter which way you are working, if one tool does not finish the job, simply use another, until you find one that completes the task.

## Tea Towel Syndrome

Even when you have completed a piece of work your clients may find they go back to a behaviour a few times before it is finally left behind. I call this the Tea Towel Syndrome and I give the following metaphor to new clients to explain it.

Have you, or someone you knew, ever changed where you hang the tea towel in your kitchen? Remember what happens then? Usually the first time you need to use the tea towel, you go to the old place. Of course, nothing is there now and you quickly remember the new place. This goes on for a few days until you only forget when you are in a bit of a flap—you are rushing around, pots are boiling over and you quickly reach for the tea towel only to discover you are in the old place. You say, 'Oh, darn,' or whatever and rush over to the new place. After a couple of weeks you no longer go to the old place even when you are in a flap. A while later a friend comes to visit and comments, 'Oh, you've changed where you hang your tea towel.' By now you are used to the new place and for a moment you had forgotten the tea towel had ever hung in the old place. You smile at your friend and reply, 'Yes, you're right, I have.'

Well, change work is a little like the tea towel. At first, out of habit you may rush over to the old behaviour, but when you do it will not have the same impact. Like the tea towel, nothing will be there and you will think, 'Why am I even doing this?' as you move over to the new behaviour. Then after a few days you only go to the old behaviour when you are in a flap—you are stressed, rushed and under pressure. Of course, when you start the old behaviour it is empty, with no impact like before, and you will say, 'Oh, darn,' and move over to the new behaviour again. In a few weeks you will no longer use the old behaviour even when you are in a flap. After a while, a friend comes to visit and comments, 'Oh, you don't do X any more.' You are pleasantly surprised to realise that the new behaviour has become so familiar you have forgotten that you used to have the old one. You reply, 'Yes, you're right, I don't.'

## ASSESSING CLIENT'S READINESS FOR CHANGE WORK

I have found my work as a counsellor, specialising in child-hood abuse, to be very rewarding. Often friends or acquaintances ask me how I cope with such a depressing subject, how I keep from sinking under the weight of the horror stories I continually hear. My answer is that if I did not witness any emotional change in clients, I would *not* be able to cope. However, with the greater percentage of clients I see remarkable and lasting change happen for them. This is an exhilarating experience, like witnessing an emotional rebirth.

It is that 'greater percentage' that keeps me going, but what about the remaining percentage?—those clients who apparently have an inexhaustible supply of 'red herrings' and seem to be avoiding the issues they say they have come to solve/change; clients who appear to generate every conceivable problem/block possible to stop or delay their progress; clients who are 'stuck'.

Thank goodness their numbers were few, because I found that for me 'stuck' clients were a major source of energy drain. They seemed to take three times as long to get one-third as far as others during which time I expended twice as much energy as usual. Therefore, when I enrolled in a Neuro-Linguistic Program (NLP) Practitioners course which offered a personal project as part of the training, I chose 'stuck' clients as my topic. I am delighted to say that I found in NLP a technique that works a treat for determining which clients are appropriate candidates for change work. It is called The Well Formed Outcome.

### Assessing Goals/Outcomes

The Well Formed Outcome can be used in a variety of ways. I will address its use to elicit information with which to determine the viability of a person's goal (or outcome) for being in therapy. There can be underlying issues (secondary gain) that your client unconsciously realises would make attaining his or her goal a loss, rather than a gain. Although that person may be aware of those issues, there is not always a conscious awareness of the connection between the issues and the goal. For instance, your client says she wants to gain confidence as a result of therapy. This may seem a useful gain, but if subconsciously your client is aware that her partner would feel threatened by the gain of confidence and, this would consequently put the relationship in jeopardy, she may sabotage that confidence goal. Should reaching the goal cause more loss than gain, it would be emotionally unsafe, and therefore the subconscious will throw in countless blocks to prevent that happening.

The Well Formed Outcome assists in determining if a goal/outcome is not safe, or will not maintain a healthy emotional ecology. If that is the case, it would not be useful for your client to engage in change work at that time. This fact will be obvious to both the counsellor and the client and therefore it will enable you to address a more appropriate direction for your client.

For clients who are ready to engage in change work, the Well Formed Outcome is a very efficient method of directing the mind towards collecting information that will be beneficial in reaching the desired goal. In fact, many times the person will take a few steps towards attaining the goal while simply answering the questions.

I have changed my client intake format to start with the Well Formed Outcome during the initial assessment session. This helps me and my client to establish clearly what is wanted from therapy. Where I had come unstuck in the past was in taking statements of 'I want to change my situation' (behaviour, feelings, etc.) at face value and starting work with my client towards change. However, if that change threatened his or her emotional ecology then a collection of 'red herrings' or blocks would start to appear whenever change was imminent.

Using the Well Formed Outcome requires people to focus on a more precise description of what change they want. In doing this, it becomes much easier and quicker to determine if that change is going to be viable. In some cases, people are primarily after an opportunity simply to 'unload' about what has happened to them, a chance to talk to someone who is not judgmental, who is caring and understanding.

Those aspects, which are only a part of what is on offer with PICT, would be the draw for that particular client, but the directive change work would have to be rejected. Therefore, it would obviously be inappropriate to attempt to engage these people in the directive change work which is outlined in this book. It would be more useful to offer clients Rogerian/person-centred counselling or perhaps to refer them to an appropriate support group.

Although I have been discussing the use of the Well Formed Outcome during the initial assessment session to determine the client's suitability for change work, please be aware that it can be used, for the same purpose, at any time during therapy. It can also be used simply to assist an existing client to clarify any desired goal.

May I suggest that you write down the answers you are given when you do this with a client. I used a printed form. It helps to have an accurate account of what can be some extremely important information.

**Congruency**
It is vitally important to be aware of how congruent your clients are when answering any questions. For instance, when giving affirmative answers, their voices should be firm, their body movements positive and eye contact easily maintained. However, if when replying positively, their voices are hesitant and questioning, their body movements hesitant or agitated and eye contact lost as they search for the answer, you are seeing an incongruent answer—you are seeing someone who has a hesitant part. If you have any suggestion that a 'yes' answer is in question, simply ask, 'Would I be right in saying that a part of you is in agreement with this and a part of you is not sure?'

Incongruent body movements may include shaking the head 'no' while saying 'yes' (or vice versa); turning the head away or down; hand up to face or chin in a 'thinking' gesture; furrowing of brows; arms locked across chest; hands clasped together; fingers drumming or twiddling; hands held or clasped between knees, under armpits, under thighs (unless, of course, it is chilly in the room). You will probably add to this suggested list as you become more aware of the movements that indicate that one part of someone disagrees with another part.

As far as eye movement goes, when the client first hears your question, you will usually see some quick eye movement as he or she internally searches for the answer. This is quite normal and necessary. If, however, when giving the answer clients search for several seconds or are unable to keep eye contact with you at all, it *might* be an indication that there is some incongruence to be explored.

Please be aware that any incongruence does not suggest that a person is lying (although those signals could also be there in that case), it simply suggests that one part of the person may not be in harmony with the rest of that person. That, of course, is useful information to determine possible blocks and therefore it needs to be explored.

## THE WELL FORMED OUTCOME

1. *What outcome do you want from therapy?*
You want your client to sum up what is desired from therapy. So, if after asking the question 'What outcome do you want from therapy?', your client looks at you blankly, rephrase the question, 'How would you sum up the outcome you want from therapy?' You are looking for one or two words or a short phrase, but if the person gives you a paragraph, assist him or her to break it down further. You will be repeating the words or phrase with each subsequent question, so it needs to be concise. You are in fact creating a blueprint to which the brain can match information, so keeping it simple will give the best results.

For this first question it is extremely important to elicit a positively stated outcome, because the brain does not recognise negatives (not, don't, won't, can't) when it does its matching up job. Therefore, if the outcome was, 'I don't want to be depressed', the 'don't' would not be recognised and the person would be left with the brain recording, 'I want to be depressed'—obviously not a good idea. If your client gives you a negatively stated outcome you might reply, 'That is what you **don't** want . . . what do you want?' If she again gives a negatively stated answer, such as: 'I just don't want to feel so isolated,' modify your reply, 'That is what you **don't** want . . . I wonder if you could tell me in positive terms . . . what **do** you want?'

Some of your clients will find making any positive statements a real challenge and you might have to give them an example such as 'So, if you were not feeling depressed, what *will* you be feeling?' If they are still stuck, offer a few options: 'I wonder, would you be feeling . . . contented? . . . complete? . . . satisfied?' Be sure to offer a few options to avoid the client using your words rather than his or her own.

Once your client makes a positive statement, e.g. 'I'd feel inner contentment', go on to question two.

*2. What would having (name the outcome, e.g. inner contentment) do for you?*
This question may seem to have an obvious answer to you, but it gives your client a chance to begin picturing 'inner contentment' in connection with him- or herself—a very important step towards gaining it.

It is usually best to avoid commenting on any of the answers, or getting into any sort of discussion over them, just acknowledge and write them down.

3. Ask the next three questions separately.
*Having (name the outcome, e.g. inner contentment), what do you see yourself doing?*
*Having (inner contentment), what do you hear yourself saying?*
[This can be to self or others.]
*Having (inner contentment), how do you feel?*

These three questions assist your client to begin embracing the goal by bringing it closer to attainment through seeing, hearing and feeling what it will be like to have it. Please use the present tense (having); it assists your client to enter into the desired state (as in our example, 'inner contentment'). It is a subtle but powerful influence.

*4. Can (inner contentment) be initiated and maintained by you?*

Your client may answer that coming into therapy is initiating her goal, and rightly so, for it is being initiated by her. Answers that indicate possible problems will be those in which the client expects that all change will be done 'to' her by the counsellor, or that change will be possible *if* her partner or family do, or stop doing, something.

It is also important to know that the client is prepared to take responsibility for maintaining her goal and not leaving it to fate or other people.

5. *What would you need to make (inner contentment) happen?*
Any clients who require other people to behave differently to enable them to attain their therapy goal (inner contentment), may not be ready for change work. In such cases, you might ask: 'What would you need to make inner contentment happen if no one else changed?'

6. *What would stop you from achieving (inner contentment)?*
This question is very useful for identifying clients who are not ready for change work and for indicating problem areas for people who are ready. Answers that suggest your clients might later sabotage their therapy goal are those which deal with identity issues, 'who' they are in life, i.e. wife, father, mother, job status, etc. If attaining their desired therapy outcome would create loss in these areas, then the part of them that protects their identity will sabotage efforts made towards the goal. For those clients, after you have run the Well Formed Outcome, explore this area with them, i.e. 'What would it be like if, gaining _____ , you lost _____ ?' If their replies suggest it would be unacceptable, and you cannot reframe the situation effectively, then it might be more useful to do something other than change work.

7. *If you get (inner contentment), what positive benefit might you lose?* [Other ways of wording this question: Can you think of any circumstances in which you would not want this desired outcome (inner contentment)? If you get your desired outcome (inner contentment) is there any negative way in which it might affect your life? Your environment?]

This question hopefully will flush out any 'secondary gain' the person's present state offers and you can later discuss if there are other ways to attain the secondary gain and still make the change possible.

8. *Is having (inner contentment) worth the cost?*
Monetary or otherwise.

9. *Is having (inner contentment) worth the time?*

10. *Does (inner contentment) match your sense of self?*
Some clients have a very little sense of self in the first place and may be hard pressed to understand this question. If so, I usually ask, 'Does this outcome (inner contentment) match your sense of the person you wish you were?'

I have coined a phrase that is very useful in explaining how to identify the person we are meant to be (who we would be minus all the problems/damage developed as a result of childhood trauma).

*The (type of) person you wish you were is who you really are, but haven't yet learned to be.*

As we look around us, we can notice many positive ways of 'being', yet we do not wish to be all of those. However, in our secret thoughts there are certain positive ways we wish we were—that is who we really are. Understanding this also gives your client permission to attain it.

## COMPLEMENTARY TOOLS

The next tool to be introduced is the Positive Resource Exercise (PRE). In this exercise, I have blended a few Neuro-Linguistic Programming (NLP) techniques which will accomplish, through visualisation, what the PICT letter series does in letter form. Obviously the visualisation will be a quicker way to work—one session vs. three or more. You may wonder why you should bother with the letter series if the Positive Resource Exercise (PRE) is quicker, but remember, some clients will need to work more slowly.

(In the first interview, these people will often keep repeating that they know it will take a long time to sort through their problems.)

Remember that you can always use one or more of the PICT letter series as a back-up tool to visualisation work if necessary. For instance, if you have used a visualisation that had good effects, but you feel your client needs just a little more input, assign a Letter TO: (on its own, without the other two in the letter series) to cover the material.

If at any time you select a tool that is less effective than hoped, just try another. You cannot hurt anyone using any of the tools, so there is nothing to lose by trying another. Each time you use a tool, you gain more information and that information will usually help you to choose the next step. If a tool seems less effective, it does not mean that the tool does not work, it simply means some further action needs to be taken on this occasion.

My students often smile when I suggest that they simply respond to unexpected developments/blocks with a congruent 'Good!' and then move on to plan B, or in some cases, plan C or D.

Also keep in mind that some mistaken beliefs are part of a system of beliefs—several beliefs that are connected by a common theme—and all will need to be changed before your client experiences full relief. So if partial relief is experienced by your client after running the Mistaken Belief Visualisation, perhaps you will need to explore more to discover if there are more beliefs in the system. (See Chapter Two.)

**Positive Resource Exercise (PRE)**
Let's first look at the steps in the Positive Resource Exercise (PRE) and then I will explain how to apply them.

You must write down some of the answers to the following questions. First write the negative feeling or limiting decision at the top of the page; then list the people in the scene, leaving space below each name to write the list of resources. When your client has completed beaming each resource over and seen the difference it has made, then tick that resource off your list. When the learning has been ascertained, write that at the bottom of the page. Without these things written down you would quickly lose track, for some clients have very long lists.

POSITIVE RESOURCE EXERCISE

1. Your client describes a recurring negative feeling or a recurring limiting decision [e.g. Negative feeling: 'I feel so afraid (angry, sad, guilty, confused.).' Limiting decision: 'I am useless (trapped, not good enough, the one at fault).'].
Ask if she would like to explore these feelings. If so: *'Just go inside and give your attention to the last time you had this feeling . . . The last time you felt* [state feeling or negative decision] *and let yourself feel the same feelings now . . . Just let me know when you have your full attention on those feel-ings . . . Good . . . now allow your unconscious mind to let those feelings of* [name of feeling] *take you back to where they really belong . . . perhaps back to the first event from which those feelings started . . . Let me know when you have that first event . . . Good . . . now open your eyes and put the scene out here* [indicate a clear space in the air—one without plants, furniture, etc.] *on a screen.'*

2. When the client indicates she has the scene on the screen, ask, *'Are you on your own or are others with you?'* Note down the individuals, leaving space under the names to write the resource list. Encourage your client to keep her eyes on the scene, gesture towards it as you speak about the scene and if she looks away ask her to: *'Just keep your eyes on the screen here.'*

3. After listing the individuals, tell your client, *'You do not need to disclose the content of this event to me, unless you feel it is somehow important to do so, but I do need to know if you are aware of the content—aware of what has happened there.'*

4. After your client has placed the scene on the screen and you have listed the individuals present, it is time to find out what resources each person would have needed to have behaved appropriately. Start first with the Child, then the secondary persons (if any) and lastly the problem person.

*'From your vantage point here in* [name the current year], *what positive personal resources/qualities did that younger you need to feel okay in that situation?'* [You are saying the name of the current year to assist your client to stay in the here and now and not to become ensnared in the former event.] For some clients, this question may be a whole new concept and they may say, 'I don't know.' If that is the reply, first ask, 'What would you guess?' If they still have difficulty, give them a few examples. A fairly good guess might be 'self-esteem' or 'confidence'.

After you have ascertained and written down the first positive resource, then ask, *'What other positive personal resource/quality did that younger you need to feel okay in that situation?'* Note down each positive personal resource and continue asking the same question until your client says the Child does not need any other resources. These will be resources children do not normally have.

5. Now you are ready to go to the other individuals in the scene. If there are more than two, start with the secondary persons. Find out first if they are important to the scene or if they are simply part of the background. If they are necessary, ask if it would be appropriate to join those who are not predominant into one unit or if they need to be considered individually. For example, one client's event included her father and two brothers. She felt that it was appropriate to consider the brothers as one unit, so we listed the positive personal resources they needed under 'brothers' rather than their individual names. Now ask, *'From your vantage point here in* [current year], *what positive personal resource did the persons need to behave appropriately in this situation?'* Finish this list out the same as you did for the client's Child.

6. Lastly do the dominant, abusing or problem person. *'From your vantage point here in* [current year], *what positive personal resources did that person need to behave appropriately in this situation?'* Some clients will feel reluctant to give the abuser any positive resources. Please explain that granting resources to the abuser is actually a gift to the Child. He or she needs to discover what a natural, loving

experience is like. In order to give this to her or him the problem person needs to have positive resources. Your client will be making the problem person into the person he was meant to be rather than the person he became. Ask, 'Would you be willing to give that younger "you" the positive experience she has waited so long for? The positive experience she deserves? Are you willing to give the younger you the opportunity to reclaim this piece of childhood, all fixed and natural, that was taken from her?'

7. After you have completed listing the resources needed for each person, go back to the Child. Starting with the first positive personal resource on the list ask, '[Client's name] *do you have the positive personal resource of* [name resource]?' If there is ANY incongruence (long pause, questioning voice tone, brow furrowing), say, '*Would I be correct in saying that you have a portion of* [resource]?' I hope the reason for asking this question in the positive, 'You have a portion?' rather than, 'Oh, you don't have much of it, huh?' is obvious. If your client confirms he or she has a portion of [resource] then ask, '*Do you know anyone who does have* [resource]?'

This could be someone known to your client personally, casually or through the media. All that is required is that the person chosen manifests evidence of the resource in question. If your client does not know if the person 'really' has the resource or is 'putting on a front', that is still okay—all that is necessary is for the person to demonstrate how the resource operates. You, the therapist, do not need to know who this person is or how he or she manifests the needed resource. You just need to know that your client has someone in mind who she (congruently) believes has the needed resource.

8. Next, your client is going to beam the needed resource over to the Child in the scene. If your client had a portion of the resource ask her or him to: '*Take the resource of* [name resource] *that you see manifested in the other person, add that to your portion of* [resource], *and* beam *that package over to the younger you and let me know when he or she has it.*'

If your client has the entire resource you would say: *'Now, beam that positive personal resource of* [name resource] *over to the younger you, and let me know when he or she has it.'* If the resource was wholly from someone else: *'Now take the positive personal resource of* [name resource] *that you see manifested in the other person and beam it over to the younger you, and let me know when he or she has it.'* When your client indicates the Child has it, say, *'Good! Well done.'* or some other positive acknowledgement. Your client is making a lot of effort at your request, the least you can do is acknowledge it. Work together with your client, be present and a part of the action, not some aloof robot offering clinical responses rather than human contact, support and encouragement.

Now ask (with positive anticipation in your voice tone) your client to *'Watch and see what changes you notice in the Child now that he or she has the new positive, personal resource of* [name resource]. *Just observe the changes that resource makes in him or her and then tell me what you see.'* This bit ensures your client is getting the benefit you are aiming for, or tells you an adjustment is needed if changes in the Child are not seen by your client.

9. Following the above format, go through each resource on the list until you have beamed all the needed resources to the Child and watched the changes each one made. [Your client will see a totally different Child when his or her resource list is complete.] Then go on to the secondary person and do the same, and lastly, beam resources to the problem person and again watch the changes made by the new resources. When everyone's list is complete, refresh your client's memory by saying: *'Now the younger you has the positive personal resources of:* [read the list]. *The* [secondary persons] *have the positive personal resources of:* [read their list], *and the* [problem person] *has the positive personal resources of:* [read his or her list].

10. It is now time to ask your client to: *'Rewind the scene to the beginning and then play the scene again,* **but this time with each person's new positive resources in place**. *Watch the*

*new scene unfold and observe what difference the new positive resources make, and let me know when the new scene is complete.'* Use the word 'complete' rather than 'finished'.

11. The new scene usually takes a relatively short time. When complete, ask your client to tell you what differences he or she observed: *'Tell me what the new scene was like.'* [She will naturally stop looking at the screen at this point, but if not please ask her to do so.] Often the former event has now become a very ordinary, everyday event—just a demonstration of being 'natural'. If your client does not use the word 'natural' in his or her description of the new scene, ask, *'Would you say it was like just being "natural"?'*

12. At this point ask your client: *'Looking at the younger you there in the new scene, tell me what positive learning, about herself, has she gained as a result of having this natural experience?'* This 'learning' will usually be in the form of a positive belief, i.e. 'She's learned she is okay', 'She's learned she can be safe', 'She's learned she has freedom'. When you reflect this learning back, put it in the first person and present tense: *'So she is now saying, "I'm okay" ("I can be safe", "I am free").'*

If your client gives a learning that is about others, i.e. 'She learned that her parents could have been nice', accept that but make a suggestion. *'So, she learned her parents could have been nice? Good. I am wondering specifically what positive learning she gained about herself.'* Write the learning down below the resource lists.

13. Now ask your client to: *'Clear the screen of the new scene and replace it with the image of the younger you with all the new positive personal resources,* AND THE NEW LEARNING OF: [name the learning].' This done, explain: *'Now, just connect that younger you there in nineteen whatever to you here in* [current year] *with a line.* [Wait for her indication of completion.] *This is a representation of your time line. You are here in now, facing the younger you there in the past. Now when I tell you to begin, I would like you to slowly bring the younger you through time. As you do so, simply watch those*

*new positive personal resources of:* [name the child's resources], *and the new learning of:* [name the learning], *re-evaluate all events from your past that were similar to, or had the same negative feelings as, the event we just changed. Simply watch all those similar events change, (in whatever way your unconscious mind represents them), coming all the way through time, all the way back to now. Okay, begin.'*

14. When your client indicates this is complete, say: *'Good. Now welcome the younger you and allow her or him to merge with you there in the chair, here in* [current year]. *Let her or him merge with you, bringing the gifts of the new positive personal resources of:* [name the child's resources], AND THE NEW LEARNING OF [name the learning]. *Let me know when that merging is complete.'* You should see a physical indication of the merging, perhaps shoulders dropping or raising, a sigh or muscles relaxing.

15. When complete, ask your client, *'How was that for you?'* and then, *'What changes did you notice when the Child was coming through time?'* After your client has described what happened coming through time, then enquire about the merging. *'How was the merging for you, what did you experience?'*

16. Now to test the work. Tell your client you are going to test the work and see how it has affected the future. Ask him or her to: *'Float up above your time line and go into the future a bit . . . to a time when a situation is likely to arise that is perhaps similar to a past experience in which the old* [name original negative feeling or limiting decision] *used to be a problem.* [Use the past tense here to assist the unconscious mind to recognise it as remaining in the past.] *It might be a work, social or relationship situation. Observe this future situation and notice how things are different now that the new resources and learning are in place. Let me know when you have completed observing the differences.'* After the client indicates that the future situation is complete, ask her or him to: *'Good, now float back into now, back to today and when you are ready, open your eyes.'* When your client has

opened his or her eyes and had a moment to reorientate, ask: *'Tell me what did you observe?'*

This test will give both you and your client information about the positive changes to expect or if there may be further 'fine tuning' work to be done. If you run into any hiccups during the exercise, or during the future test, first ask, 'What stops you from . . . ?' Next ask, 'And what would you need to accomplish this?' or 'What would need to happen to allow you to accomplish this?' then make whatever changes are needed.

### Positive Resource Exercise (PRE) vs. Letter Series

Now let's look at how the Positive Resource Exercise is similar to and different from the PICT letter series.

Should your client be talking about a recurring difficult problem in life *today*, you can use the Personal Resource Exercise to (a) take him or her back in time to where the problem started, (b) resource the individuals involved, (c) change the experience through finding the learning, (d) bring that change through time (affecting other life circumstances) to become a part of your client today and (e) test out the change work experienced.

The three steps of PICT are also found in that formula. In essence, (a) connecting the 'today' problem with an experience from the past allows the Child to tell how what happened then was significant and needs addressing, as in the Letter FROM:. One big difference is that with PRE you can work with or without your client disclosing what the actual content of the experience was. This allows your client to choose whether or not to disclose the content and details of the original experience. The Child will be telling the Adult, but not the counsellor—the client will know what the incident was, but you, the therapist, will not have to know if the client chooses not to say anything.

Giving personal resources (b) accomplishes the same goals as the five steps of the Letter TO:. Positive personal resources are positive personal qualities, such as: confidence, self-esteem, assertiveness, 'having a voice', sense of self, responsibility, sense of identity, ability to love, understanding, caring, courage, strength, selflessness, etc. You cannot accept negative answers such as: 'needs not to be so selfish', 'not domineering', 'not cruel'. If your client offers resources stated negatively, ask her: 'If they were not so selfish, what would they be?' or 'If he were not domineering, what would he be?' until you get the resource stated positively, i.e. 'They would be caring (have selflessness)' or 'He would be understanding'. You may offer descriptive words if your client gets stuck, but never use a word that *you* think describes the resource better *unless your client agrees congruently*.

When all the individuals from the past event are given the personal resources needed, and the old scene is replayed in a positive manner, the Child is given the positive and needed experience of emotionally healthy interaction. It restores a portion of your client's 'lost childhood'. It also automatically disconnects the mistaken/limiting belief, because the negative event never happens, so the mistaken belief does not form. (This is accomplished by point four in the Letter TO: and the Mistaken Belief Visualisation.)

It is best to start with the Child when your client is first choosing what resources are needed and later beaming those resources over. The Child's needs must come first. If there are several people in the scene, start with the Child, go on to the secondary person or people and end with the abuser/ problem person. Also ask if the other people (two or more) can be made into one unit or if, in fact, they even need to be included in the resource giving. For instance, if the scene takes place in a classroom, it may only be necessary to attribute resources to the teacher and Child because they are the principals in the scene. On the other hand, if the scene is a family one, perhaps other siblings could be one unit needing the same resources, leaving the Child and parent to be treated individually as usual.

On some occasions resources may be given to the Child only. This is done when your client needs to gain a sense of his or her own personal power. In that case, you will be employing the same aspects of the Child Fantasy Escape. You may decide to do the scene both ways: first grant resources to each person and the second time only to the Child.

Finding the learnings (c) also has the same effect as the Mistaken Belief Visualisation in that it changes the effect of the event on the client's identity.

The results of playing through the new scene, after all parties possess the necessary resources/qualities, also accomplishes the same goal as the Rescue Scene. It changes the former experience. Remember, the memory of what originally happened is not changed, but by changing the experience of what originally happened, you change the feelings about it and consequently the attaching problems. Our goal is not to wipe out people's memories, but to change their negative reactions to those memories.

Bringing the experience back through time to the present (d) is also a function of the Rescue Scene (although covertly), but we now can add a new element—testing out the change during the session (e). Formerly, this would be experienced during the time between sessions. Now we have the opportunity to give the client a taste of change before he or she even walks out of the door.

## TRAUMA RESPONSES

When you gain access to a repressed memory with your clients, it is usually an emotional experience. It is important for it to be so, because it will be evidence that the memory is something they have experienced. For instance, we all feel emotion when hearing, or describing, a distressing event that happened to someone else, but that emotion in no way compares with the gut reaction felt when we too have *experienced* a similar event. It is usually the gut reaction emotion during the memory retrieval that is evidence that the event remembered is a strong representation of, or is an actual experience.

To illustrate this gut reaction emotion, ask your client to recall a time when he or she felt a very strong emotional reaction upon hearing about someone else's experience that was in some way similar to one of his or her own. Compare those feelings with the times when sorrow, sadness or distress was felt when hearing about someone else's horrific experience that was *not* similar to anything that had been personally experienced. Your client will find the former will carry a much bigger emotional 'punch', often experienced in the pit of the stomach—a gut reaction.

Your client is free to label the uncovered memory as a 'representation' or an accurate account. Using either label the uncovered memory can be worked with and your client will consequently experience freedom from one or more symptoms. There is no way to prove any uncovered memory is accurate, unless you have the perpetrator present to verify it, i.e. 'Yes, that is exactly what I did to you'. Since that scenario is highly unlikely, you will need to look at the emotional 'punch' and rely on the knowledge that working with a 'representation' is just as effective as working with an accurately recalled event.

**Strong Emotion vs. Trauma Response**
Strong emotion/gut reaction will usually be demonstrated by tears or sobs, hands over face or arms wrapped around knees or chest. However, when strong emotion turns into a trauma response you need to bring your client out of it. A trauma response is demonstrated by hyperventilation (tears and sobs that turn into long or short gasping breaths); posture with arms that were wrapped around the knees or chest becoming more foetal position rocking; the memory recall turning into memory *experience*. When the memory is re-experienced the client may choke, attempt to push something away, frantically brush something off, recoil into the chair, curl up and try to hide.

Strong emotion is useful for verifying the uncovered memory and, technically, I suppose you could say that a trauma response can serve the same purpose. I personally feel that it is unnecessary and irresponsible to allow a client to stay in a trauma response state, but there are other dissenting opinions in the therapeutic community.

**Dorothy's Trauma Response Technique**
To bring people quickly out of a trauma response state I have developed another handy tool from NLP, which I call the Separation Technique. I have adapted this tool from the Molecule Technique created by Robert Dilts. I have

renamed it because it varies quite a bit from the original and I didn't think Mr Dilts would appreciate my very simplistic model wearing the same label as his sophisticated original. The simplistic model makes it easier to remember when you are suddenly faced with a client who has gone into a trauma response. It can also be used for decreasing any strong or unwanted emotion or for dealing with confusion.

It is a process of directing the client to separate out the overwhelming conglomeration of feelings, pictures and sounds originally experienced into different locations. We have a trauma response because the feelings, pictures and sounds of the event are collected together in one big bundle which is overwhelming and confusing. The Separation Technique separates the three and the emotional impact is immediately reduced.

Before I list the steps of the Separation Technique, I shall first give you an example of how it works, using Dorothy's experiences. Dorothy, if you remember from the chapter on Anger, had experienced ritualistic abuse. As is true of many people who suffered ritualistic abuse, Dorothy had repressed most of the horrific experiences. During one session, when we were exploring a past event, we suddenly tapped into one of the horrific experiences.

Dorothy began to breathe rapidly, squirming and recoiling in the chair, brushing frantically at her arms and torso and crying out repeatedly, 'Get them off! Get them off!' She no longer responded to my regular voice tone. Her emotions increased. Her face showed expressions of extreme revulsion. Her eyes often rolled back. She was practically recoiling into the back of the large chair she was in. Her breathing was ragged and laboured. She cried out, 'The snakes! The snakes! Get them off! Get them off!,' as she used her hands to frantically brush the remembered snakes off her body and arms. Obviously, Dorothy was no longer remembering something, she was now *re-experiencing* it.

I first adopted a firm, strong voice tone and volume, and using Dorothy's name I called her. 'Dorothy! Dorothy!' Once I had gained her attention, I directed her, 'Look down here. Keep your eyes down here!' (Indicating down and to her right and keeping my hand in that position.) She struggled for a few moments, but was finally able to look where I was indicating. 'Good! Now put all the feelings down here. Place all the feelings of the snakes on you, down here. Let me know when the feelings of the snakes on you are all down here.' [External sensations.] In a moment or two she nodded and looked up at me. 'Just keep your eyes down here, Dorothy.' My hand was still placed down and to her right. 'Now, put all the feelings of revulsion down here. Right down here. All the feelings of revulsion down here.' [Internal emotions.] She seemed to be struggling more with this one, so I kept encouraging her until I could see her feelings grow calmer. 'Place them here, put them down here. Let me know when all the feelings of revulsion are down here. Good! Very good. Just leave all those feelings down here. Good. Is there any other feeling to remove?' Dorothy shook her head no.

I then moved on to the pictures. 'Okay, Dorothy, now look up here.' (Indicating up and to her left.) It did not take as long for her to bring her eyes to the location this time. 'Good. Now place all the pictures here. Place all the pictures you are seeing right here. Pictures of the snakes, people around you, whatever you are seeing—place those pictures here. Every one of them, right here. Let me know when all the pictures are up here . . . Good!' Again her distress levels were dropping markedly.

'Okay, Dorothy, now put your eyes down here. Just look down here.' (Indicating down and to her left.) 'Good. Now just put all the words down here. All the words down here. Those words, "The snakes. The snakes. Get them off. Get them off." All those words down here.' Dorothy nodded, 'Good. Now all the sounds. Put all the sounds in that memory, all the sounds that were there, put them down here. The sounds of you crying out or other sounds you may be aware of, put the sounds down here. Let me know when all the sounds are down here.' By now Dorothy was calm and breathing normally (after a few sighs).

'How is that for you now?' Dorothy took a couple of deep breaths. 'That's better, but now something else seems to be coming up, a different part of the picture.' The memory sequence continued and she again had similar reactions. We went around the circuit again, just as before, placing the feelings in the feeling place, the pictures in the picture place and the words/sounds in the sound place. On this occasion we did this four times, until nothing else surfaced.

'How is that for you?' I asked.

'Better, much better! Gosh, that is like magic. I like that. Putting everything in a different place really helps.'

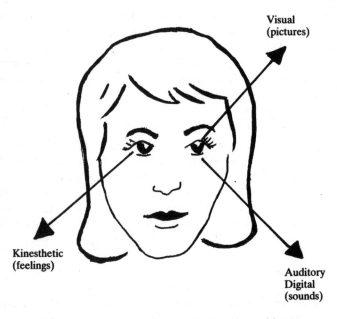

*Eye Accessing Patterns: Feeling, picture and sound locations*

As illustrated in the model of eye accessing patterns, the feelings are placed down and to your client's right, the pictures are placed up and to your client's left and the sounds are placed down and to your client's left. Most people will follow this model. However, it may be reversed for those who are left-handed. In that case, the feelings place will be down and to the left, the picture place will be up and to the right and the sounds place will be down and to the right.

Occasionally, a person will have just the picture place reversed or just the feeling and sound places reversed. Any time your client is having difficulty 'letting go' and leaving the feeling, picture or sound in the location you are indicating, simply switch to the opposite side. So, if you are indicating up and left for pictures and nothing is happening, say, 'Good . . . that tells us that your picture place is on the opposite side. Just look up here now. (Indicating up and to the person's right.) Place all the pictures up here . . . Good.'

On very rare occasions you will find a person whose eye accessing patterns are completely jumbled. In that case, simply test each location until you find where the person *can* release feelings, pictures and sound. It would be useful to make a note of those places for the next time you may need to use this exercise with that person.

Please do **not** at any time say, '*Try* and put the picture (feeling, sound) here', because that is what your client will do: *try*. Be direct, simply say, '*Put* the picture here.' Delete the word 'try' from your therapy vocabulary, unless you are actually wanting the client to 'try', rather than 'do'. Another preface remark that it is not helpful to use is, '*Can you* put the picture here?' Again I would suggest that you drop the 'Can you', and accompanying question mark, and simply say, 'Put the picture here.'

## SEPARATION TECHNIQUE

1. First adopt a strong, firm voice tone and volume. Using your hands indicate in the air the position you want your client to look at. Ideally you want her to keep her head relatively straight and to move her eyes to the specified point. You might say: '*Keeping your head facing more or less straight ahead, just move your eyes to look here*' (as you indicate with your hand). '*Just turn your eyes so that you are looking here.*' Keep your hand in the desired location the whole time you are running the exercise and if your client looks away, direct her back. '*Keep your eyes here. Keep looking here*', while gesturing with your hand.

2. It is a good idea to start with the 'feeling' place first

(Kinesthetic Accessing Point), because this will calm your client quickest. Indicating down and to your client's right, say, '*(Name), look down here. Just move your eyes to look down here. Good. Now put those feelings of* [name feeling you see evidenced] *down here. Place them right down here.*' The feelings include emotions and sensations; name each (as in Dorothy's example) and ask your client to put them in the feeling place. With each feeling named, ask your client to indicate when she has completed the process. '*Let me know when all that feeling of* [name of feeling] *is down here.*'

3. Next go to the picture place. Indicating with your hand up and to the person's left, say (Visual Accessing Point), '*Look up here. Look up here. Good. Now just put the pictures, all the pictures up here. Put everything you see up here. Let me know when everything you see is up here.*'

4. Now go on to the sound place (Internal Dialogue Accessing Point), again using your hand to indicate the appropriate location and your words to assist your client to look in the correct direction. '*Look down here, down here to the sound place. Put all the words* [repeat the words she has been using] *down here. Good. Now put all the sounds around you and the sounds you may be making, even your thoughts, put all the sounds down here. Let me know when all the sound is down here.*'

5. When you have completed this sequence, ask, '*How is that for you?*' If it was insufficient to restore your client, she will indicate that some aspect is still there to be dealt with. If an additional memory is surfacing, your client will indicate that she is now experiencing something else. Either way, simply repeat the process, starting with the feelings once more. You will be finished when your client has no more traumatic recollections and is feeling and remaining calm.

## MEMORY RETRIEVAL EXERCISE

In addition to the Personal Resource Technique, you can also use the Memory Retrieval Exercise to assist clients to uncover repressed information. The Memory Retrieval

Exercise paints a more detailed and fuller picture. It can be used to uncover totally repressed memories or to clarify fragmented ones.

It is also very useful for enhancing a client's happy memories. Many people who have lived in highly dysfunctional families have little recall of happy times. Often they tell you there were no happy memories. However, even in the most dreadful of childhoods there will be some occasions when the person experienced happiness, even if it was for a short time. These occasions may not be with their immediate family, indeed often these occasions are with friends, or perhaps at school, a sport event, school trip or maybe a party. It is very useful to enable your client to remember and enhance these happy times. The Memory Retrieval Exercise is great for doing just that and I suggest to students that they use the exercise regularly with their clients.

First I will explain how the Memory Retrieval Exercise is used to clarify repressed or fragmented memories in clients with no knowledge of abuse, but who have many of the classic abuse symptoms, and in clients who have vague or patchy memories of abuse. Keep in mind that your client will be associated in the Child [be experiencing the event as the Child] for this exercise, and therefore will have a much stronger experience of feelings. It is your responsibility to monitor the situation and bring your client out, if he or she goes into a trauma response. (See Separation Technique.) However, there is another tool to try first: simply ask him or her to leave the Child and float to the top of the room to observe what is happening. (Most people with abuse backgrounds will have no problem doing this.) It will reduce the impact of the emotions because the person will be dissociated [out of the body]. Do not be too quick to rush in and stop strong feelings, for in doing so, you may rob your client of a valuable piece of evidence concerning his or her past. However, do rush in when you see that strong feelings have developed into a trauma response.

**Memory Retrieval Steps**
1. First ask the client's permission to explore areas containing strong feelings and explain that she can expect tears and feelings of fear. Give reassurance that you will monitor the

situation closely and can interrupt the process if needed.

[Use step 2 for totally unknown, repressed memories only; for fragmented memories go ahead to step 3.]

2. You need a 'stepping in' point for repressed memories. This is done through feelings. Our conscious mind may have forgotten the traumatic event, but our unconscious mind still has the event logged in. It tries to let us know about it through the feelings we had at the time, because our unconscious mind strives towards resolving repressed material. Therefore, people with repressed material will on certain occasions have feelings (usually very strong) that they cannot explain. These feelings are often intense fear or panic and are usually connected to an abuse event of some nature that has been entirely blocked out. All that remains is the last memory from just before the abusive event started.

I have mentioned Priscilla who could not bear it if someone closed the curtains on a sunny day (perhaps to enable the television screen to be seen). Her fear and panic feelings would take over and she would have to rush over and open the curtains again. This reaction was puzzling to Priscilla because she did not know why she had these strong feelings. When she came in to therapy, and we were using the Memory Retrieval Exercise, it finally emerged that she had been severely abused immediately after the abuser closed the curtains on a sunny day. The memory of the abuse had gone, but the warning stayed: 'Curtains closing on a sunny day means something horrible is going to happen.'

Another client, Hannah, whenever she was in a small to medium size room with the door closed, would panic and have to open the door. This was convenient at home, but not so useful at someone else's home or a public place. When we retrieved the memory connected with the feeling of panic in a small to medium size room, she recalled a time when she had been abused by her grandfather. She had to wait in the room, watching the closed door, knowing that when the door handle turned and the door opened, abuse would happen. The memory of abuse had gone, but the panic of watching the closed door remained.

To gain access to one of these repressed memories, just ask your client: *'Have you ever experienced any "over the top" reaction to a simple everyday event, a reaction for which you have no reasonable explanation?'* You can give the example of Priscilla or Hannah if needed: *'For instance, one woman experienced a strong sense of panic whenever someone closed the curtains on a sunny day.'*

Ask your client to: *'Close your eyes and remember the last time you experienced the over-the-top reaction of:* [name the reaction].' For example: 'Priscilla, give your attention to the feelings of panic you experienced the last time someone closed the curtains on a sunny day.' *'Just remember those feelings and allow yourself to feel them now.'* Watch her physiology. If she is not experiencing the feeling very well, ask her to: *'Remember another time you had this same reaction and allow yourself to experience the feelings fully.'* For example: 'Priscilla, now give your attention to another time someone closed the curtains on a sunny day, and remember the feelings of panic. Allow yourself to experience the feelings fully.' Watch the physiology until the responses show that the feeling is clearly being experienced. [NOTE: This may take one to five goes depending on the person. If you accidentally overload someone (access too many examples of the feeling), the feelings will just shut off. If this happens, explain that it is very helpful because you now know the shut-off point, and start again—obviously stopping short of where you were before.]

3. For fragmented memories, ask your client to: *'Give your attention to the fragment of memory. Allow yourself to see whatever picture you have, letting your eyes linger on those things significant to this event; now add in whatever sounds there may be; and finally, just allow yourself to experience fully the feelings attached to this memory fragment.'*

4. Once your client is clearly experiencing the feelings, use a gentle, but firm, hypnotic voice tone to assist him or her to move back in time.

For totally repressed memories use the following sorts of phrases: *'That's good, Now . . . just let your unconscious*

*mind* **scan back** *through time* . . . **Follow these feelings** . . .
*We don't know how far that will be, just let your unconscious
do the work* . . . *knowing that your unconscious can take
you* **back to another time** . . . *perhaps the* **first time you
experienced these feelings** . . . *Don't try to think about it,
just let your unconscious* **follow these feelings** *and guide you*
. . . **back in time** . . . *Good* . . . *When your unconscious
stops at the* **appropriate time** *you may experience a sense of
"stopping" or a sense of being somewhere* . . . *or maybe you
will know you are there by having a* **picture in your mind** *of
being in a room or perhaps being outside somewhere* . . .
*Maybe you will know you are there because* **you can hear
something** . . . *maybe someone's voice, music, your own
voice or some other sound* . . . *Let me know when you are
there.'*

For fragments of memory: *'Just comfortably* **float back
through time** . . . *let your unconscious mind take you* **back
to that event,** *just let your unconscious mind* **follow those
feelings,** *which your conscious mind does not* **clearly recall**
. . . *back to* **that earlier event** . . . *Just float* **back to that time
when** [describe the fragment that the client has given you]
. . . **Let me know when you are there.'**

[NOTE: The bold print indicates the key words to guide the
unconscious, drop your voice tone slightly on these words.]

5. When your client indicates she has some sense of something different (whether detailed or foggy) say, *'That's
good!'* Then begin exploring. When you explore, do not lead
the client. Make your questions objective and start by *slowly*
building the surrounding picture first—if you start by trying
to get right to the abusive event she may simply blank out.
Have pen and paper ready and write down what your client
is telling you—*do not* try to keep it in your mind—she may
want to know the details of the room, as well as, the event
later.

6. Find out if your client is indoors or out of doors. *'Are
you inside or outside?'* Next you want to discover her physical location in the scene: *'Where are you in the scene?'* After

you have determined the position, ask your client to be associated (be inside the body looking out of her eyes, rather than observing the scene from a distance). Once the person is associated in the scene, concentrate on the room or surroundings. You want to build the picture from the floor up. In doing this you will be making an outline; filling in the details of the picture; and finally putting the picture into action and consequently revealing what happened in that scene.

If your client is outside, ask about the ground covering within the boundary of the scene: *'What is the ground covering around you, looking only as far as is important?'* To build the frame, ask about ground, sky, season, time of day and large stationary objects (trees, bushes, cars, buildings, water)—enquiring about the colours, sizes, shapes, distances, and temperature of each of these. To fill in the details of the picture, ask about the plants, animals, outdoor furniture, stones or shells, sounds and smells or background people and their colours, sizes, shapes, and distances apart.

If your client is indoors, to build the outline, start with the floor. *'Can you tell me what the floor covering is?'* Notice you do not ask, 'Is there lino on the floor?' because it is important not to lead the person. Make your questions as generic as possible. Continue with the following questions (of course, leaving time for your client to answer each one): *'Is the floor covering (wall covering, window covering, furniture, clothing, etc.) light or dark?'* *'Does it have a pattern or is it plain?'* *'Is it old or new?'*

Sometimes your client may not make mental pictures very clearly and say, 'I'm not sure, it isn't very clear.' Respond with: *'That's fine, just tell me what you sense it to be.'* Carry on in the same detailed manner (light/dark, pattern/plain, old/new) with the wall coverings; ceiling (light fittings, light/dark/colour, plain/patterned); placement and description of doors and windows (shape, size), including window coverings. If your client says she does not know or simply cannot see a particular item, respond with, *'Good . . . that's fine'*, and go on to the next item. Seldom is every item clearly defined.

Next, to fill in the details, move on to the furniture. *'Is there any furniture in the room?'* If you receive a simple 'yes' or 'no' answer to that sort of question without any attempt to give more details, it is probably simply a signal that your client is well into a state of trance. Just ask a more specific question, such as, *'What piece of furniture is closest to you?'* Again, go through the detailed description (light/dark, pattern/plain, old/new) with each piece of furniture. When you complete one piece of furniture, ask, *'Is there any other furniture in the room?'*

Continue and ask about pictures on the walls (using shape, size, etc. questions) or possible heating units or plants and even if there are any toys or other items about on the floor.

7. Once you have completed a picture of the surroundings, you are ready to concentrate on the client. Ask: *'What foot covering, if any, are you wearing?'* Then move on to her clothes (colour, texture, pattern, style). Ask what her hair is like. Lastly, ask the person's age.

8. Next you move on to other people. *'Is there anyone else in the room with you?'* Occasionally your client will access/ recall a scene just after or before the event actually took place. If there are no other people around, ask if it is before or after the event. Simply ask your client to move the scene like a video, ahead or back to when the event was happening, so you can get a description of other people involved.

When you have established that there is another person or other people, don't ask, 'Who is it?' Instead, continue with the same generic technique—*'Is it a man or a woman?' 'Is he short or tall?' 'Fat or thin?' 'Old or young?' 'Is his hair light or dark?' 'What is he wearing?'* and finally, *'Do you know this person?'*

Of course, your client may already have said who the person is, but if not, it may be because the person's identity is too painful to know or it may be that the person was a stranger (although the client usually states that, e.g. 'I don't know his name, he was just the man who lived in that house'). If the abusing person was known, your client may need to continue to block out his identity. If that is the case, do not press the point, you can still do the work without knowledge of his identity.

9. Once the outline/frame, details and people are in place, you are ready to discover what happened in the event. Ask your client to operate the scene like a video and rewind to the start of the event and allow the event to happen. *'Let the event begin, staying associated there in the Child and tell me what is happening around you.'*

What you are aiming for is the abuse situation itself. However, once there, only stay long enough to ascertain that abuse happened, continuing to fast forward five or ten minutes at a time until you reach the end ('Now, just move ahead ten minutes and tell me what is happening there.'), just dipping in to see what is happening along the way, but staying only as long as needed to understand the event. It is not necessary or helpful for your client to recall every gory detail, the highlights will be sufficient.

10. Now, ask your client to: *'Rewind the scene to the beginning, to the time when the abusive event just started to happen.'* When your client has done that, tell her to: *'Now allow the event to happen again, but this time watch as your strong, resourceful Adult comes forcefully into the scene.'* [If your client's Adult is too frightened of the abuser and cannot do this, you may engage 'George' for assistance.] Ask her to: *'Watch the abuser's reaction of surprise and fear. Notice the relief you feel as the Adult pulls you away from the abuser and holds you protectively.'*

Now ask your client to: *'Listen as the Adult holds you comfortingly and explains that nothing that happened is your fault, and also explains that you are not alone any more, and says, "I love you".'* Ask your client to: *'Tell me when the Adult has completed this.'*

Now, ask your client to: *'Listen as the Adult tells off the abuser and let me know when this is complete.'* When your client indicates it is complete, ask what the Adult said to the abuser. You will be listening for at least two of the points listed in the Letter TO: 1) abuser was wrong; 2) how the abuser should have behaved.

If either is missing, say, *'Perhaps it would also be useful for the Adult to remind the abuser that . . .'*. [Give the missing points separately, allowing time for your client to implement each one—client nodding after each is complete.]

11. After that tell your client: *'It is now time for the Adult to take you away to a safe and happy place. Just let me know when you are there.'* When the client indicates, ask her to: *'Just take a few moments for you and the Adult to enjoy the scene and to celebrate the new freedom properly—let me know when the celebration is complete.'* When she indicates that has happened, ask her to: *'Have a snapshot taken of the happy scene* [wait for a nod to show it is done]. *Accept the photograph from the Adult and embrace lovingly together.* [Wait for a nod.] *While you are embracing simply merge together, going inside to your safe place. When the merging is complete and you are one, come back to this room . . . when you are ready . . . and open your eyes . . . maybe you would even like to stretch.'*

You can then discuss the experience with your client.

**Memory Retrieval for Happy Time**
1. Ask your client to: *'Make yourself comfortable in the chair and remember a happy time from your childhood. It may be with friends, it may be at school, a club or a sports event, it may be a time with a pet, or perhaps a time with relatives or immediate family. It may be a clear and distinct memory or it may be a fuzzy, vague fragment.'*

2. Next ask your client to: *'Give your attention to that memory and the happy feelings associated with that memory. Now just allow your unconscious mind to follow those happy feelings and take you back to that time, to just float along your time line to that event—and let me know when you are there.'*

3. Once there, just as in the unknown or fragmented memories, slowly build the picture around the person—AFTER **first ascertaining if it is inside or outside, the client's location**

**in the scene and making sure she is associated (in her body looking out of the eyes).**

Now to build the picture (depending on whether the scene is inside or outside), **start with the floor/ground coverings** (light/dark, pattern/print, old/new); **then the wall coverings/ surroundings; next the ceiling/sky; windows and doors** (location, shape, size); and **the furnishings/houses, vehicles, plants, trees, etc.**

4. Next have your client describe herself, **foot coverings**, if any; **clothing** (colour, light/dark, pattern/plain, texture, old/ new); **hair** (colour, short/long, style); and **age** (if you don't already know).

5. Now ascertain if there **is anyone else in the scene**. If so, **start with the person located closest** and have your client describe his or her: **height, weight, build, hair** (colour, length, style), **foot coverings, clothing**—just as you did for your client. If there is more than one other person, do each one separately **starting with the one located closest** and moving out from there. You may not always get clear descriptions of everyone, just note what there is and move on.

6. After everything in the scene has been described (surroundings, people), ask your client to **draw her attention to the surrounding sounds**—distant sounds first and then closest sounds. Next ask your client to **give her attention to the surrounding scents, fragrances and odours around**. If there is any food in the scene, have her **give her attention to the taste of the food**: *'Just allow yourself to taste again the (name of the food)'*. **Allow a few moments for each of these to be experienced**.

7. Now that the event is fully accessed, ask your client to: *'Now experience the event from the beginning, taking as long as needed. Let me know when the event has been completed, but stay there in the event because there will be one more step to complete.'*

8. When your client indicates that the event has been completed, ask her to: *'Choose one scene that will represent the happiness of the entire event best and take a photograph.'* When the photograph has been taken, ask her to: *'Place that photograph inside where you keep all your valuable treasures—knowing that whenever you take the photograph out you can again experience the scene fully, with all the happy feelings.'*

### Heather's Sample of Memory Retrieval

Once clients have experienced and are familiar with the tools used to explore memory or beliefs, it is perfectly acceptable for them to use the tools on their own. Pamela's client, Heather, after several experiences of the memory retrieval exercise, used it on her own to explore an issue she was having trouble with. I have included an edited version here. It is more leading than a PICT counsellor would present it, but Heather was more aware of the content than a counsellor would be and was also clear about what was acceptable to the Child.

*Heather's memory release about Grandad*

Hello Sweetheart. How are you feeling? Now that you are so much stronger and have faced and dealt with a lot of your fears in a very brave and honest way, I want you to have a look at one thing which I know still upsets you. Let's see if we can find a way, together, to help you be less upset and hurt and confused by it. Remember, I am with you all the time and you are safe. If you do manage to remember something nasty connected with this, try to hold on to the fact that it is only a memory and can't hurt you any more, because I am here all the time and I will keep you safe because I love you. So, in your own time, if you can, I want you to tell me how you feel when Roy [husband] says to me, 'I want to kiss you all over'. Ready? Off you go.
    **My tummy feels screwed up and tight. I want to run**

away. I don't like wet mouths. It makes my neck wet. I can't breathe. I dread it.

There's a big shadow. I don't want him near me. He frightens me.

It is all right, sweetheart. I'm here and you are safe now. You know who it is, the shadow, don't you?

**Yes. Grandad.**

And can you tell me where you are?

**In bed. In Nanny's house.**

Is it light or dark?

**Nearly dark. There's a light outside.**

And what is Grandad doing. Can you tell me?

**He's kissing my face and my neck and my chest. He's opening my pyjamas. His big face is horrid. I hate it.**

Is he talking to you while he's kissing you?

**Telling me to be quiet.**

Anything else?

**No. Just groaning, sort of.**

Is it just your chest he's kissing?

**And my tummy and arms.**

Nowhere else?

**No.**

And he's not trying to touch you anywhere else?

**No.**

It's okay, my darling, you have been very brave to tell me all this. You know, from what I have said before that none of what happened was your fault, don't you? I don't expect you find that very easy to believe at the moment, but it really wasn't. Your grandad is the one at fault. He was very wicked to do that to you. He knew it would frighten you, but he did it anyway, just because he wanted to. He was a nasty, cruel, wicked man to make you so frightened, but I am so glad you could remember and tell me about it. Now we can start to sort it out and you will start to feel better about it and not be so confused and frightened about being kissed any more.

Kissing another person's body is something grown-ups do for each other, not something any grown-up should do to a child. It is wrong behaviour and no child should have to put up with it.

I love you very much, you are a very special, brave, good little girl who has done nothing wrong. You were used to doing what grandad said and not arguing with him and that is all you did on this occasion. He was the one who did something wrong, not you, and you will never again have to put up with that—I shall see to it that you don't because my precious little girl deserves much better than that and I'm going to see to it that she gets it. You are warm and safe now. I will always stay with you. Be at peace now.

# 6 The Nature of Repressed Memories

## ASSESSING MEMORY RECALLS

A common question that is asked is: 'Do people ever make up memories?' In our experience, this happens rarely and when it does it is for a very understandable reason.

Most counsellors feel very bad when they experience feelings of disbelief concerning a client's information. They tell themselves off for disbelieving. Unless you consistently disbelieve people, my suggestion is to accept your feelings as a signal of incongruence in your client. Try then to identify that incongruence, i.e. physiology, voice tone, flushing, etc. You might ask yourself what it is that you are noticing that does not add up for you. It is not necessary to jump to an immediate conclusion; first simply assess what you have noticed, observing any further signals, until you have a fuller picture to assess—perhaps by that time you will have enough information to decide the matter.

## TWO MEMORY GROUPS

You will be concerned with two kinds of memories. The first is spontaneous memory recall—those memories experienced outside of either the presence, or assistance, of a counsellor. The second is memories elicited with the assistance of a counsellor. In both groups there are three basic measurements to be aware of; in the second group you will also be able to witness any incongruence.

The three basic measurements to consider are: 1. (*For sexual abuse*) Details of surroundings vs. detail of genital contact. 2. Rejecting memory vs. welcoming memory. 3. Gut response vs. head response.

Let's look at the first one—details of surroundings vs. detail of genital contact. For most children, while being sexually abused it felt safer to concentrate, or focus, on things around them or even to dissociate completely, than it did to keep focused on the genital contact. Most of them still knew what was going on with their bodies, but they had simply moved their mental focus to something else. Therefore, people who actually experienced such an event will usually retain detailed information about their surroundings or the surroundings they dissociated to. When you do a memory retrieval, there will be full information about the surroundings.

As you saw when using the Memory Retrieval Exercise, the surroundings were filled in first in order to link up to the traumatic experience, demonstrating, if you like, that the surroundings are still more easily recalled. Therefore, if your client brings information concerning a memory that is very vague on the surroundings and heavy on the genital contact—I find that very curious. If the information on the genital contact is extremely explicit and the client is comfortably repeating those graphic details, with dramatic flair, that is a red flag waving. Something is wrong: you may not have meaning yet, but this is not congruent behaviour for someone recalling a traumatic sexual abuse event. For someone who has actually experienced a sexually abusive event, the sexual details are uncomfortable and discussed as the last resort. *Note*: It is congruent for some clients to smile ruefully or bitterly laugh while discussing abuse events.

The second point is rejecting the memory vs. welcoming the memory. Without fail, the first reaction to a retrieved traumatic memory (whether spontaneously or with assistance) is one of disbelief, 'This can't be true. This couldn't have happened to me. I must be making it up.' That is a very natural response to the arrival of a previously unknown, unpleasant piece of a person's life, particularly if it involves loved ones behaving in an unacceptable way or involves abhorrent experiences.

People make that statement in the face of *any* traumatic event, even one they are witnessing in the present. You even hear the phrase 'Oh no! It *can't* be true!' repeatedly in dramas. Therefore, when a client *immediately* embraces a trauma and seems actually to be welcoming it and pleased to know it, you have another strong signal that something is wrong.

Please note that I am not referring to the person who initially says, 'This can't be true, I must be making it up', but after the initial shock is glad or relieved to know about it. All that person is demonstrating is the relief of finally being able to understand feelings or behaviours that did not make sense without the final puzzle piece. This acceptance can take place in the space of a few minutes or a few days.

The final point is gut response vs. head response. Any time a person has a strong 'kick in the gut' reaction (see Separation Technique, p. 175), it is an indication that she may have experienced the same or similar trauma or that some aspect of the trauma is similar. If there is no truth at all in the memory, there will be no gut reaction.


WHY MAKE IT UP?

I have experienced clients inventing sexual abuse in order to avoid facing the real trauma. Some people cannot face looking at what actually happened to them, so they create something else to distract themselves and the counsellor.

A good example of this is a young woman who was physically abused by her father. She was very uncomfortable with the intensity of the anger she felt towards her father and could not accept the information given to her that her intense feelings were a normal reaction. Before long she arrived at her counsellor's with a great smile on her face and eagerly explained to the surprised counsellor that she at last understood her intense anger. 'I've remembered that I was sexually abused!' she confessed happily, welcoming the memory, 'No wonder I was so angry.' The young woman then launched into her story of the sexual abuse experience. It focused mainly upon sexual details and was told with flair and animation (points one and three). When asked about the surroundings, general information was given, but deemed unimportant by the young woman (point one). She expressed anger and some tears as she told the story, but did not show the same gut reactions observed when she had spoken about the physical abuse (point three). She summed up the story saying, 'I want to start to work on this right away!' (point two).

The counsellor did not immediately disclose all the incongruent points she had noticed, she simply said they would put this memory on the end of the memory list, and, at the moment, finish where they had started. The young woman was disappointed and argued that it should be done now, but the counsellor persevered, asking that her judgment be trusted on this matter, and consequently they carried on with the physical abuse memories.

When those physical abuse memories were completed and the counsellor asked if the woman now wanted to look at the sexual abuse memory, the young woman smiled sheepishly and said, 'I don't know whether that was actually real or not, besides which, it doesn't seem very important any more.' The counsellor said 'fine' and simply congratulated the young woman on the hard work she had done on those physical abuse memories.

On that occasion the counsellor used the information the signals gave her to sidestep what was simply an avoidance ploy. The young woman was so uncomfortable facing the real experiences that she created something else (sexual abuse) to distract attention from what was really frightening (physical abuse memories containing the strong feelings). It did not seem to be done on a conscious level and the counsellor did not feel it necessary even to point out that, in her opinion, the sexual abuse memory did not happen.

More worrying was the following experience with a would-be counsellor. A woman came to see me before I started the PICT training courses with a desire to become a counsellor in the field of sexual abuse. I saw her periodically, sharing information and answering questions she had. One point that she kept coming back to was the fact that she did not think clients would find her credible since she had not been sexually abused, as I had. I assured her that simply being abused did not make a credible counsellor, in fact, someone who has not resolved his or her own abuse material could be a dangerous counsellor. I explained that what made a credible counsellor was one who had all the appropriate information about resolving abuse issues, and one who could share that information congruently and empathetically.

Unfortunately, she was not able to understand and assimilate that information and I was appalled one day to hear her excitedly tell me that she had just remembered that she had been abused. She came bursting in the door with her story, smiling, animated and, as was her style, very dramatic. The incident was particularly sexually graphic and when I interrupted to ask what sort of bed covering was there, she looked at me as though I was really stupid and replied, exasperated, 'I don't know!' I persevered, 'Was it a duvet or blankets?' By the look she gave me, I think she reckoned I had taken leave of my senses, but she obliged me with an answer, 'I don't know . . . a duvet, I suppose.' 'Print or plain?' At this point, she simply ignored me and carried on with her graphic rendition of what had happened to her at an early age at the hands of her father, summing it up with the statement, 'Now I know how it feels to be abused and I think that will help my clients. I think I will now have more credibility as an abuse counsellor. I can be a wonderful role model.'

I had not experienced anything quite like this woman before and I admit I was a bit speechless, I knew I needed more time to think all this over before I tried to put anything into words. However, in a few days, I got an excited telephone call from her to say that she had had a further memory release. This memory allegedly involved herself and her brother apparently having a sexual relationship over several years—again graphically told. In her words, 'I guess I never remembered it before because it did not seem bad, it was a very loving relationship. We had intercourse and did everything! At first I was surprised to know this, but now it is like I've always known it.' (pause) 'So, I guess I've had childhood experiences that are even different to *you!*' She remained animated and happy throughout the disclosure.

When she had rung off, I put the phone down in a daze. Later, when I had collected my thoughts and relayed to the woman my opinion concerning her incongruent signals, she did not accept it. That was the end of her visits to learn about my methods.

## WHY DO MEMORIES SURFACE?

It takes emotional energy to keep memories repressed. It also takes emotional energy to deal with any current stressful life experiences. In the present, if we experience several concurrent life crises (divorce, moving house, job loss, illness, death or separation, etc.), the emotional energy we were using to keep memories repressed will need to be used to cover the present-day crises. Whenever that happens, the memory comes closer to the surface until eventually it comes into consciousness. Consequently, you often hear people say, 'Why did I have to remember this *now?*'

This can also happen when a person goes into therapy. Although the presenting problem may seem to have nothing to do with abuse, whenever exploration to resolve the presenting problem begins, the repressed memory can pop up.

Sometimes repressed memory surfaces when the abuser dies. Perhaps it somehow feels safer to 'know' when the abusing person can no longer hurt or be hurt. For a few people who were abused by their father, it is not until both father and mother die that the repressed memory surfaces. It is as though there is no one left to hurt or be hurt and the victim can finally 'know' what happened.

## WHEN DOES REMEMBERING STOP?

When the symptoms end, the remembering usually ends. There may be other traumatic events in the person's life, but the point of remembering is to give the person information to facilitate healing. The unconscious mind will give us a flash of information to help us piece together enough information to enable unresolved issues, which are causing emotional havoc, to be resolved. When enough information has been gathered to accomplish this, we no longer need to know any more.

In other words, when the symptoms that represented the unresolved issues are gone, there is no longer any need to know further information. Our unconscious mind chooses the memories to reveal to us, which, when resolved, will cause other similar ones to be resolved also. Therefore, we do not have to go through every traumatic memory from our childhood. It is the same principle used when you collect the trauma memory list from clients who have conscious memory of their childhood.

In poetry and scripture, humans have been likened to vessels. To be of proper use, all vessels must be whole and able appropriately to contain their valuable contents. However, some vessels are also works of art: not only can they make useful containers, they are also magnificent in some way. Perhaps time has been taken to polish and shine these vessels until they are a delight to behold. Similarly, on occasions, there may be more memory recalls at a later date. These will simply be efforts on the part of our unconscious to polish and shine the vessel, and they will not usually be memories of the intensity of the first ones. This sort of memory recall also happens for people who had conscious memories of the major events.

## WHEN CLIENTS CAN'T BELIEVE

As already stated, it is quite natural for a client to say, 'This can't be true!' when you have done a memory retrieval exercise (or an event is spontaneously remembered). While accepting that this is quite natural, it is also important for you to reframe the experience to help your client to resolve it.

First explain that there is no accurate memory—only a representation of the event. Any time you are remembering an event from a dissociated position or you are not able to see every detail and vivid colour (as you can if you stop now and look around you), you are experiencing a representation of a memory—because *all* the original bits are not there or are not in the same perspective. So, there is no accurate memory—only a representation of the event. *However, it is only necessary to deal with the representation to secure a resolution.*

The second half of the reframe is in story form. Tell it in this format, obviously changing the gender as appropriate:

'Let's just pretend, for the moment, there is a six-year-old girl who has disclosed to you that her grandfather has sexually abused her. [Or whatever the nature of the client's abuse.] You are the only person this child can trust and the only person who actually understands this child's language.

So, being the caring person you are, you take the child to Social Services and the police, to get justice done. At first, the authorities are very interested and start working immediately. The grandfather turns out to be a pillar of the community, vicar, scout leader, all-round good citizen, *and* he denies all the allegations. In fact, he is so distraught and concerned for the child, *you* almost believe him! 'The poor little thing,' he says. 'Of course, I didn't interfere with her in any way! I would never harm a hair on her head. There must be some terrible problem with her mind for her even to make up such a story. Please, we must get help for her—I will be happy to pay for whatever treatment she needs. I just want her to be well.'

So, with the grandfather denying all charges and no physical evidence to go on, the authorities finally tell you there is nothing more they can do for you and the case is closed.

Now, you are back home with the child explaining the situation. She hears you out and then looks at you with great sadness and wails, 'But he *did* do it! I'm not lying, honest! Please believe me.' In your heart you know the child is telling the truth, but there is nothing more you can do to get help for her. What do you do now? Do you say, 'I'm sorry, I have done everything I can do. You will just have to put it all behind you. Just forget all about it', and carry on with your life leaving the child to suffer alone? [Pause at this point and wait for your client to take this in.]

Or will you say, 'Honey, I am so sorry that no one has been able to help you so far, but I am still here for you. I believe you. I will do my best to help you get over this and feel okay about yourself again. You are a lovely little girl and it is not fair for you to go through the rest of your life with this dreadful experience affecting you. We will do our best together to solve this.'

I have never had a client say she would not help the child in the story. When she has said yes, I then quietly and simply ask, 'Would you like to do the same for your own inner child?' No one has refused yet.

I then explain that we will work with the information given in the memory recall as the truth, using either the letter series or another tool. I do not ask my client to say it is the truth, simply to work with the information *as if* it were the truth. Assuring him or her that since all memory is only a representation anyway, it will not matter, it will be just as effective as if we could prove it. I also remind him or her that the only way any abuse allegation can be *proved* is if the perpetrator admits to it. Since that is highly unlikely, it is best to get on with resolving the issue without *proof*.

The following letter to the Child is a result of the reframe.

### Jill's Letter to Child
### (80 per cent) Belief

Dear Little Girl,

Baby, it's a long time since I talked to you like this. It's a sign of how far we've progressed in our relationship with one another over the past eight months that you and I have managed a good, happy time over this past month. You keep reminding me, though, that all is not quite at rest with you just yet. You are still anxious quite often. You are getting better at withdrawing from anxious situations, and allowing me to take full charge, which is, of course, how it should be.

But you do still have concerns. One such concern regards your old uncle, Harry. During a visualisation exercise recently, you were able to bring up a picture of him, with yourself, many years ago. It was a picture which concerned and distressed you, but in fact was not the first time that you had experienced difficulties in your relationship with him.

I understand how difficult you find it to give information about people in this way. I know you had guilty feelings,

feelings of having 'made it up', but I'm not interested in those feelings. These pictures emerged, my darling, and that's enough for me. Factually, perhaps, they mightn't be totally accurate—NO! I take that last sentence back. A 'factual' recount of an experience depends very much on your position in the event. What I mean by that is, this version you visualised may be different, say, from your uncle's visualisation. That is of no importance, the 'factual' part; it is the feelings you retained as a result of this experience which interest me. Darling, you don't have to 'prove' that any of that happened. It happened—your body and your heart retained evidence of that experience, and that is what I want to talk about. There were probably other incidents too, which left you with bad feelings. It is those bad feelings I want to work on.

Those guilt and shame feelings which you had as a result of that experience (and perhaps others too) were a normal reaction to the experience you had. The visualisation featured a scene of abuse. As a child, then, you were treated in a way which was wrong, certainly not in your best interest. You were in a situation of abuse. There were probably other times, too, when you were abused, or ill-treated, by someone who was in a position of authority, whom you were told to respect, who was always automatically right, whereas you (the child) were automatically assumed wrong. In such a situation, darling, it is *normal* to feel guilty, ashamed. That's how the adults get away with it. They unite together, and by using/abusing the love or trust we have in them they convince us that they are in the right, and that the problem is our responsibility, that the fault lies with us. CRAP! The reverse is true, 100 per cent true. It is the responsibility of the adult to set a good example of behaviour, and to allow the child to have a right to his own feelings, to give a child confidence to express those feelings.

Where children aren't listened to or respected, where their parents don't reciprocate the trust and confidence their child has for them, then the child is bound to feel confused, guilty and ashamed—to feel that it's all their fault. You know now that whilst the feelings of guilt and shame were a natural reaction to your abusive situation, you needn't have those feelings with me. As your special adult person, I trust you entirely. I know you would never do anything bad. Anything that you may feel guilty about having being involved in (notice I avoid saying 'having done'), I know wasn't your fault. It was caused by the badness in an adult, in someone else who should have known better, and who was able to involve you because you were a naive child without the confidence to fight for yourself. Therefore it is not your fault!

In a way, I just described the kind of proper, healthy behaviour an adult should show. An adult should have trust and confidence and respect for a child, so that the child can in turn have enough confidence in an adult to be able to say or ask anything, and that child, in the long run, will be confident, healthy, strong, and believe in him- or herself. That is the kind of mutual love, trust and respect relationship which an adult should develop with a child. That's appropriate behaviour.

To show appropriate behaviour, your uncle might have taken some interest in the toy you were playing with at the table. He might have encouraged you in what you were doing, encouraged your dexterity and mental development. He might have taken you in his arms and hugged you, given you the proper kind of hug, one which is a wonderful exchange between two humans. A hug would have been wonderful, had you ever felt safe, secure, loved by your uncle. But you never did. You always felt strangely nervous, self-conscious, self-aware, afraid of him. Because his behaviour was unsuitable throughout.

As a result of his bad behaviour, of his inability to respect you, to love you, and because you didn't have the self-confidence and information which you have access to today, you developed a mistaken belief, the belief that it is dangerous to be sensual. You developed a nervousness, a difficulty interacting with men, because of the fear that they are all attracted to you when they look at you and that unless you're careful they will hurt you—a difficulty to look men in the eye, feelings of shame, dirtiness, being bad deep inside where no one could see it but you, and a deep unease about the sexual act.

It's to your credit that you've been able to battle on this far with all these feelings inside you. You've had this one visualisation (two pictures in all involved) and there is every possibility that these were not isolated incidents. It's a measure of your strength, intelligence, resourcefulness, and ability to recover that you were able to give me that quite painful information. Thank you so much. Thanks for listening to this, even if I haven't been able to explain things too clearly. I'm always here to listen if you need to talk about anything else.

With love,
Jill


'BEING STUCK'

There are occasions during a session when you hit on some material that causes your client to go into an emotional 'stuck' place. They will have physical sensations and feel very confused; often they define their condition as 'being stuck'. When you enquire about what they are experiencing, the replies can be very interesting. A few samples we have heard are: 'I'm trapped in a bunker.' 'I'm stuck in a fog.' 'I am trapped in something like an eggshell.' 'I am stuck behind pink cotton wool.' 'I'm trapped behind a wall of membrane.'

These types of replies can be very confusing to counsellors as well as to clients. What is generally happening is the unconscious mind is offering symbolic language definitions of an emotional state. Your client is trapped or stuck because the material being discussed is touching a tender area; the stuck condition is a diversion from that tender material.

It is usually easy to recognise the difference between the 'being stuck' condition and a sudden memory release, because the 'being stuck' condition is completely unrealistic—i.e. eggshells, membranes, pink cotton wool, etc. The bunker example could have been a memory release, but when I enquired I could see that the scene described was unrealistic. I have included the session notes and information to end this chapter.

*Note*: I need to point out here that should your client disclose ritualistic abuse, the scenes may also appear unrealistic if you do not have information about what is involved in ritualistic abuse. It is, therefore, a good idea to do some research on the subject so that you can tell the difference.

If your client is suddenly in 'stuck' condition, to assist his or her release use the same symbolic language as the unconscious is using to describe the stuck/trapped situation. I will first give you an example of this using the man who was stuck sitting in an eggshell.

'John, just look around where you are sitting and you will see a hammer, tell me when you find it.'

'Okay, it's here.'

'Good. Now just pick up the hammer and hit the eggshell and watch it shatter.'

'I've done it, but the eggshell is too thick, it won't break.'

'That's fine. Put the hammer down and notice to the left of you there is a sledgehammer. Let me know when you have found it.'

'Yes, it's here.'

'Good. Now just use the sledgehammer in the same way and watch the shell shatter.'

'No, still too thick.'

'Okay, good. As you set the sledgehammer down, notice there is a blowtorch next to it.'

'Yes.'

'Fine, now use the blowtorch and melt the eggshell away.'

'Okay, that did it. Now I can see the other side, but I need a knife to chip a hole big enough for me to get out through.'

'Good. Just look to your right and you will notice a knife just the right size. Use it to chip a bigger escape hole.'

This may all sound just a bit airy-fairy, but it is very real to your client when this experience occurs. Now let's have a look at Peggy's 'being stuck' experience. First are the notes I wrote on the day and then the homework I assigned to follow up what we did in the session.

### Peg's Scene of Child 'Being Stuck'
Counsellor's Notes:

'During a joint session Peggy's husband described her sexual responses as often like a 'rag doll'. Later in Peggy's regular session I enquired about her reactions to sex, her feelings and behaviours, and it soon became clear that 'Little Peg' was in charge of the sexual side of Peggy and 'Little Peg' still believed she was with her father.

My explanation of this had a dramatic effect on Peggy and she reported she felt she was splitting into two people. She saw herself in a 'bunker'-type place with several pairs of herself as a child and her father, lying around on the floor in varying degrees of decay. She was very disoriented and said in a very Child-like voice, 'I'm stuck in here, I can't get out.' When I suggested that her Adult could assist her, she said the Adult could not reach her, because she was trapped inside and there were no doors or windows. She said all the walls were covered with thick creeper vines, there was no way out.

I suggested she fix her gaze on the vines and beam her hidden power over them and then watch as the vines began to dissolve. Once all the vines were gone, she could see a door that was hidden behind them. Again with her gaze she beamed her hidden power over to release the door. Once the door was released and opened she could join the Adult and they could leave the bunker behind to be destroyed. I also assigned a written version of the visualisation (and a drawing) for her homework, because when we finished, she was worried that the experience could happen again and said she didn't think she could stay free.'
[Written work always secures information more thoroughly.]

The next session Peggy brought her homework back incomplete. It ended after the creeping vines that covered the inside of the bunker had been destroyed. The child was unable to continue, thinking her parents were too needy of her to be able to leave them. We discussed this problem and Peggy went back to work on it armed with more information. The second attempt was very successful and turned out to be easier to accomplish than Peggy had imagined it would be.

### Peggy's Second Attempt at Bunker Scene

Hello darling, I'm back again. I'm so sorry it's been a long time before I came back to get you love. You see I know how scared you are about trying to leave your concrete, walled world where it seems safe and I didn't know what I should do. I don't want you to feel scared any more love. I know what I'm asking you to do is scary but I also know that if I don't ask, if I don't help you out, you will be stuck in there forever. *I will not let that happen! I will not sit by in my sunny world whilst you suffer in your grey prison. I will not!*

Peg, I feel so angry that your parents have put you in that place and lied and lied to you so that you daren't come out. *They are telling lies.* The world beyond your prison is a wonderful place Peg, it's just as I said—full of trees, flowers, birds, animals, warmth, streams—and all bathed in sunshine, full of love, full of new things to do and see, adventures to have, things to achieve. It is a place where you will be *free*, a place where you can bask in my love and feel the energy of your own life growing, feel proud of yourself, like yourself. Please darling, let me bring you out. Let me get you free away from your pain and their tricks and lies.

*I can't—where is the way? Where is the way, help me, please, help me. I can't, I'm stuck. Daddy says . . .*

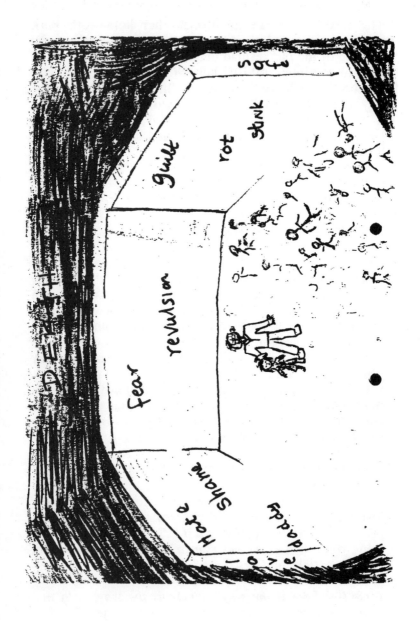

Never mind what daddy says love, that was all lies. Lies to trap you. My love will free you, darling, I promise you. I will always love you Peg.

Now then honey, can you see the wall? Good girl. Walk a little closer love, so that you can see properly. Do you see the marks left by the vine creeper? Do you remember how you looked and it all shrivelled up and you got stronger and stronger and the wind came and blew all the bits away? If you look hard you can just see the shadow it left.

Look at that my love. Do you see through the shadow to the wall? Yes, that's right and as you look the shadow fades and now you can see the door. It was quite well disguised, wasn't it? But now you've found it and under your gaze all those bits of wood start falling away, each rusty old nail falls to the ground. That's it my love. Oh, you are doing well darling. There goes another piece. Well done honey, you're so clever love.

Now as you look, the slats start falling faster, under your gaze they fall and turn to dust. The last one is just going. That's right love, give it a good stare. Hurrah! There it goes, well done, my darling, well done!

Now all the dust is settling and as you concentrate the cool fresh breeze comes again and blows away all the dust, which is all that's left of the wood and nails. Now you have a clear view of the door. Isn't it lovely, a big old door with a round iron latch on it. Do you see the latch love?

*Yes, it's all painted black with a pretty pattern on.*

That's right, darling. As you are watching and looking at the round latch handle, you can see the pattern quite clearly. It's a magic pattern darling, it is the code that makes the door open. It works when it is really concentrated on by good people. If you look at it closely, look really hard, you will be able to make the magic pattern work and the door will start to open.

*Me? Really? Can I?*

Oh yes, darling, you certainly can. That's why they hid the door in the first place, because they knew you could open it. If they thought you couldn't do it, they wouldn't have bothered hiding the door would they? See how mean and sneaky they have been?

*Mmmm. Okay.*

That's my girl! Let's go love, look hard at the door.

*They want me back. Daddy will die. Mummy will cry. He's falling and crumpled up.*

Honey, that's another trick to try and make you stay. That is your bad daddy crumpling up as he deserves. You can't do anything about them. They must choose for themselves love, and they chose to trap you, to hurt you and trick you.

It's okay darling, you can come out now. Look again at the latch. What do you see? That's right, the handle is all shiny and bright. You did that love, well done. Keep looking and you will see the handle lifting up. Very good love. Now it's turning, and turning and the latch is off. Oh, well done darling, very well done. Now as you are watching, the door starts to swing on its hinge, very, very slowly at first but it is opening.

Now you can see something strange, can't you? That's a shaft of sunlight shining through the gap. It looks grey on your side because it has to shine through the dust in the air from all their tricks and lies. That's good honey. As the door swings further open, more and more lovely sunlight is shining your way. Try going a little closer. Reach out your hand into the sunlight and feel how warm and strong it is. Good girl. Now the strength from the sun is flowing up through your arm and into your body, filling you with its warmth and strength. You are so strong now that you can push the door the rest of the way open.

Well, hi there! I'm so glad you can see me now. You

look lovely darling. Come my love, you can come to me now. Reach out and take my hand. I love you so. That's right love, just a couple more steps. There! Your hand feels so good in mine. I'm so happy to hold hands with you.

There, you're out! Come, walk a few steps with me. That's it, our steps match, don't they, and each one makes you stronger. There honey, look how far you've come. Look at all the wonderful things around you, feel the warmth on your skin, hear the sounds of life in this wonderful place.

Now look back behind us. Do you see the walls? The door is closing again now, keeping all the pain, lies and poison locked away from us. It will never touch you again. There, the door is locked. Hey, look at that, your new dress is growing. How do you like it? You look so beautiful and your hair is shining as bright as the sun touching it. I love you so much, my wonderful girl. I love you.

Look back again. The walls are starting to crumble now. With dull thuds and crashing, the prison turns to rubble, as you watch the rubble turns to dust. An insignificant pile of dust. And now comes the lovely cool breeze, blowing away the dust. Nothing is left but a bare patch of earth.

As you look, you see the grass seeds sown by birds flying overhead. The seeds begin to grow now really, really fast. Little green shoots push their way up and strengthened by the sun, and your gaze, they quickly make a green lawn to mingle with the rest of this great place. The flowers start to grow now, bluebells and buttercups. It looks so pretty, doesn't it? Oh look, the rabbits are playing on the grass there and a bird is making her nest in the new tree you grew, her eggs have hatched and she is feeding her baby birds—do you hear their chirping?

The life has spread out now. The happy forest lives there now as it does here. We are one. We are free and I love you. How about walking with me and I'll show you your new world. You can feel the grass on your toes. We'll paddle through the stream and over to my house. You can see it over there with flowers all around it. Tea is ready on the table and your room and bed are made ready too. There's toys and clothes and books and a warm bath, a clean nightie and I will light a lovely fire which we can sit in front of on a rug and have hot milk and toasted marshmallows.

*Oh yes, yes, let's run, let's run. I love you too! . . .*

# 7 The Role of Assertiveness

Assertiveness plays an important part in the recovery of your client. It is one way to assist a person to recognise, build up and strengthen their Adult. Most people who experienced life in a dysfunctional family do not have much of an understanding of assertiveness, and, therefore, do not have much of an understanding of how an Adult speaks, feels or believes.

It is vitally important for your client to develop as an effective Adult. As already discussed in Chapter One, the Adult part needs to be strong enough to take charge; strong enough to defuse any damaged Parent or Child messages; strong enough to make it possible for the Child part to 'tell' repressed memories; strong enough to carry out the jobs of the Adult part—gather information, have a strong assertive voice, manage life circumstances effectively, make realistic assessments of self and others, and be the decision maker over the other two aspects (Parent and Child). It is obvious what a crucial role assertiveness plays in achieving this effective Adult status.

Since effective Adult role models may have been scarce in your client's experience, assertiveness gives a clear example from which to model—with plenty of information and classes available to learn from. However, because you are going to be giving information to your client about the Adult role, you need to be congruent. It is therefore very important for you also to be a role model of assertiveness for your client. It would not be wise to leave that responsibility strictly to outside sources.

As a counsellor you will need to be clear on this subject in order to share assertiveness information effectively with your clients. It is also useful to have some information sheets to hand out to your client, and some knowledge of books and assertiveness courses to which you could refer your client.

I would suggest that if you have not experienced an assertiveness course yourself, that you take this opportunity to do so. Take as many as you need to get the subject well integrated, and suggest that your clients do the same. I took six assertiveness courses before I felt I 'knew' and could quickly draw upon the skills. Therefore, when I hear clients say, 'Oh, I took one of those once. It didn't work for me', my suggestion is to take it again, until it does work. I remind them that they kept getting back on their bicycle until they had mastered that skill, and I challenge them to do the same to gain the vital and life enhancing skills of assertiveness.

## REFLECTIVE LISTENING

It has always puzzled me why reflective listening skills are not taught in school, and why they are only available to those of us who have taken special courses. I teach reflective listening skills to clients regularly and I also encourage them to take assertiveness courses when they are available.

One aspect of reflective listening is being able to reflect back what you think someone said, to be sure it is what they actually said, before you launch into a reply. It is a rather useful communication tool, one that most people would benefit greatly from. Too often people get stuck into an inflexible stand during disagreements, and even when they do discover that there was simply a misunderstanding of meaning to begin with, they cannot climb down from their entrenched position. Learning to reflect (repeat) what you *think* you heard, to be sure that it is what was *actually* meant, would stop many disagreements in the bud, e.g. 'So you're saying that you think I am not interested in what you're talking about because I don't look you in the eye when you speak?'

Reflective listening also includes being able to reflect people's feelings back to them. Someone tells you that the assertiveness class she signed up for was full and you respond/reflect: 'You must be feeling really disappointed', rather than, 'Oh well, there will always be another one'.

Most people try to make others feel better with that sort of comment, but nothing is less comforting than some cheerful, 'Oh well . . . look on the bright side' statement.

People first need to be acknowledged. With our feelings acknowledged, we will then be in a position to look naturally for our own bright side. If our feelings are not acknowledged, we often continue pushing for that to happen, which in turn stops us being able to take that next step of looking for the bright side. If others knew how to acknowledge our feelings, we could very naturally move on to that next comforting step. So, although people think they are 'helping' by starting off with cheerful statements, they are actually retarding the moving on process. Just think how much easier family interactions would be if that one skill were in operation.

Reflective listening also includes being able to sum up people's statements in a sentence or two, to ensure they know they have been heard. When people know they have been heard, the conversation can also move along. If this doesn't happen, they will repeat themselves until they know you have heard them. This is particularly true in disagreements. Assertiveness teaches this very useful skill.

What usually stops us from naturally reflecting back what someone has said in a disagreement is that we think we would be agreeing with them and we are not happy about doing that. However, we can reflect back *without agreeing* and therefore facilitate negotiation in a much shorter time. For instance, in the case of someone trying to get you to agree to do something you do not wish to do, he or she might say, 'You are so boring. You never want to have any fun. Come on, go to the cinema tonight.' You could respond with, 'You may be right, perhaps I am boring to you, perhaps it seems as if I never want to go to places that you find fun, but I am still not going to the cinema tonight.' You have not actually agreed with the person's statements, but you have reflected back the essence of what was said and he or she no longer needs to keep repeating it.

Your clients may feel a bit wooden at first as they are learning to use reflective listening and assertiveness skills, but the more they are used, the more fluid they become.

## ASSERTIVENESS CHECKLIST

a. *Assertiveness creates adult behaviour and 'voice'.*  Most clients come from dysfunctional families where passive or aggressive behaviour is seen as normal. Therefore they will not have had much in the way of positive behaviour role models. Learning assertiveness will give clients knowledge of how to stand in their own space as a person *without* having to bully others with aggressiveness to do so. It will also give them the ability to stand in their own space *without* having to give that space up to others 'more worthy' or more pushy. Knowing how to present their ideas and opinions in an assertive way will give them an adult 'voice', for nothing sounds more childish or parental than people who are speaking passively or aggressively. An adult 'voice' and adult behaviour will be needed not only to regain emotional balance (sorting the damaged Child/Parent parts), but also to maintain it.

b. *A strengthened Adult assists the inner Child to disclose repressed memories.*  Many times children keep abuse information to themselves because they feel their parents are too fragile or explosive to be told. The same feelings are often reflected in those with repressed memories: the Child part keeps all the abuse memories to enable the fragile Adult part to have a life. When, however, the Adult part is strengthened, then the inner Child can finally disclose.

c. *The strengthened Adult has more coping skills and personal power.*  The strengthened Adult having more coping skills does not need explaining, but I would like to say something about personal power. The term 'personal power' is often categorised with the term bully, but personal power is just what a bully lacks. It is having confidence and self-esteem—without which people feel vulnerable. Bullies deal with vulnerability by 'acting powerful'. Pushing others around gives the bully a sense of power, since he has no personal power (confidence and self-esteem) he has to compensate by using the only power he knows how to tap into—power over others. Of course, power over others does not give the kind of satisfaction that personal power gives, so the bully tends to keep trying harder to secure his prize. Unfortunately, it is a losing battle—it is like a hungry person trying to satisfy hunger by solely drinking water. The stomach would be full, but the hunger would continue. Personal power is the essence of assertiveness.

d. *Reflective learning skills assist Adult communication.* What is reflective listening? It is the ability to rephrase people's statements to ensure that what you heard is what they actually said. It is the ability to reflect people's feelings back to them to ensure that they are acknowledged. It is the ability to sum up and reflect the essence/gist of people's statements in a sentence or two to ensure they feel heard.

e. *A strong Adult/assertive 'voice' makes identification of damaged Parent/Child self-talk messages easier to monitor and stop.* The stronger the Adult 'voice', the more obvious any damaged Parent/Child messages are and the easier it will be to exercise a 'stop'. However, if the Adult part is weak and ineffective, damaged messages will seem normal and the ability to stop them will be weakened.

f. *Be sure YOU have assertiveness, for your clients will learn more from what you ARE, than from what you say.* As a counsellor, you have a unique opportunity to be a role model for emotional health. It is sad when counsellors/ therapists do not personally apply what they teach, for they are then simply being a role model for incongruence.

g. *Assertiveness handouts.* From books on assertiveness, you will find plenty of information that will convert into useful handouts for your clients. The basic information to cover is:

- Assertive Human Rights (included in most assertiveness books)
- Assertiveness Means (*Assertion Training—A Handbook for Those Involved in Training*, Anni Townend, FPA Education Unit, 1985)
- Four types of behaviours (*A Woman in Your Own Right*, Anne Dickson, Quartet, 1982)
- Nonverbal Components of Self-Assertion (included in most assertiveness books)

## EMOTIONAL BLACKMAIL

Most of us, at one time or another, have experienced someone who frequently uses ill-health or personal difficulties to
manipulate others. Often, much as we resent and dislike
what we are being asked to do, we find ourselves unable to
say 'no' because the other person is in a weaker position.
Often we are not even aware that this behaviour is finely-
tuned manipulation. Sometimes our lack of awareness is due
to the fact that the person is frequently apologising for 'putting us to so much trouble' or is 'so sorry for having to ask'
and we begin to believe that the situation cannot be helped.
Other times we feel obligated by a close relationship to the
person, e.g. 'I have to do this, she *is* my mother'. In any case,
the presupposition is that the other person has no choice but
to make demands upon us, and that we also have no choice
but to cooperate.

Weak or dependent people do not necessarily play upon
others' guilt, nor are their ploys as calculated as they seem.
Their behaviour is such an integral part of their emotional
make-up that they are not always aware of what they are
doing. Of course, as long as their behaviour gets them what
they want, why would they even consider changing it?

Everyone feels needy at some point in his life. What separates normal neediness from unhealthy dependency is the
way the neurotic person employs his or her suffering to elicit
guilt or pity from others. The person who uses feelings of
failure or inadequacy to *get* attention and love is identifying
with his weakness in a damaging, unwholesome way.

Negative behaviour patterns are usually learned in childhood. Children of neglectful parents learn unhealthy dependency because the lack of parental support and love leaves
those children with a sense of inner emptiness—a bottomless
pit of need.

Children who have been overprotected have often experienced parents who had an exaggerated need to feel powerful
and literally cultivated dependency in their offspring. Over-
protection often damages a child's self-esteem so severely
that he or she evolves into a chronically weak adult.

When people learn that their inadequacy and neediness

can secure attention and love, they may deliberately avoid gaining strength or experiencing positive change. Why would they desire to change a pattern that works? Unconsciously, they may believe that strength will lead to abandonment or isolation, that without inadequacy and neediness they would have no way of 'connecting' with others.

**The Helper**
Chronically needy people target their helpers carefully. They will look for signals (recognised on an unconscious level) to identify the person who would be most likely to play the helper role in harmony with their needy role. If they tried playing the game with the wrong person, the response might be instant dismissal, as some people care enough about their own lives not to allow themselves to be used.

The type of people who respond most readily to the call of the needy are sometimes called the 'strong ones'. People who are always the 'giver', always the one who is together, always the strong one. These people are apt to have an unacknowledged and unexpressed sense of neediness. They cannot reach out to say, 'I'm hurting. I need comforting', for they would feel too vulnerable. Their own frightened and helpless inner child gets projected onto others. By playing the role of the tower of strength or the helper, such individuals are attempting to heal themselves. Those roles offer a good many rewards—they are seen not only as good and caring but as competent, even powerful. The problem with these roles is that the tower of strength or helper cannot ever let down his or her guard or assume the role of the receiver.

The difference between people who have a healthy desire to help or have empathy for others and the 'strong ones' is that the latter cannot say 'no' to the demands of weaker people. They need to feel super-adequate to conceal their own hidden desire to lean on someone else. This imbalance sometimes develops from a family background in which one parent was seen to be abused by the other. A child's frustrated desire to save the victimised parent may result in a need to help other weak people.

Those children who are pushed out of the nest too soon

and forced to behave independently before they are ready are sometimes driven to compensate for that loss. They often are too embarrassed and uncomfortable to admit to their need for help and nurturing and are driven to prove that they can cope against all odds. They are often trapped in unequal relationships, constantly giving succour.

Emotionally healthy people in good relationships may also be quite strong, but they are not compelled to comply with excessive demands. They have the ability to say, 'no, that's enough'. They are naturally using assertiveness skills. Your clients may find themselves in either the 'helper' or 'needy' role.

## USEFUL BOOKS ON ASSERTIVENESS

*A Woman in Your Own Right*, Anne Dickson (Quartet, 1982).

A book with good examples of the personality types for 'passive', 'aggressive' and 'assertive' behaviour. It is useful in deciding which area a person errs in most often and provides a positive Adult behaviour (assertive) example.

*When I Say No, I Feel Guilty*, Manuel J. Smith (Bantam, 1976).

This book provides good dialogue examples for your 'Adult voice'. Although it has American overtones, in most instances it is easy enough to adapt to your own conversational format. A very useful book to learn how to exchange assertively with someone who continues in an aggressive manner.

*Assert Yourself: a Self-assertiveness Programme for Men and Women*, Gael Lindenfield (Thorsons, 1987).

Written in a personal and friendly style. Easy to read and simply explained, with helpful exercises for either groups or individuals.

# 8 Sexuality

Those people who had parents who were rigid and inflexible concerning the subjects of bodies and sex usually have difficulty in finding their own sense of being natural in those areas. Consequently, you will find clients who have never been sexually abused, but who have similar sexual difficulties to those who have been sexually abused. As we know, children usually take on their parents' belief systems; sexual dysfunction without a personal experience of sexual abuse is a good example of that.

## REFRAME AND DEFUSE GUILT AND SHAME

Most people who carry guilt and shame are loath to bring up the subject and start happily chatting about it. It is not helpful or necessary for a counsellor to wait for that to happen. It is more responsible for the counsellor to bring the subject of sexuality into the conversation. It is suggested that this be done in a casual, easy way. If anything in the client's conversation can lead naturally onto the subject, use it. If not, bring it up yourself.

'I thought we might chat a bit today about the issues of guilt and shame most people face who have experienced abusive childhoods. Of course, these may not be problem areas for you, but I think it will be useful to understand what can happen.

The issue of shame is usually strong if the person ever experienced physical pleasure during abuse. Most commonly, that person believes that experiencing pleasure means that they must have wanted the abuse to happen or that they are now "just like the abuser". On some occasions, the abuser will even say that to the child, "Oh, you liked it, you must have wanted it."

Of course, neither of those beliefs nor that statement is correct. The truth is that our bodies were designed to respond to touch. Our genitals were designed with even more sensitivity to touch than other places on our body. The nerve endings in our body responsible for our response to touch do not have the ability to differentiate between appropriate and inappropriate touch—they just respond. The differential is made by our perceptions: if the touch is experienced with someone we love and there are no "rules" (to our knowledge) against it, we perceive our response as pleasant and acceptable. If, however, the touch is experienced with someone we either do not like, or someone we like but do not want this particular touch from, we often perceive our response as bad—perhaps thinking that our response somehow connects us with the bad in the event.

As you can see, the response is neither good or bad, it is simply a response that our body was especially designed to give—just as it does when our knee jerks up when the doctor hits it with his small rubber hammer. If the doctor hits the right spot, we cannot stop our knee jerking up. If the abuser touches the right spots, we cannot stop the pleasurable responses. The response is not bad, the "bad" is that a grown-up chose to interact sexually with a child.'

If your client is demonstrating any acknowledgement of this sort of experience (either verbally or non-verbally), you might gently ask at this stage, 'Did you ever experience any feelings like that?' If the answer is yes, you might say, 'I wonder . . . have any questions come up that you would like to know the answer to?' If she says no, just reply, 'Oh, that's good. I'm glad you are clear on that issue. There is another area I feel it is also important to explore. Again, you may not have experienced this, but it is useful to know.'

'First of all, it is our parent's responsibility to behave in such a way that we feel special and important. All children (and adults) need to experience this. Feeling special and important is as necessary to our emotional health as food is to our physical health.

We are all familiar with stories of people who were so desperate for food that they ate things that would normally be repulsive to them. In fact, I reckon that if you or I had not had anything to eat for a month, we would be fighting over the contents of my rubbish bin, rather than engaged in meaningful conversation. The contents of my bin would appear as treasures, not rubbish. The smell and deterioration of the food will seem a small price to pay if we could partially fill our hunger.

That is what happens to people who are desperate for food, but what can happen to people desperate to have their emotional needs, of feeling special and important, met? Many times children whose parents cannot usefully demonstrate their love will settle for abuse attention (from parents or others), because for that short time they feel special and important. For that short time the focus is on the child, even if the focus is of a sexual or painful nature. The accompanying guilt or shame will seem a small price to pay if it partially fills their need to feel special and important. Those times with the abuser may appear as treasures, not abuse.

When our food or emotional needs are adequately met, we do not have any desire for poor alternatives. There is no shame or guilt attached to settling for rubbish to eat or settling for abuse attention—you were simply surviving the only way you could find. If shame or guilt is to be placed anywhere, it should be at the feet of the parents, whose responsibility it is to meet their children's physical and emotional needs.'


BLAME

As with shame and guilt, your client will seldom be able to bring up the subject of blame. This is another opportunity for you casually to introduce it. Always use terms such as: 'some people'; 'many people'; 'there are people'; 'often people feel'; 'I have found that people can feel'; 'there are those who feel'. Please do not start off by asking or expecting your client to disclose his or her feelings, or by connecting your comments to your client—make your comments random, talk about 'others'. When you display a non-judgmental attitude, and reframe the blame experience, then your client can feel confident enough to disclose if she has had a similar event happen in her life.

Blame often takes the form of having a chance to 'tell', but not taking it. For instance, perhaps a child's teacher, Scout leader, authority figure, relative or friend's mother caringly and lovingly asked the child what was wrong—and the child did not tell about the abuse. Often children grow up feeling that the abuse is all their fault because they did not tell when they had the chance, feeling that they have no one to blame but themselves, and they usually do just that.

Of course, as mentioned in Chapter One, most children are afraid of getting their parents in trouble; not being believed; being put into care; going to prison; becoming a social outcast/being rejected. A child who does not take the opportunity to tell is simply a child trying to survive: a child trying to protect him- or herself the only way he feels safe, by keeping the abuse a secret. In other situations, it is often too much for the child to bear the responsibility of being the one to 'tell' and change the family in such a profound way. Often these courageous children bear the pain themselves, believing that by doing so they are saving the family.

## NORMAL RESPONSE

Always explain to your client that whatever sexual dysfunction he is experiencing, it is a normal response to abusive situations. It is important for your client to hear you say that his or her problems are a normal reaction (even to emotional abuse). It is appropriate to give your client examples of the kinds of different, and similar, problems others have faced (obviously observing confidentiality if it was a personal client). Doing so gives your client an opportunity to put his own experience into context.

Once you have openly, and non-judgmentally, discussed the shame, guilt and blame issues, it is appropriate to enquire if your client has any specific area of question that has not yet been mentioned. It is most helpful to do this all in one session, so that your client can speak up while the atmosphere is most welcoming.

## CONTROL POSITIONS

Sometimes your clients will be reluctant to do any work on sexuality issues for fear of facing the shame. It would be remiss of you not to mention the fact that while they do not face and solve the issue, they leave the abuser in a control position. Not facing and solving the issue means that the abuser is still controlling your clients' sexuality, inwardly telling them what they can or cannot do. It is almost as if the abuser were in a client's bed, perhaps between your client and his or her partner, perhaps even laughing about how much power can be exerted over your client's life. At this point of the explanation, your client should be squirming with discomfort. Then ask, 'What is it like to think that your abuser is in control of you in that way? Would you like to pull the plug on the abuser's power? Would you like to kick the abuser out of your bed?' Looking at the situation in that light, normally, your client will see the benefit of addressing the sexuality issue.

## FIRST SEXUAL EXPERIENCE

In the natural course of events our first sexual experience happens after puberty and after we are able to give informed consent. It is meant to be a loving, pleasurable experience between two people who have mutual respect and desire for one another. At that time our brain logs in the location; type of person involved; activities involved; accompanying scents, tastes, sounds, sights and feelings. Our brain does not give this experience a 'good' or 'bad' label, simply a label that states 'first sexual experience'. In the future, any situation that has similarities to the details logged in our memory bank will cause us to experience mild or strong sexual arousal, because the brain will immediately have retrieved the matching elements from our first sexual experience. The brain's formula is: some matching elements = sexual stimulation.

You can see the benefits of this formula when the first sexual experience was a pleasant, natural one, as described above. Unfortunately, the same formula is in practice when the experience was not pleasant or natural, because, as stated, the brain does not give a 'good' or 'bad' label. Therefore, those of us who had our first sexual experience as a child, unable to make informed consent, and without mutual respect or desire, are stuck with the same formula—some matching elements = sexual stimulation.

This formula can be present during an actual experience, while reading about a similar experience or while watching a film about a similar experience. Remember, it does not have to be an exact replica, it only needs some matching elements to trigger the reaction. Even reading other victims' accounts of their abuse, in a book designed to be of help, can trigger sexual stimulation—much to the reader's dismay. It is a very confusing and frightening experience—wide open for misinterpretation.

My own experience of this was in my thirties, when I first read *Forbidden Flowers* by Nancy Friday—a book containing a variety of favourite sexual fantasies donated by women. Some of the fantasies I found to be hilariously funny and wondered how anyone could find them sexually stimulating. Others I found really repugnant and again wondered how anyone could find those sexually stimulating. Some were just boring. Then there were the ones that affected me with sexual stimulation. There were a few fantasy categories to which I responded sexually, but only one category worried me—fantasies which involved an adult and a child, and most specifically a female child and her uncle. I panicked at first, thinking it must mean that I was a child molester and did not know it yet. I knew that I had never had any sexual interest in children, but I feared that this newly discovered response must mean sexual interest in children was just dormant, waiting to erupt.

Fortunately, I decided to look into my response and explore other possibilities of meaning, before I made plans to jump off the nearest bridge. As you can imagine, I was greatly relieved to learn that my response was quite normal, given the fact that my first sexual experience had been at two years old with my uncle. My response did not mean that I was an abuser.

If your client is aware of sexual stimulation in regard to adult/child sexual scenarios, she will probably be reluctant to disclose any information about it. On the other hand, she may not yet be aware of this phenomenon. Either way, it is kinder for you to offer this information, casually and relaxed, utilising the same non-judgmental attitude as before, i.e. 'Oh, by the way, here is some useful information you may be interested to know. Some people experience an unusual phenomenon . . .'

## USING LETTERS

If you have used the Personal Resource Exercise, the Mistaken Belief Visualisation, or the above information to reframe the issues surrounding sexuality and still your client cannot shift the problem, use either the full letter series or just a letter to the Child. Below are samples of letters about sexuality. The first is a full letter series from Sally. The second is a letter series from Peggy. Both will make useful samples to share with clients when needed. Encourage them to 'nick' whatever phrases they find useful and use those phrases in their own letters, if desired.

*Sally's Letter Series*
*Letter FROM: Mother not speaking about sex*

Dear Child,
    As we grow up we all find that we need to talk to someone about the things we see around us and don't really understand. For a lot of people this is easy, but I think that maybe you need someone who can listen to you and explain to you the things you don't understand. I would like to do that for you because I can be here whenever you want. I won't ignore you or be embarrassed by what you say. I won't laugh at you because you needed to ask.

I will just talk to you and let you talk to me about whatever you want.

I understand that this may be difficult to start with because you don't usually talk to grown-ups about yourself, how you feel or about your body, but perhaps you could tell me why you don't do this.

*Nobody talks about those things at home, so I don't think I should. I never hear mum and dad talk about people's bodies; not when I'm there. Sometimes it's like we don't have a body, just voices. It's all secret, but other children know about their bodies, because they say so at school. Their mums talk to them, but I daren't ask my mum. How can I if she never talks about it? It's just not allowed. But I feel shut out because they all know, all the others at home and at school. So why can't I know? What's wrong with my body and me that no one tells me? I know because I've read about things and talked to my friends, but I want mum to tell me, to share something with me, not leave me out.*

[Mistaken belief was: I am bad because I know about bodies and sex.]

Thank you for telling me that. I'm sure your mum didn't mean to make you feel left out or ashamed about your body, but you see, she was embarrassed. Perhaps when she was little no one talked to her either and so she didn't know what to say to you.

You don't ever have to feel bad about growing up and changing. It's quite natural. You are allowed to know about your body—everyone has to, it's part of life. So don't forget I can talk to you about this whenever you need me.

> *Sally—Letter TO: Speaking About Sex*
> *Child belief was 90 per cent*

Dear Sally,

You remember how you told me about how no one ever talked to you about bodies and sex and how you felt

ashamed about those things? Well, I want you to understand that any child of your age needs to know about her
own body and any child would have needed that information given to her by someone she trusted—like her
mum. However, if that information only comes from hearing other people talk, or looking at grown-up books, or
watching TV, then the child is going to be unsure of what
she should know—of what is 'okay' knowledge. It is quite
normal that you felt that way.

If that child then tries to get that same information from
her mother, but her mother reacts by being embarrassed,
then the child will finish up feeling guilty and embarrassed
about the little she does know. She becomes ashamed of
her body and feels embarrassed when she hears others
talk about bodies and sex and the feelings of guilt get
worse. This is what has happened to you. It is wrong that
it did happen and it is not your fault.

The person who was wrong was your mother. It is part
of her role as a mother to guide you and talk to you about
growing up, about your body and how it changes. These
things are normal and natural, they happen to everyone
and you don't have to feel bad about wanting to know or
about what you do know. You *should* know, and it was
your mum's job to tell you in a way that you were able
to understand and to feel comfortable with.

Just because she wasn't comfortable about her body
does not give her the right to make you feel bad about
yours. There is nothing wrong with your body, it is quite
normal. But as you become older, and more aware of
your body, you want to know more and it was up to your
mother to realise this and to find a way and a special time
to talk to you—so you both could share the knowledge
openly and you could feel good about yourself.

Because these things did not happen you began to
believe you should not ask about or talk about bodies or
sex, believing other people would be embarrassed like
your mum. So, you kept quiet and hid the knowledge that
you had. You also began to believe that because no one
openly told you about sex, you couldn't talk about it
because they might ask how you knew and that in turn

would reveal what your brother had done to you. You worried that if no one talked about sex, and grown-ups were only allowed to have sex, what would they do if they knew about you having sex, because you were not allowed?

This all adds to the belief that all that you do know—whether you found out from friends or from having sex with Marvin—was bad. It was all information that to you was wrong, it was part of your guilt, but you were trapped because you couldn't get rid of what you knew. All of that made you believe: I am bad because I know about bodies and sex.

All these beliefs are wrong, very wrong, and they are making you feel bad when you don't have to feel that way. Your mum might think that talking about sex with a child is embarrassing, but that's her problem, not yours. Marvin might be afraid that if you talk about what you know it might mean being found out, but he caused you to know so he can only blame himself. He shouldn't have made you carry his guilt. You're right to find out about your body and what you know can help you to feel good about your body and what you know can help you to feel good about yourself, if you let it. So, let your mum and Marvin sort themselves out, leave them to worry and let go of your fear, it doesn't belong to you anyway. Give the 'bad' and the fear back to them.

[Mistaken Belief Visualisation done here.]

There, now you know it's okay and you don't have to feel embarrassed any more. Just remember that I am here now and I can help you and be there whenever you want—because I love you and you deserve to be cared for because you're so special to me.

### Sally—Rescue Scene: Speaking About Sex

Even before I opened the door, I knew what I would find. I was so angry with her mother for not seeing what she was failing to do. I pushed hard at the door and felt a jolt of power as it banged back on its hinges. The mother was standing at the sink and looked up startled. Immediately she opened her mouth to protest, but I was determined—not this time.

'No!' I said. 'No, don't bother to speak. I don't care what you say. Just for once don't make excuses, just come and look at your child and see what you've done to her.' I pulled her towards the playroom door, not listening to her protests of how she had to get the dinner on.

I pushed open the door and herded her ahead of me, still holding her arm. There little Sally sat on the floor. She had her head down, knees folded up to her chest. I could feel her confusion and her need to talk and ask questions. As the door opened she looked up, and as she saw me, her face changed. The anxiety faded a little and she began to smile at me.

'There,' I shouted at her mother. 'Now can you see? She's scared and she's confused. She needs to know about growing up, but who can she ask? Certainly not you. Oh, no, you're too embarrassed, too busy, too useless. You're supposed to care for her, support her, give her the knowledge she needs to help her grow up confident about her body, but not you. You just go on pretending it'll all come to her in some kind of dream. Well, it won't. You're messing things up and we've had enough. Little Sally and I are leaving. We're going away and together we'll answer all the questions you never even heard her ask.'

Sally had risen to her feet now and all the anxiety was gone. She was already moving towards me, her face eager and full of anticipation. Her mother just stood there. She still had no answers and I pushed her aside in contempt as Sally reached out her hand to mine.

Together, arms around each other, we walked out of the door and into the sunshine. Everywhere was warm and light. The garden looked so fresh, so inviting. Sally ran ahead, touching the flowers, laughing, and I followed her. Together we wander along the paths, looking at each border, each pond, each tree, sharing each discovery.

*Peggy's Letter Series*
*Letter FROM: Sleeping*

Hello again my precious love. How are you feeling now? A little bit rested I hope. Come, sit with me darling. I want to talk with you again. You have been such a very brave girl to tell me some of the scary things about your daddy.

Well, honey, I would like you to tell me some more about the time when you were seven years old and you were all curled up in bed pretending to be asleep and daddy came in. It's okay, love, you will be safe, you are here with me and I will keep my arms around you, loving and protecting you while you talk. Go ahead, sweetheart, I'm here for you now, listening with love.

That's right, darling, you are seven years old and you're in your room, curled up on your side, in your bed. What happens now, love?

*Daddy . . . daddy's coming. I can hear him up the stairs. He's big and they make a noise. It's all dark in my room except where the landing light comes through the top of my door. There is a special glass part for it, high up.*

*I am in my bed behind the door and I am curled up like the nurse showed me when I went to have my tonsils out. I can do it on my own now without her fingers in me to twist me up.* [See note at end.]

*Daddy creeps in the door quietly and I am all curled up to be asleep, but he is leaning over me. The edge of my bed goes down and I hold tight to the covers in my fist and screw up my eyes tight. I am asleep, really I am, but he is leaning over me. I look asleep. I don't even breathe but he is on the bed and it goes down more. His hand is on my face, moving my hair and touching my cheeks. (Go away, please, please daddy, go away. I am asleep, please go away. I am a good girl, please go away. I am a very good girl, I am, I am. Daddy, daddy please, I am, I am a good girl. I didn't do anything, please don't . . .)*

[*Note*: Child's words in parentheses represent her

thoughts, not spoken words. Adult interrupts at this point to comfort distressed child. Child's writing had become very large and scrawling, while Adult writing is normal. While writing, Adult holds and cuddles a teddy bear, as a representation of the child. The actual handwriting changes can be seen in Chapter Three.]

Shh, honey, it's okay my lovely one. I am here and you are safe. There now, there now, I am here with you. It hurts you so, I know that, baby, just take your time. Let me hold you, darling. I love you so very much Peg. It cannot happen again, it is a memory this time, love. Just a bad memory, I promise it is not real now. I will not let him do that again. Try, my love, try to tell me the rest. It's okay, you are safe.

*Daddy is pushing the covers up into a heap on me and it feels cold on my back and my bottom. I want to be asleep but I can't because he's still here. (Oh, please don't daddy, I am a good girl. Mummy will hate me. I am a good girl, mummy will be horrid. I am . . . I am . . . I am . . .)*
*Daddy is pushing me. He is pushing my nightie up. It is pretty pink with white lace neck and a pink daisy and daisy buttons.* [Child tries to escape pain of event by concentrating on the detail of her nightdress. Dissociation in a variety of forms is a common experience for children during abuse.] *My neck is slobbery wet and hot breathing. (Go away, please, go away.) Where's my mummy? She will hate me. I am a good girl, daddy, please love me. I am a good girl. Oh, no daddy, please, don't.) Pushing his fingers in my legs and wetting on my neck and cheek and hurting me underneath and pushing my legs over and up and touching and my bottom's out. (Don't, don't. Go away please, don't.)*
*I am a dirty girl, a bad, bad dirty girl. Mummy has told me before I am a bad girl. I should set an example. I am a bad girl and I know better.*
*He's pushing up at my bottom. (Go away, please go away.) Big finger in my bottom. I want to be asleep. I am good. I love my daddy. (Don't, don't. I love my daddy.*

*Go away, I hate you.) Wet and slobbery and hot breath and horrid and horrid grunt, grunt, piggy grunt. Grabbing me, grabbing my bottom like squeak piggy squeak. A game like squeak piggy squeak and I am blind and it is HIM. I love daddy, I hate HIM, he is doing it.* [Child dissociates from the reality that this is her father, she splits the father she loves off from the father doing this to her. This father becomes 'HIM'.]

*(Ow, no, no, no, no. Ow, ouch, ow. No, please, no, no.) I curl up like the nurse showed me (No, no), I curl up tight. My bottom's sore and cold and I have gone stiff and dead. He is gone and the covers are tidy. I am dead, I am gone.* [Mistaken belief was: I am bad.]

Peg, my beautiful little girl, you are fine now. So very brave, so very lovely. You are the best little girl I know. I am so very, very sorry that your daddy did that to you. It was very wrong of him. Have a little rest now honey, I will hold you and keep you safe and when you wake up we will talk. I love you darling. xx

*Note*: The experience with the nurse happened when the child was four years old and a nurse inserted her fingers into the child's vagina, and then twisted to cause the child to pull her knees further up to her chest to facilitate the use of a suppository.

## Peggy's Letter TO: Sleeping

My darling,

What a good little girl you were to go up to bed and try to go to sleep like that. It was so bad of your daddy to come and push the covers away. It made you cold and very frightened. I know honey, I know. It's okay, love, it's over now and it won't happen again.

Your daddy did those things to you because it made him feel good and powerful, darling, and he was very bad to do it. You are a good little girl and you did nothing to make daddy be bad. You couldn't have done, darling, children cannot make grown-ups do bad things and they can't stop them either.

You did all you could, darling, I know that. I know you couldn't call for mummy because she would not help you, she was too weak and afraid herself. It was bad of her not to be stronger for you and stop daddy from forcing his bad behaviour on you. She should have stopped him.

You were right, love, she did know already. She was just not a strong enough mummy to face what he was doing so she pretended not to know. That was so very, very bad of her. I am so sorry that you had the bad luck to have such a weak mummy. She did love you, darling. She was just too scared to act on that love when it really counted and she should not have been. It was not because of you. Just like it was not because of you that daddy kept on doing sexual things to you. They were *both* at fault, my love, you were not, you never were.

I'm so sorry that daddy made you feel all slobbered on with his wet kisses. These were not proper daddy kisses, they are the sort of kiss a man gives to a woman who he is making love with and he should not have inflicted them upon you, a little girl. It is normal for a man's mouth to be a bit open while kissing when he is sexually aroused. It was not a weird thing to happen, but it was wrong, very wrong that he made it happen to you. That sort of kissing is only good between grown-ups who choose to do it.

It is the same with the way he touched you. It was so wicked of him to force your legs up so that he could touch your bottom and vagina. This is something that should only happen between grown-ups. It is a normal part of adult sex. I think your bottom felt so cold because he took away the covers, my love, and I think it felt sore on the outside because his hand squeezed at your buttocks. The part that felt sore inside was not really your bottom, sweetheart, it was what is called your vagina.

Between your buttocks (the outside of your bottom) is a hard tight hole where you pooh from (you can touch it and see later if you like). You will know the hole I mean because it feels sort of hard and you won't be able to get your finger in very well. That is called your anus and we all have one, girls and boys, ladies and men. It is the same as the part you can see under Rex's tail [Peg's dog] where he poohs from when he goes to the bottom of the garden.

The other hole, the one that hurt you inside because of what daddy did, is called your vagina. It feels warm and soft and you can get your finger in quite easily. It is more in the middle, between your legs. This is the place that babies come out of their mummies and it is also where a man puts his willy when grown-ups make love. It is a good part of you and not at all dirty like mummy thinks. She thinks that because she is a bit confused about it. She does not really know much about vaginas feeling good and being precious. I don't think she ever learned that, but I did and so now I am helping you to learn it too.

Your vagina is not the same as where you wee from; that is only a very little hole, only as big round as your little white lolly sticks, so you can't see it very well. It is higher up than your vagina, just underneath the little bumpy bit that goes warm when you touch it; you can just see it if you look carefully in a mirror.

The warm bumpy bit is called your clitoris and it is especially there for you so that you can have that warm, safe feeling whenever you want. When you grow up you can share it with a special man as part of making love or just touch it on your own. Either way will feel good and both ways are right when you want that to happen. This is another thing your mummy never learned about and she thinks it is bad. Some grown-ups quite often think things are bad when they don't understand them and are too afraid to try and learn. This is just one of those things for your mummy. So don't worry about what she thinks. She doesn't have the information we do, so she makes mistakes.

Darling, you are a wonderful, wonderful child. I love you so very much. Remember that I am here for you now. I will always be with you, loving you. Try not to worry about your mummy's mistaken ideas about your body, love. We now know how it really is, don't we? I love you, darling, rest safely, sweetheart. Your 'special person' is here now, and I am yours, in love for always.

[This letter series does not include the Mistaken Belief Visualisation because it was written a few years before I incorporated the MBV into the Letter TO:.]

## Peggy's Rescue Scene—Sleeping

As I park outside No. 76, I know that Peg's father is on his way upstairs; whilst her mother sits downstairs behaving like the three monkeys all rolled into one and failing miserably as monkey No. 3.

I push the front door open, the glass cracking with the force of meeting the hall wall. In a couple of bounds I am upstairs and along the landing. As I kick open the bedroom door, my hand snaps on the light.

Her father looks shocked and very, very frightened as the power of me advances upon him. To Peg I say gently, 'It's okay, my love.' Then my strong arm reaches for him, gripping him in a vice-like hold around his neck. A flick of my wrist spins him, smashing him through the glass of the window to land broken and torn through the trees, onto his precious spiky fence.

Gently I stoop to Peg, my arm changing to a strong yet loving, gentle support. 'I'm here, honey, I'm here, you're safe now.' As I lift this beautiful child her little body relaxes against me as her face lights up with the joy of being loved and safe.

'Come on darling, let's get you some warm clothes and you can come home with me.' She is happily chattering about my house: 'Where is it?' 'What is my room like?' 'Will there be a fire?' 'Shall we have warm milk and chocolate biscuits?' Peg dresses and we leave her room.

The frightened 'monkey' downstairs is immobile, trying not to 'see' or 'hear' any evil. We enter the room, holding hands. 'We're going now, you useless, stupid woman. This is my child now, not yours. She will live in love and security with me.' We turn and leave, the broken door creaking pathetically behind us.

At my house we spend our time getting Peg's room just

how she likes it. All her toys, books, pictures and clothes are there with a brand new bed and a big grown-up dressing table with a proper winged mirror. I tuck her up between the fresh, sweet sheets and we share hot chocolate and a plate of chocolate biscuits before she sleeps a deep, peaceful sleep. Her glowing face and smile reflecting her new and everlasting joy.

How I love this child, I will treasure her always.

At the end of this rescue scene Peggy was feeling very angry with her father. She then got another piece of paper and wrote the following anger letter:

*Peggy's Adult Anger Letter to Father—Sleeping*

You huge turd. How dare you do that. An *innocent* little child, *your* child. You don't deserve her. She's far too good to be with you. You will *never, never* see her again. She's with me now; safe, warm and loved and if you *ever* try to come near her again I *will kill you. Do you hear me? Do you understand?* Keep away or I *will kill you.* I will flush you away like the shit you are. You will gag and drown on your own piss. *Is that clear?*

## DIFFERENT DIRECTIONS

There are times when your client is sent off to do one piece of homework, but comes back with something completely different. Do not despair. It may contain some useful information that the unconscious has delivered. The following extremely important work was done in just such a way by Peggy.

She was unable to complete her assigned homework and in frustration just wrote her feelings down instead. She brought that along to me to show just how confused and muddled she had been. However, something much more important was there between the lines. My title was: Damaged Parent, Damaged Child Exchange from Peggy; but Peggy's original work did not have any heading. The parts

that I have put into italic print were simply separated by
space in Peggy's letter.

*This is ridiculous! Why can't/won't I do this homework?*

I'm tired. I've had enough. Why do I have to do all
this? Why does he [husband] yell so much? Why do I stay?
Why would I go? I want a rest. I want to run and hide
somewhere. I don't want to care for everyone else. I want
someone to care for me. Why can't I go back? Why can't
I have it over again, but properly? Cindy [daughter] is no
better than I was, why can she have it and I can't?

*What did I ever do to end up being betrayed like that?*
*Nothing. Why do I feel so pathetic? This isn't me. I don't*
*really feel so weak, surely?*

Oh, yes you do. You feel weak, you are weak, you're
scared and gutless. Too pathetic to carry on, aren't you?
Aren't you? Go on admit it, you're pathetic, more pathetic
than you said Matthew [husband] was. You just don't
want to lose your daddy, do you? Well, I've got news for
you, you never really had him. That wasn't love, that was
using you. You like that do you? Being used? Well go
ahead then stay as you are, but don't come whingeing to
me when you don't like it any more. Quit now and you're
just asking for it really, aren't you? *Aren't* you?

*No, No, I'm not. I didn't do anything. I can't help it. I*
*was only a kid, wasn't I?*

You're not a kid now are you? You are a grown-up.
You are a mother and a wife and you are a woman above
all that. If you'd only let go of your precious bloody father.
But no, you want to sit around feeling sorry for yourself,
don't you?

*Well, why shouldn't I? I have to do everything and I*
*don't want to. I want a rest. I want some peace. I'm too*

*tired to do this any more. Look around, look at my house.
It's won. Look at my husband, he's won. Look at my
kids, they'll win too eventually. I can't do it any more. I
can't. I have to stop. I have to go away. Why can't
they all just leave me alone? Whinge, whinge about
their problems. Where's the care and support for mine?
For me?*

You cannot be serious!! You are your support and if
you don't do something about it you'll never get free. Do
you hear? NEVER. Still, I guess that suits you, doesn't
it? Daddy's girl!

*Go away, I hate you!*

Good, because I hate you too. You whinge and moan
and act pathetic and it spoils my life too. You are being
very, very selfish. You should pull your finger out and do
your homework. Why do you think Penny set it in the
first place?

*I can't. I'm too tired. Daddy wouldn't love me. I'd have
to have sex with Matthew. I can't. I'm too tired. I want
someone to look after me. I can't do it and you can't make
me. Go away, I want some help, not you yelling at me.
Leave me alone. I'll be fine.*

(*My notes on the day*) Peggy still looks a bit weary, but I'm
not surprised. She attempted to do her homework, but
ended up doing something altogether different. A dialogue
between her P/C voices. She didn't think it contained much,
but actually it was very informative. The biggest piece of
info was that the 'Child' is reluctant to give up her perception
of her daddy. She felt more special than anyone else in the
family because of the sexual abuse attention. She enjoyed
the 'most loved' status. To now give that (connected to her
sexuality) to Matthew would threaten the identity she has
always felt safe with.

I assigned a letter from the Child enabling her to confess
her love for her father (so we can begin to work with those

feelings) and a return letter from the Adult explaining that love.

### Peggy's Letter FROM: About Loving Daddy

*Peg my love, how are you feeling now? This afternoon with Penny was really hard, wasn't it? It was really good too because she helped us both realise some more of how you feel about your daddy and how much you need his love. Could you please tell me some more of how you feel about that, Peg? I feel that we have to talk about it in order to really get our hands on the freedom we have come so far to find.*

Okay. Well, my daddy is mine. He's all mine and I'm all his. My daddy loves me very, very much and I am his best girl. He calls me his girl. I am my daddy's girl. Daddy is everything. He helps me when I am stuck with something. He explains things I can't get. My daddy is my friend and he plays with me. He loves me very, very much, so I don't mind about the other because it makes daddy happy and shows how much I am special and he loves me.

Mum can't do some things, but I can. I can look after dad. I want to. It shows I love him back. I love him so much. I want to make him happy. I am lonely without him. When he has to go away for his work, I miss him very much. I don't moan like mum does because I am stronger than her.

I help with jobs and Jon and Sally [younger brother and sister], he knows I can manage while he's away and he'll love me when he comes back. I feel safe and warm with my dad. He loves me very much and I love him very much. I want to be with him because I feel very special then.

He talks to me like a grown-up. He thinks I am very good and can do lots of things. I want to do things that make him feel good, like when I rub his back or do things so mum won't have to, like iron his shirts or the hoovering. He says I mow the lawn best so I like to do that too. He lets me help him with his jobs on the car or doing things in the house and I am happy because I am helping him very much. I am a big help.

About when daddy comes in my room or somewhere and we do that, well, some I don't like really but daddy does and I like to help him so he is happy and loves me. Some I like. It is warm and I know he loves me best. I don't have someone else who loves me that much. There is only my daddy and I am glad to be his girl. He keeps me safe and warm and makes me feel special so I love him very much and it doesn't matter if some things he likes, I don't. I can still do them. It's only for a little while and then daddy still loves me and it's not often, after all it's doing me no harm. Daddy just wants to love me properly, that's how daddies do loving. I know that.

He doesn't love mummy like he loves me. He pretends he does, but I know he doesn't really. He just pretends so she won't mind about how much he loves me. I don't want to lose my dad. He would be so hurt if I didn't love him and I don't want to stop. I would be alone and scared. Daddy would be very sad, so I don't want to stop. Me and my dad will stay together. We will always love each other. I am his and he is mine and I like it that way. Can I have a rest now and talk to you later please?

*'Of course you can, sweetie. I'll talk with you later after you have rested. You have done very well.'*

Later . . .

### Peggy's Letter TO: About Loving Daddy

Hello again, my love, are you feeling more rested now, darling? I had another look at what you told me the other day. How wonderful to feel so much love for your daddy and to know he loves you too. I think that's lovely, honey. With daddy loving you so much, of course, you want to keep it that way. No one would want to be without all that love, would they?

You love your daddy so much honey, no wonder you can't imagine any other love feeling so strong or so long lasting. It feels so safe to have your daddy love you and know you will always have that love to share.

You are absolutely right darling, daddy will always love you, but he will not always be the only one who does. You are such a wonderful person that there will be many others who love you too. You feel that because there is only daddy right now it will always be that way, just you and him. If that were so it would mean all the other people who will love you won't be able to if you don't let them because you still only want daddy.

You know daddy loves you right? And he always will and nothing will change that honey, nothing. Daddy will love you and so will other people. Daddy will feel glad that you are such a lovely person that others see that too and love you for it. He will be glad that you are so full of love that you can love them back too.

You know how much you love daddy and you love Grandad and Aunty Jane and Rex [dog]? And they all love you too, don't they? Well that doesn't mean you and daddy can't keep loving each other does it?

*No, but it's not the same. It's not the same as daddy. I love daddy. I am his girl.*

Yes, honey, you do love daddy and that's great, really great. Right now daddy is the only man you can live with and love and so you love him best. When you grow up and are a woman, you will probably meet another man who you love very much, only in a different way than you love daddy. It will be the same sort of strong love you feel for daddy and he will love you back the same way.

*Daddy says he's* [future love] *a monster. He is chasing me in the woods and I am running. It is up to me, it is my dream, my monster. I will not let it get me. I will keep away from the monster and daddy will help me, he is in the woods too. I will find him and the monster won't get me, he won't, he won't. I will run to find daddy, who will always love me best.*

[This writing was ended with strong, angry scribbling.]

When I enquired about the dream mentioned, Peggy explained that Little Peg used to have a recurring dream about being chased in the woods by a monster—knowing her father was somewhere nearby but unable to find him to help her. When, as a child, she told her father about this dream, he told her the monster represented the man that would someday come along and take her from him when she was grown-up. In light of that information, it is no big surprise that Peggy had such difficulty completely giving her love and sharing her sexuality with her husband.

After the above letter ended in angry scribbling, Peggy took out more paper and wrote the following anger letter to her father.

*Peggy's Adult Anger Letter to Father*
*(Written quite large and taking up three sheets of paper)*

HOW COULD YOU!! YOU PIG, BIG BLOODY PIG! YOU SPOILED IT! YOU SPOILED MY MARRIAGE. HOW DARE YOU!!

How do you expect a child to adjust to that? How can a child understand your jealous love? How can she understand that you got it wrong? You WILL NOT keep me. I will fight. Matthew will love me and I will love him.

I WILL BE MY WOMAN NOT YOUR GIRL!

MY WOMAN!!

AND I'LL SHARE THAT WITH MATTHEW, I LOVE HIM.

YOU COULD SHARE TOO IF YOU'D LET GO.

LET GO. WAKE UP!

Peggy brought the three above letters to me next session, feeling very despondent. I explained that this particular bit of work was the weakest point so far for her and that she was just not able to pull forth all the 'goodies' (appropriate information) from her Adult to combat the powerful beliefs left by her father. We discussed the 'goodies', which Peggy was able to grasp, reporting that now it all made perfect sense. I assigned an Adult letter to Child to include the information discussed. That subsequent letter (below) was completely successful.

### *Peggy's Letter TO: Child About Enjoying Sex*
### *Child's Belief 95 per cent*

Hello love, how are you feeling? Still pretty confused I expect. I feel that I'd really like to talk to you again about your feelings on sex and you. I don't think I explained it very well last time we spoke so I'll try again, okay?

Firstly, I think it's important for you to understand where all the confusion and bad feelings came from. When you were little you didn't really get many loving hugs from your mum and dad, did you? That was because they aren't much good at being loving, remember? Well, you also remember that sometimes your daddy would make you feel really special, he would really spend time with you being gentle and loving. It felt so good to know your daddy loved you, didn't it? And he did love you, you know, but the way he chose to show it was not right. He would cuddle and touch all of you, wouldn't he?

You had thought what you experienced with your dad felt so good and now you find out it was bad, so you now believe you are bad for enjoying parts of it. This is not true. It was bad of daddy to be having sex with you, but not because you, or sex, is bad. The reason it is wrong is that you are a child and he is an adult, your father. He should have shown you his love in a non-sexual way. He should have sat you on his knee and hugged you, kissed you a proper loving good night kiss when he tucked you in and read you stories. Those are the ways for a dad to show love to his little girl, sex is not.

Sex is for adults to share to show how much they love each other. It is not for children. It is an activity for adults only. Your dad was very wrong to say that it showed your love for each other. It didn't. All it showed was that he didn't give you proper love as he should have done and that he tricked you into thinking that the sex between you was loving and right. It wasn't.

It will be that when you are grown-up and are with someone you find special, who you want to show your love to in that way. With daddy you would rather have had love in another way, wouldn't you? So what he did was wrong.

You find you feel uncomfortable when daddy tells you that you do like this kind of love with him because your body shows that you do. Of course you feel uncomfortable. He is telling you a lie. You know you don't like it, you'd rather have a gentle hug instead. Your body does not show that you 'like' or prefer this kind of love with daddy. Your body simply responds to the touch. All of our bodies do that! Remember when I told you about your clitoris and the warm feelings you can get from touching it? Well, our whole body responds that way if it is touched right, our clitoris does it most strongly, that's all.

When we are touched like that and we get the warm feeling, our vagina gets wet too. That is natural and how it should be. It is to make it feel good to have a man's penis go there when you are a grown woman making love to a man (or just on your own with your fingers or a vibrator). Our bodies do that automatically. It is not something we decide about or choose, it just happens. Like when you go to the doctor's and he can make your knee jerk up by getting the little hammer on the right spot. You can't stop your foot going up, can you? If it doesn't, it just means the doctor missed the spot, didn't get it quite right.

It's the same with sex and touching. If you respond with your body going warm, or wet, or both, that means the touch got to the right place to make that happen. If you don't, that means the touch missed, so don't be fooled into thinking you can stop it happening because you can't. And what is more, that is nothing to be ashamed of either. You're a lovely girl with a body that can feel good and I am pleased about that. It means that when you choose to, you can enjoy sex with a partner who is also an adult like you will be.

Don't feel bad honey, daddy lied again. You are right and he is wrong. You don't like it, you would rather have a cuddle. Yes, your body does work, but as a child it shouldn't be being made to work by him, an adult, so it feels wrong, that's all.

[*Adult now addresses the inner 'young woman' the child grew into*] When you do find your body responds, and you want it to because you are with someone you choose and you are enjoying the close loving touching, you find you feel guilty, don't you? That's a normal reaction, love, anyone who had been tricked and lied to as you were would feel that way. The guilt you feel is a result of the tricks and lies from your father. It is because you fear that the things you are enjoying are bad, so you feel bad to like it.

This is not the case. The things you are enjoying are good, are enjoyable, so naturally you enjoy them! The guilt is a leftover from when you found you had liked daddy touching you, because of feeling loved, and then finding it was incest which is bad. Now (today) sex isn't that. It is something you choose, something for you to enjoy with Matthew [husband]. There is no place for guilt there. The place for the guilt is with your dad for introducing sex, which is for adults, to a child. That was wrong of him, but you hold no guilt. You were tricked, that's all, and it would be the same for any child. It's easy for an adult to trick a child and he was bad to do that to you.

It is this same guilt that makes you feel like you are 'in the spotlight' when you touch Matthew sexually, especially if you are making love. That is because it seems to feel like you are showing on purpose that you are enjoying the sex and you fear you are encouraging him in a bad thing.

Yes, you are showing you like the sex. Yes, you are encouraging him. THAT IS WHAT SEX IS ABOUT IF YOU ARE WITH SOMEONE SPECIAL WHO YOU CHOOSE TO BE WITH. You are doing very well to enjoy it, you are doing a wonderful thing to share that by touching. You are not showing something bad or shameful about yourself. There is nothing bad or shameful there to show. The bad and shameful thing was your dad, an adult, tricking a child, having sex with her. That is for him to feel guilt and shame for, not you.

You, my love, are lovely. You are free to enjoy your sexuality alone or with someone special like Matthew. That is your choice, your pleasure and so it should be. Don't let dad steal it from you and replace it with his guilt and shame. His lies are lies and you know that now and so does he, so there is no more game to play. It is over.

Let it go now and share your non-sexual love with your dad and keep your wonderful sexual love where it belongs—for you to share when you want to with Matthew. I love you honey, go ahead, have fun, you deserve it. Dad can fuck off!! He has lost. We have won. Hooray!! Hooray—I love you! I love me!

## USEFUL BOOKS ON SEXUALITY

Have a list of books on the subject of sexuality that you can refer your client to. It is often much easier to learn about some of the more tender issues from a book—it is also a good idea to ask your client to jot down any questions or points she would like to discuss further. I usually suggest that you have books on sexual subjects available to loan out, because some people will find it very difficult to ask for or purchase these at a book shop or the library.

Here is a list of the books I normally lend out to people. You may also have others you find useful. I have listed these in the sequence that I usually suggest people read them.

*Questions of Sex*, The Diagram Group (New English Library, 1989). An excellent book to clarify the information victims have about sexual and personal subjects. A source of answers for big or small questions. Some drawings. Often a good step one book for clients—if they already have the information offered, they then have the opportunity to feel pleased with the fact that even in the face of their difficulties they were able to learn about an important and essential subject. (That is the reframe you can offer if they say, 'There was not much in the book for me because I knew most of that stuff'.)

*The Mirror Within: a New Look at Sexuality*, Anne Dickson (Quartet, 1985). A book about female sexuality and body image. Simply written and easy to understand, with useful exercises. Do not make the mistake of offering this book only to female clients. It is important for both genders to know the problems faced by their sexual counterparts. Suggest your client read the book about his or her own gender first and the opposite gender second.

*Men and Sex*, Bernie Zilbergeld (Fontana, 1980). Explodes myths about, and explains reasons for, male sexual problems. Written in a down-to-earth manner, with self-help exercises. Well-written, excellent book.

*Treat Yourself to Sex: a Guide to Good Loving*, Paul Brown and Carolyn Foulder (Penguin, 1979). A straightforward look at a delicate subject—good practical information. Simply written, easy to understand, no drawings. The authors give information about the typical questions regarding sex and go on to give information of the enjoyment, delight and pleasure that two people can give to each other if they know how. Excellent for your client who is now ready to learn about sex, but do not give it to the client who has not even been able to acknowledge that his or her own body exists.

# 9  Therapy Blocks

## FOUR BASIC BLOCKS

The first basic block is being stuck in the victim role, or as I referred to it in *Rescuing the 'Inner Child'*, being the 'poor thing'. The second is 'getting even', people who are sacrificing their own lives to punish the abuser or parents who let them down. Thirdly, we have clients who simply feel overwhelmed by the backlog of childhood material and the often similar material from adult life. Lastly, there are those people who are simply not ready for change work. Sometimes these people need a long period of 'unloading' or just telling about what happened to them and the devastating effect it has had on their life before they are able to engage in change work. For others there seems to be an inner time clock that indicates, 'now' or 'not now', when it comes to change work.

### Poor Things
These people will demonstrate their condition in one of two ways. Either by the familiar 'downtrodden' attitude and posture or with 'angry child' behaviour and posture. Both see themselves as being taken advantage of by others—others always win, leaving the poor thing as the loser.

You will hear many 'always', 'everybody', 'everything' and 'never' statements from these people, because there is a strong leaning to generalise their experience. 'I'll always lose' and 'I'm not good enough' are typical limiting beliefs that operate their life. As we know, the brain works very hard to match up our life experiences with our beliefs ('There's one, there's one') and automatically discards those experiences which are a mismatch to our beliefs ('That's not one'), so it is not really too surprising that 'poor things'/ victims generalise and can only recognise events which substantiate their 'poor thing' identity.

As a result their lives are usually full of self-sabotage and their conversation full of 'I can't' statements. Healthy Adult behaviour is seldom evidenced, the damaged Child is the star performer. The Child demonstrates as helpless, wanting people to rush to the rescue (as the Child needed during abusive situations). They appear to be small children dependent on adults, but operating from the emotional standpoint of a small child does not work for a grown-up. Most people do not automatically rush to the rescue, in fact, many people become annoyed and try to force the 'poor things' to help themselves.

Those people who do consistently rush to the rescue are usually running off their own limiting beliefs, 'I must always help others', 'My needs come last', etc. It is not surprising to see 'helper' and 'poor thing' as marriage or co-habiting partners. It is even less surprising to see those relationships break apart if one of the partners actually engages in change work.

Seldom are 'poor things' able to take responsibility for their behaviour. It is seen as coming from 'out there'. Other people do these things to them. When they come forward for therapy (which is often), they usually want one of two things: the therapist to make others stop victimising them or they want a willing audience to talk to about how horrible life has been. When change work is approached, they will either stop therapy or throw in one block after another.

The idea of giving up their 'poor thing' identity is very threatening. How would they ever relate to anyone without their 'needs' as the focal point? How could they operate in life without others to help? What would happen if they had to come out from behind the safety of the 'poor thing' identity?

When you run the Well Formed Outcome, the 'poor thing' problem will be obvious. It is very useful to know this problem exists early on, rather than running the gamut of blocks put forward while you struggle on trying to engage in change work with the person. You may feel this person would benefit more from working in a strict Rogerian format, where he or she is able to unload without the 'directive format' utilised in this change work.

If you are happy to work following a strictly Rogerian format, then carry on with these clients in that manner. If, however, you are not at your best in a strict Rogerian format, refer your clients on to someone who is. You might say, 'From the information you have given me, I feel you are now ready for the task of unloading. Ready to explore and talk about the experiences you have had and the resulting problems. To do this properly, I think you will benefit most from a strict Rogerian therapist, where you will have an empathetic and unconditionally respectful listening ear, where you can explore these issues for as long as you need. The work that I do has much less focus on exploring your past experiences and moves along at a much quicker pace—I don't think you would benefit from that format. Let me give you the name of Mr/Ms . . .'

If you think that your clients may be able to shift the 'poor thing' identity, and what they want from therapy (first question of the Well Formed Outcome) matches with a change from that identity, it is a good idea to explain beforehand what to expect. Explain that you will be building up their Adult and working with their beliefs about 'self' to enable them to learn a new way of being—[insert here their wording for their positive outcome]. Explain that engaging in this work will result in consistent and profound change and enquire as to whether they are prepared to engage in this way. If, at any time during the therapy, you feel they are throwing in constant red herrings and blocks (that you cannot reframe effectively), it is advisable to stop work. Explain what is happening and that you feel other work needs to be done before they are completely ready for what you offer—then refer them on to the strict Rogerian therapist.

**Getting Even**
These people are well into punishing their parents/abuser. They may be punishing for abuse that they experienced or for the lack of love and nurturing they experienced. Often this punishing is done in an indirect way, either by withdraw-

ing from close contact or, most often, by carrying the symptoms of abuse. It is a belief that the problem people will be reminded of their failings every time they see or hear about your client's symptoms and emotional problems.

The sad fact is that those problem people have usually learned many years ago to project their personal responsibility onto others. Therefore, when they see or hear about your client's problems they feel nothing personal. It is a futile effort on your client's part, a great waste of his or her life. When I hear clients using statements that imply that the problem people in their lives 'know why I'm like this' (or any 'know' statements), I often ask, 'What is it that tells you that they know?' Their answer usually gives a clear outline of the assumptions being made and gives you the opportunity to share some accurate information to counteract those assumptions.

It is not unusual during therapy for clients to realise that they had secretly enjoyed their parents' distress concerning their emotional problems (client's), because it was a way of getting their own back. Not a conscious thought, but a controlling one and one that would sabotage efforts to end the problems. Even people who have not experienced severe abuse sometimes have the same need to retaliate over hurts and disappointments concerning their childhood, but no one can get better, or reach their full potential, while solely bent upon punishing their parents or problem people.

People with this need to retaliate as their main focus often want to have significant others participate in their retaliation plan. They attend class after class, see counsellor after counsellor and read book after book, all without shifting their problems, because their need is to have others know what 'shits' (a technical term) their parents/problem people are— a 'see what they did to me' theme. The presenting problem (phobia, illness or negative behaviour pattern) chosen may be aired and shaken out from time to time, but any change work will be quickly avoided and the problem clutched tightly again.

These clients often need to air their feelings through anger work, giving them a way to write out retaliation scenarios on paper rather than acting them out in symptoms/problems.

Another useful tool to help clients recognise that they are actually keeping their problems to get back at problem people, is to have them make two lists. The first is headed, 'Advantages of Being Emotionally Healthy' and the second is headed, 'Advantages of Being Emotionally Unhealthy'. The results are usually very surprising and insightful to clients. (See page 157 of *Rescuing the 'Inner Child'* for one example.)

**Being Overwhelmed**

It is not surprising when people who have a host of problems think that the state of their life is too much to face. They want to be different but the task seems too difficult to tackle. It reminds me of a time many years ago when I used to sell handcrafted jewellery at craft fairs in California.

It was very nice sitting in the sun, chatting to customers and selling jewellery, until an occasional stiff breeze would catch the board displays and throw them to the ground. Invariably, the chain necklace boards would be the ones to fly through the air and land in the most tangled mess you could imagine. Ten or 12 fine chain necklaces would be all knotted together in a tight ball. The chap I worked with had little patience and would immediately shove the tangled wad at me with orders to, 'Do something with that!' I would find a place in the shade, take a fine needle and slowly begin to pick gently at bits of chain to see if anything would move. It was slow, tedious and frustrating work and many times I wanted to give up and say, 'It's just too difficult, I can't do it!' However, after a little break, I would continue and after about 35 minutes, the first necklace would come free. I would feel so pleased that I was tempted to stop people walking by and shout, 'I've got one free! I've got one free!' The remaining necklaces would be easier and quicker and usually within two hours I would have completed the job. What a feeling of accomplishment that was! I was so pleased with myself that it was always tempting to tell people how I had just done a seemingly impossible task, but fortunately my better sense kept me from making too much of a fool of myself.

The seemingly impossible task of solving traumatic childhood issues can become slow, tedious and frustrating work and many times people want to say, 'It's just too difficult. I can't do it!' It is very useful, therefore, to explain to your clients that you will work on one piece at a time and with each piece they will feel delighted and pleased—even though there will be more yet to do. Each piece solved will make the rest easier and quicker until suddenly the task will be completed.

Many people think that they will not feel any better about themselves until the therapy has finished. It is useful to tell these people that they will begin to feel better and better as they go along. Knowing there is respite along the way diminishes the feelings of being overwhelmed.

**Not Ready**
It is true that people have to be ready to begin work on childhood material. Change does not happen when people come into therapy because their partner or family members think they should. Change happens when the individual wants it and is ready for it. Looking from the outside, it may appear that some people's lives are in such dire straits that they would, of course, be ready for change—sadly that is not always the case. Often it ends up being the old 'horse to water' problem.

I know of nothing that can 'make' a person ready, but having said that, you cannot lose anything by offering a few reframes or information. On occasion I have seen a few people make a decision towards therapy, who started out hesitant. The important thing is to remember that you must gracefully let the person go if the reframe or information is not taken up. Do not labour the point. To do so usually ends with the person being convinced that nothing will help his or her problems and he will perhaps not come forward later when he *is* in a ready state.

These people often come into therapy not knowing that they are not ready, but when the work starts to get near the bone, that realisation becomes clear and they usually stop therapy. One young woman was a good example of that. Anne came to see me because she had been arrested for a petty crime and the shame of that arrest brought her childhood shame to the surface. She disclosed her abuse experience to her mother-in-law, who was very supportive and suggested she see a counsellor.

We worked together for four weeks, but during that time it was clear that Anne was avoiding every issue that suggested pain or possible disclosure of any feelings. She made very telling statements like, 'I want to do well in this therapy, because I would feel dreadful if I let my mother-in-law down'. Anne was not in therapy for herself. She was trying to please someone else. She was simply not ready to do any work; although she needed change, she was not ready to face it.

Other people think they are ready but find the reality of facing difficult issues (no matter how quick and relatively painless) too much. Usually they drop out of therapy early on, some after the first session, others after a month or so. Having said that, using the Well Formed Outcome will assist you and your clients to determine their 'readiness' and give them a clearer understanding of their experience.

Not being ready today does not necessarily mean those people will never be ready, it is only a reflection of where they are at this moment in time. It may be a matter of days, weeks, months or, in some cases, years until they knock again on a therapist's door.

## PROBLEMS FOR COUNSELLORS

There are a few common mistakes made by counsellors that become a block for the client.

1. The first one, and perhaps most important, is when the counsellor does not have enough knowledge concerning the subject of abuse. When that is the case, the counsellor is unable to understand some of the responses received and may misinterpret the clues given by their clients. Not having enough knowledge also prohibits the counsellor from anticipating some of the difficulties that could sometimes be sidestepped.

2. It is disastrous for the counsellor to believe that children are guilty of all or part of the abuse they experience.

A common example of that would be the situation involving a child going back to the abuser's house, knowing that abuse was probably going to be on the agenda. When that happens, it is only a statement of how emotionally needy the child was—s/he was settling for abuse attention. It is not a statement about the child's guilt. Counsellors must be clear on these issues or they will not be equipped to assist their clients to let go of misplaced guilt. It is always the responsibility of the adult to ensure that the relationship is appropriate; children do not have the power or the knowledge to take on that responsibility.

3. It is also a problem when the counsellor does not understand the connections from the childhood experience to the present-day behaviour. This generally refers to recognising how limiting beliefs start (child trying to make meaning of experiences without appropriate information) and carry on ruling the person's behaviour and attitudes. It is vital for clients to be able to see the connection because this will prepare them for the 'letting go' of limiting beliefs.

4. It is slow work when a counsellor expects childhood abuse clients to overcome their limiting beliefs or negative feelings by logic. Years are sometimes spent in therapy trying to talk and 'logic' the behaviours and negative feelings away. Of course, logic does work on some limiting beliefs, but it will not touch others; other tools must be utilised.

5. It is most helpful when the counsellor offers information (in conversational style) about subjects that clients are usually too embarrassed to disclose, particularly concerning sexuality or body issues. By presenting information that applies to 'most people' or 'many people', rather than focusing directly on the client, the counsellor can give the needed information without sacrificing the client's dignity. The client then has the choice of exploring the subject further or not.

6. Some therapy methods suggest that the counsellor remain aloof and personally distant from the client. Often the client does not know anything more than the counsellor's name. This way of working is not suitable for the childhood abuse client group. That does not mean to say that the counsellor should spend great amounts of time chatting on and

on about self. However, if you have a personal piece of information that is pertinent, please feel free to share it— obviously keeping it brief and to the point. It is useful for your clients to feel natural with you, rather than experiencing a 'clinical' relationship. It will be helpful for them to know you as a person, rather than an 'aloof professional being'.

7. It is surprising to me that there are still trained counsellors who respond with shock or sympathy to details of trauma experiences. Neither of those responses is helpful to clients. Shock response can cause clients to hold back further information, thinking that you are out of your depth upon hearing new material. If you seem upset upon hearing their material, clients will automatically protect you from the worst. You will be operating like many colluding parents who could not hear about what was really happening.

However, it is appropriate to state calmly that you find certain material shocking, as long as you refrain from emotional responses such as gasping, quickly covering your mouth with your hand, shaking your head, looking upset and saying, 'Oh, dear, you poor thing!' That may sound over the top, but according to clients there are still counsellors out there who are reacting in that manner.

It is also appropriate if on occasion you have tears upon hearing heartrending material. In fact, your clients usually feel supported if tears happen. Just make sure you are only shedding tears and not going into a sobbing display. You are allowed to have feelings, but it is not helpful to be over the top in expressing your feelings. You can also verbalise your feelings, such as: 'I am sorry you were hurt in that way', 'I feel sad for that little child trapped in that situation', 'I feel very moved by that experience' or any other simple expression of how you are feeling. However, it is not helpful to make 'poor thing' comments of any nature. Express your sorrow for clients without labelling them 'poor things'.

8. Most people who have worked for long in the field of childhood abuse will tell you that the 50-minute therapy hour is neither appropriate nor applicable. Some childhood abuse counsellors work two, three or four hour sessions with clients, others an hour and a half to two hours. If you work

for an agency who expect you to use the 50-minute therapy hour, it would be advisable to collect and present some information and ask for an extension of time for abuse clients.

9. Please respond to all the client's abuse scenarios with equal concern. Do not make the mistake of treating emotional abuse as though it had minimal impact. The same goes for 'only touching' as compared to 'full intercourse' in the area of sexual abuse. All abuse has equal impact on people; there is no such thing as minimal abuse which can be defined by the acts committed. Minimal abuse is only defined by the meaning given to it by the victim, **at the time that it happened**.

10. It is vital to establish rapport with your client, for without rapport you will simply be going through the motions. Without rapport the best tools and techniques become clumsy and ineffective.

11. The last item on this list is about 'inappropriate touch'. I hope it goes without saying that to touch a client in the interests of your own sexual gratification is absolutely wrong. Therapists who sexually exploit the vulnerable are in need of therapy themselves and in need of a different profession.

Some therapists/counsellors have been known to begin dating a client. This changes the therapeutic relationship and diminishes your effectiveness with the person. If you think you are developing a personal interest in a client, you need to stop working with that person immediately and refer him or her to another counsellor. You could develop a personal relationship with the person, but it is NOT in his or her best interests while you are that person's counsellor.

Some counsellors seem to have a need to hug all their clients and other counsellors keep themselves at a definite distance from clients. It is best to hug, or not, according to your client's needs. Some clients will have a problem with touch and you need to keep your distance to enable them to feel safe. Other clients will have a need to be hugged because if you keep them at a distance they interpret it as a rejection.

If your client is crying, do not automatically assume that he or she wants to be hugged; most often the person needs

to be left alone physically, so just use your voice in a supportive, caring manner. However, if you think your client does
want to be touched, *ask* first: 'Would it be helpful if I held
your hand or put my arm round your shoulder?' If the person
would rather have a supportive arm around his or her shoulders, it is wiser for you to offer one arm rather than to hold
the person in both arms like a child. You are meant to be
offering support, not parenting.

Sometimes, at the end of a particularly significant session,
you may feel it is appropriate to offer your client a hug. If
so, it should be warm and brief. If your client is of the
opposite gender, be very, very careful about hugging. On
some occasions it is appropriate, but only very infrequently.
For any client, hugging should be offered for specific reasons
(usually support or celebration) and should be infrequent.

If you are a counsellor who frequently hugs your clients,
you might ask yourself if it is for your benefit or theirs. If
you are a counsellor who is purposefully distant from your
clients, you might ask yourself the same question. A counsellor should be able to hug or not hug appropriately, according
to the client's needs.

## COUNSELLOR'S EMOTIONS

There are times when you will be moved to tears by letters
from the Child. I still have tears on occasion. In fact, I hope
I never get so hardened to suffering that I cannot experience
tears. Clients are not harmed by knowing that you are moved
by their experience and you can express your feelings about
their letter as well, e.g. 'I am very moved by your letter. I
feel sad that you had that scary and uncomfortable experience.' Clients usually experience the counsellor's expression
of feeling as validation of their pain. On these occasions I
have heard statements such as: 'When I saw that you had
tears, it made me think that maybe I wasn't making a mountain out of a molehill after all.'

When I say tears, I am not referring to sobs. It is not
helpful for the counsellor to break down; clients would then
feel a need to protect and start holding back some of their
painful material. Counsellors need to settle their own *known*

personal painful childhood material *before* embarking upon work with clients in the abuse field, otherwise they may find that client's material will push buttons and sometimes cause a 'breakdown' or 'gut reaction' impact.

This can also happen when the counsellor has repressed material. In this case, the counsellor's reaction will have the strong 'gut reaction' impact and he or she will want to move quickly on past the subject. If the counsellor is ready to 'know' about the past experiences, flashbacks or dream material may also begin. Depending on the individual, he or she may or may not need to stop working with clients while the past experiences are faced and solved.

## LETTERS FOR THE COUNSELLOR

At times when I have continued to feel anger towards someone's abuser, I have used the anger letters myself. If you read my book *Rescuing the 'Inner Child'*, you may remember Richard. I am sure you remember Richard's aunt, Ellen. She was the recipient of a few anger letters from me (obviously I am not referring to posted or delivered letters). You can also share your anger letters to the abuser with your client. In Richard's case, he was moved to see that someone was standing up for him and also commented that it helped him realise that what she did was really bad. When you are used to abusive behaviour, it tends to seem 'normal' and you often reckon you are making it much bigger than it was. My anger about Richard's treatment enabled him to say, 'Yes, what happened to me WAS as bad as it seemed.'

On occasion, when a client is having difficulty bonding with her inner Child, I have written a letter to that Child. In the letter I have acknowledged the Child's feelings, explained that the problem people were wrong to behave as they did, described what healthy parenting would have been like, explained that as a result of those experiences several mistaken beliefs were developed, that those m/bs affected life in restrictive ways and that we would be working towards changing those to positive beliefs. I explain that often the m/bs are about 'being bad' or not worthy of help or love, but that I know that all children are worthy of help and love and that 'being bad' was simply wrong information learned from the damaged adults in their life. I end the letter saying that the Child deserves support, information and love and that I think he or she has been very brave to carry on so long without it. I **do not** say I will give it, just that it is deserved. Most often, clients find the letter a useful bridge to enable them to begin connecting with the Child.

Counsellors can also use the anger letters (or physical anger exercises) if they are feeling frustration towards a client. Before I had the Well Formed Outcome to assist me with identifying clients who were ready for change work, I would run up against frustration. Most counsellors experience frustration when working with clients who seem to throw every red herring available to personkind into the works. Often the counsellor thinks it may be her lack of expertise that is stopping the forward movement. However, after much soul-searching and implementation of different skills and tools, the counsellor begins to feel frustration towards the client, because the counsellor believes that the client wants change but is sabotaging it. At that point, frustration can evolve into anger.

Obviously, it is not particularly useful to carry around anger towards a client, for it will be sensed on some level. The anger exercises work very well to help you vent your frustration and regain your sense of balance. It is not useful to share these letters with your client, any more than it is to share anger letters with problem people. Anger letters are to vent personal feelings in an 'over the top' manner, and therefore, they do not make useful communication tools. However, since I have used the Well Formed Outcome, I am no longer faced with the frustration experienced with clients who are not ready for change work and therefore have not needed to use the anger letters in that way.

# Summary

I was recently asked when the poem, ' Sexual Abuse' (which is at the end of *Rescuing the 'Inner Child'*) was written, and if I still felt the feelings described in the last paragraph.

> But, still, when I hear the stories
> Of others like me, I cry.
> There seems to be a terrible grief inside,
> A howling cry that would finish me
> If I let it out.
> Grief for innocence and freedom
> I never knew as a child.
> Grief for the others, not as lucky as I,
> Whose loss may consume them.

I wrote the poem in 1986, the year before I began to write my first book. I no longer have the 'terrible grief' inside; it was connected to the need to write the book. Once I had written and published the book, I felt I had 'delivered my soul' of the message I needed to share. It is my opinion that the 'terrible grief' was there to assist and motivate me to record the information I had for other people to benefit from. If I had not accepted that responsibility, it would be like someone who had a cure for cancer and only used it on him- or herself—not sharing it with other cancer sufferers.

In 1991 I again became increasingly uncomfortable. This time it was in the form of sleep disturbances. I would wake up in the middle of the night and have imaginary teaching sessions. I was teaching the PICT course a few times a year at that time and I reckoned the sleep disturbances were just related to improving my teaching abilities. However, they seemed to increase and were beginning to affect my ability to concentrate during the day. Boy, did I wish I had an 'off' button to stop the constant thinking so I could get some sleep.

I mentioned my sleep problem to my colleague, Pamela Hayes, and she said, 'Maybe you ought to get up and write down what you are thinking.' Her words really hit home, and as I began to write, it became obvious that I needed to write a training book for counsellors. The sleep disturbances did not stop until I had completed about one-third of the manuscript. At that point my publisher rang me and asked if I had considered writing a second book. I laughed and said that I was in the process of doing just that. They asked for a copy of what I had completed and later contacted me to say they were interested in publishing it and we set up a deadline date. With a deadline date to work towards, the sleep disturbances ended—as the job to identify my goal and motivate me towards it was complete.

It is my wish that this book will be used by counsellors and therapists to learn more about the subject of childhood abuse, increase their skills and add more 'tools' to their toolbox. For those who wish to add practice to theory, there is a PICT Advanced Practitioner Training course.

This thirty-four day course (two-day sessions held once a month over 17 months) offers unique tools and skills to enable practising therapists or counsellors to work quickly, competently, thoroughly, confidently and compassionately (which means without taking clients through details of traumatic experiences). The course contains the 'Trauma Resolution Experience' (TRE) which students report as being the most powerful and useful overall PICT tool (not featured in this book). The PICT Advanced Practitioner Training manual contains handouts for clients and has every exercise scripted for ease of use.

Students will gain knowledge and techniques to deal with all aspects of the damaging results of emotional, physical and emotional childhood abuse, as well as, a wide range of other emotional problems, such as eating disorders, OCD, DID, self harm, ritual abuse, anxiety or depression, Post Traumatic Stress Disorder, phobias, agoraphobia, working with abusers, grief and loss issues (including murder, suicide, abortion, still-birth and miscarriage, pets), and have the ability to assist with Critical Incident Debriefing (witnessing/experiencing highly traumatic events).

The course includes training in the PICT Quick Change

Therapy format. Mrs Parks has been using, perfecting and teaching this style of intensive PICT therapy since 1996 with very positive results. In comparison to traditional weekly, one hour sessions, this intensive therapy model offers the equivalent of five months work in five days. Successful students will be qualified to practise the PICT Quick Change Therapy with their clients.

There are currently PICT trainers in Suffolk, Essex, Berkshire and Teesside.

PICT students have reported that the tools they gained are invaluable:

'*It* (PICT course) *gave me confidence to work with childhood abuse issues.*' CPN

'*It is a structure that is easy to follow and it works! With the scripting of exercises I never feel at a loss.*' Community OT

'*Up until now, I have felt I was working in the dark with abuse clients, the PICT method is like at last having a light turned on.*' Social Worker

'*It works quickly and it's easy to use. What used to take six months now takes six sessions.*' CPN

'*PICT transforms the way you work with clients, because you know you can get through very traumatic material in a relatively short time.*' Psychotherapist

'*The PICT method is not only humane (easy and gentle for the client), but because it cuts down the time spent with clients it is very cost-effective.*' NHS Therapist

Perhaps it would be appropriate here to paraphrase the 'sense of self' motto I created to accompany the Well Formed Outcome:

> *The counsellor you wish you were is who you really are,*
> *but just haven't yet learned to be.*

Warmest regards,

Penny Parks

For more information on the PICT training course, seminars, workshops or personal therapy please contact:

The Penny Parks Foundation
Mount Pleasant
Debenham
Stowmarket
Suffolk
IP14 6PT
Tel: 01728 860490
Email: info@ppfoundation.org
Website: www.ppfoundation.org
A list of accredited PICT therapists can be found at:
www.pict-therapistsdrectory.org.uk.

# Index

Penny Parks was abused as a child and developed her unique Parks Inner Child Therapy (PICT) from her own experience of self-recovery. An American by birth, Penny has lived in Suffolk since 1982 and founded the Penny Parks Foundation.

The Foundation provides a comprehensive and fully supported training in the PICT model for counsellors and therapists through the PICT Advanced Practitioner Training Course (university accredited). The Penny Parks Foundation also oversees the PICT Association, which provides supervision for accredited PICT therapists and a directory for the public.

More information and resources are available on the website: www.ppfoundation.org

The PICT Advanced Practitioner Training Course extends the knowledge of *The Counsellor's Guide to Parks Inner Child Therapy* to an advanced level.